W9-BUN-888

Career Solutions for Creative People

How To Balance Artistic Goals With Career Security

by Ronda Ormont, Ph. D.

ALLWORTH PRESS
NEW YORK

05   04   03   02   01   5   4   3   2   1

Published by Allworth Press
An imprint of Allworth Communications
10 East 23rd Street, New York, NY 10010

Cover design by Douglas Design Associates, New York, NY

Page composition/typography by
John Cole GRAPHIC DESIGNER, Santa Fe, New Mexico

ISBN: 1-58115-091-1

Library of Congress Cataloging-in-Publication Data:

Ormont, Ronda.
Career solutions for creative people: how to balance artistic
goals with career security/by Ronda Ormont.
     p.cm.
Includes index.
ISBN 1-58115-091-1
     1. Job hunting. 2. Creative ability. I. Title

HF5382.7 .076 2001
650.15—dc21

                                        2001022262

Printed in Canada

To: *My daughter: Perri Ormont Blumberg*
        My husband: Henry Blumberg
        My parents: Irving and Sylvia Ormont

"Ah, but a man's reach should exceed his grasp,
Or what's heaven for?"

—Robert Browning, "Andrea Del Sarto"

Acknowledgments

The publication of this book would not have been possible without the wise counsel of my friend and agent Wendy Lipkind, the tireless efforts of my editorial assistant Suzanne Fox, and the patience and understanding of my family.

The editors wish to thank Patch Schwadron, Career Councelor at the Actors' Work Program, for her invaluable suggestions.

Contents

Preface ix
Introduction xi

Section I: Finding—and Creating—a Better
             Creative/Career Balance 1
Chapter 1:   Are Your Creative and Career
             Commitments in Balance? 3
Chapter 2:   Overcoming the Barriers to Change 19
Chapter 3:   Reassessing Your Values, Skills, Motivations,
             and Decision-Making Style 47

Section II: Exploring and Expanding Your Work Options 77
Chapter 4:   Employment versus Self-Employment:
             Which Is For You? 79
Chapter 5:   Understanding the World of Work 95
Chapter 6:   Discovering a New Career 105
Chapter 7:   Popular Lifeline Careers for Creative People 125

Section III: Building a Better Balance through
             Lifeline Employment 145
Chapter 8:   Your Personal Selling Tools: The Personal
             Commercial and the Resume 147
Chapter 9:   The Official and Hidden Job Markets: How
             To Get The Job You Want 177
Chapter 10: A Guide to Successful Interviewing 197
Chapter 11: Restructuring Your Current Position 225

Section IV: Building a Better Balance through Lifeline
             Self-Employment 243

Chapter 12:   Envisioning and Establishing
              Your Own Lifeline Business 245
Chapter 13:   Your Business Selling Tools 267

Afterword: Congratulations and Closing Thoughts 289
Resources 291
Index 297

Preface

Ronda Ormont has given us a unique and valuable addition to the vast library of career books. She has accomplished this through her considerable experience working with creative people and by bringing her own creativity to the content and structure of this book.

The concepts of the career-counseling process are familiar to most professionals in the field, and there is no shortage of books advising job hunters. It is rare to find the kind of innovative approach presented here. The reason for this is that the focus of traditional career counseling has been matching individuals with careers that fit their interests, skills, and values. While consideration is given to juggling jobs or changing careers to fit various life exigencies, rarely do counselors address the possibility of permanently combining two career tracks. Yet this is precisely what may be the perfect "career solution" for creative people.

In this book there is both a sensitivity to the creative personality and a detailed, pragmatic plan for finding the balance between creative expression and making a living. The author values creative people and affirms her belief that the world does, too. At the same time, and with respect for individuality, she guides the reader through the process of decision-making and job hunting. She does this with specific, practical suggestions. At the same time she demonstrates an appreciation for that special balance necessary to allow creativity to flourish. This is truly a balancing act in itself!

In each chapter, the reader will find excellent examples of how this process has worked for people in the creative art fields. The life stories and career strivings of these individuals enrich and inform each step of the process. Easy-to-follow exercises will help the readers to test themselves and determine their own goals.

The traditional concepts of career decision-making, such as self-assessment, researching career options, and job hunting, are adapted to the special needs of creative people. But many of the chapters, such as "Employment versus Self-Employment" and "Understanding the World of Work," will be appropriate for many job seekers. The detailed creative suggestions on preparing for and going after the job you want (in Section III) will benefit all job hunters.

Ronda Ormont was a longtime member of the Career Development Specialist Network. As a participant in our programs she both received and gave support and encouragement. Her enthusiasms and insights enriched our meetings. Her untimely death grieves all who knew her. She will be missed as a professional devoted to her field of work and as a friend to all her colleagues. This book will be a monument to her memory.

Carol Feit Lane, Ph.D.
President, Career Development Specialists Network
New York, NY
November 2000

Introduction

How To Use This Book

In order that people may be happy in their work, these three things are needed: They must be fit for it; they must not do too much of it; and they must have a sense of success in it—not a doubtful sense, such as needs some testimony of others for its confirmation, but a sure sense, or rather knowledge, that so much work has been done well, and fruitfully done, whatever the world may say or think about it.

—W.H. Auden

As a creative or performing artist today, you can find scores of books written to help you identify the sources of your creativity, hone your gifts, and improve your skills in the artistic discipline you've chosen. Many of these books are wonderful. Some are even listed in the Resources section at the end of this volume. Yet in the course of over a decade of providing career-related counseling to thousands of creative people, I have become convinced that the biggest problem facing artists is actually *not* a creative one.

Instead, it's a practical dilemma. Specifically, *how can creative people find the time and freedom necessary to pursue their art, while also making a sufficiently stable and rewarding living?*

All too often, they can't.

This is a problem that faces thousands of gifted people throughout this country (and, indeed, the world). *It is perhaps the single most common reason that creative people fail to flourish or succeed.* Yet no books specifically address this dilemma.

This book has been written to fill that gap.

I am a career counselor with a Ph.D. in counseling psychology and over twenty years of experience in working with diverse groups of individuals, including students, executives, individuals in midcareer transition, and senior citizens. In 1986, I cofounded the Actors' Work Program (now a division of The Actors' Fund of America), an employment and training program for entertainment industry professionals such as actors, singers, dancers, musicians, set and costume designers, directors, and writers. As Director of Training and Counseling Services there, I have personally interviewed over 5,000 such artists and developed a broad range of career-related counseling services to meet their diverse needs. My frequent lecture and speaking engagements across the country, as well as the articles I publish in professional and trade journals, all build on this hands-on experience. Even more importantly, so does this book.

It is not my aim to fix what isn't broken. This book takes for granted that you, the reader, are already highly creative. I do not consciously try to make you more so—although you'll find that the kind of balance and security I help you to achieve may well enhance imagination and creativity as a side effect. Instead, this book is designed to help you, the creative individual, to understand how important it is to balance your creative and career commitments and then to help you find the type of balance that works for your needs and your life.

I have filled the book with a wealth of hands-on exercises, tips, and facts. I have also filled it with people. I have changed names and combined or altered some basic facts to respect their privacy. Though the details have been changed, the basic situations are all true. They show you how other creative people have struggled with unequal investments in their creativity and their practical lives. They show you how those imbalances have been resolved. Most of all, they show you that you are not alone.

I hope that these stories will demonstrate the rich range of possibilities available to creative people, inspire you to new and effective action, and—most importantly of all—prove to you that you can have a satisfying, fulfilling life as *both* a creative artist and a citizen of the practical, everyday world.

This book is designed to speak to creative people struggling with two common life dilemmas: the "starving artist" who's tired of panicking every time the rent is due, and the well-compensated professional pining for some time to devote to his or her art. Whichever group you are in, you should read the text and complete the exercises in Sections I and II. Section III is designed for those who choose to seek a better life balance through salaried employment, while Section IV focuses on self-employment and freelance strategies.

The process of readjusting the creative and practical balance of your life is a unique, challenging, and exciting journey. As you begin the process of reassessment and exploration described in the pages that follow, you may wish to keep a journal that records your responses to your new insights and experiences. It need not be formal or detailed. It need not even be written—one printmaker I know journals by doing an "autobiographical drawing" each day. You'll certainly want to keep one or more new career files to hold the new information you'll accumulate. Finally, you should hold on to all of the exercises and checklists you complete. Put them in your journal or career files. Together, they create a detailed professional picture of yourself at the time you complete them. Having them may come in handy, either during your current transition or at some later point when your career needs shift again.

And shift they will, most likely. Though my focus in this book is to guide you through a single type of career transition—into a newly balanced artistic and practical existence—the truth is that the delicate balance between your creative commitment and what I'll be calling your life-line career will probably still need smaller adjustments over time. I believe you'll find that reviewing relevant chapters, or simply rereading some of the creative life stories I've related, will provide both assistance and reassurance during all of those transitions as well.

Section I:

Finding—and Creating— a Better Creative/Career Balance

Chapter One

Are Your Creative and Career Commitments in Balance?

If you have built castles in the air your work need not be lost; that is where they should be. Now put foundations under them.
—Henry David Thoreau

When God wishes to destroy, He first makes you successful in show business.
—Francis Ford Coppola

To regret deeply is to live afresh.
—Henry David Thoreau

Creative people are, by their nature, highly distinctive. Each and every one of the clients I have worked with over the years has had his or her own unique and memorable gifts, needs, and interests. Yet their situations also reflect shared problems and dilemmas. *In fact, virtually all of the artistic clients I have counseled on career issues first saw me in response to one of only two basic problems.* I see these two types of situations so often I have come to think of them as archetypal patterns for artists (or those who desire to be artists) in our culture.

The stories below are composites that bring together the most typical features of each of these two situations. Read them and see if either sounds familiar to you. You may be a composer or poet rather than an actor, a lawyer or salesperson rather than an accountant. You may have less or more financial need, fewer or more family commitments, than David or Shelley. But if you have picked up this book, I suspect you'll see aspects of your own situation in either one or the other of their stories.

Ever since he saw his first play in grade school, David has had a passion for the theater. He'll turn his hand to almost any kind of work, from scenery painting to ushering, that lets him be around a play in progress, but his special gift is for acting. Recognizing this need from the start, David has never taken a restrictive nine-to-five job. Instead, he's worked as a waiter at a series of restaurants, leaving each job when he lands a new part. In the beginning, this life seemed fun and adventurous, and dreams of becoming a star kept him going. But recently, if he's honest with himself, he'll admit that the constant difficulty of making ends meet and working at a menial and unchallenging job is actually draining energy from his acting. Usually happy, he suddenly finds himself feeling bitter about the difficulties of auditioning, envious when a friend is chosen for a role, and resentful about being broke all the time. At thirty, he's started to worry about how he'll support the kids he wants to have, what will happen when he doesn't have sufficient funds to retire on (being a struggling actor doesn't yield pension benefits), and how he'd take care of himself if he got sick (being a struggling actor doesn't offer paid sick leave or medical insurance, either). The struggle makes him feel exhausted. Often, he's tempted to just give up. He secretly feels that it would actually be a relief to happen upon some other, more predictable kind of work. But he's not sure what that work would be or whether he has any talent at all outside the performing arts. He also feels as though searching out a better second career is admitting failure, something he's still reluctant to do.

•

Like David, Shelley had an artistic dream: she always wanted to be a writer. She published poems and stories in her college magazine and excelled in the many literature and writing classes she took. When she graduated, though, Shelley reluctantly gave in to her parents' admonitions that being a writer was "no kind of life." Immigrants who had struggled to make a living themselves, they urged Shelley toward a lucrative white-collar field and showed that they were ready to help fund her professional education. How could she turn them down for a talent she might not even truly possess?

Putting her writing on the back burner, Shelley took advanced courses in accounting and then passed the C.P.A. exam. She now works for a prestigious tax firm. It's exactly the kind of career her parents wanted for her: predictable, lucrative, respectable. She enjoys the security her career gives her and the stable lifestyle it helps her family to enjoy. Yet it all feels flat—like something is missing. She is frustrated and, truth to tell, bored with the work that consumes much of her life. That missing something, she knows, is her writing. Instinct tells her that if she's ever going to be a real writer, it's now or never. Just taking a course or writing a short story here and there—all that her busy professional and personal life has let her do—no longer feels like enough. Yet with her gift for financial analysis, she knows that quitting her job just isn't a practical option. Instead, she keeps working, getting more and more disheartened.

The Problem: Lack of Balance

The life situations of David and Shelley seem to be diametrically opposed. Yet different as they may seem, they are actually two sides of the exact same coin. At their core, they both represent the same problem: *an imbalance between the creative imperative and the need for career security in everyday living.*

For David, the imbalance reflects too much weight placed on *creativity.* Ironically, it's his willingness to sacrifice for his gift that is now draining him of creative fuel. If he had a dependable source of income, he wouldn't have to spend so much of his time and energy just struggling to survive. He'd also have more confidence, knowing that he had a marketable skill other than his acting to fall back on. In order to fill up his creative "gas tank" again, David must *balance his creative commitment with what I call a "lifeline career"*—a career that would anchor him in the turbulent sea that is the world of the arts by providing him with practical necessities such as food, shelter, money in the bank, security, a stable schedule, and—ideally—benefits and a retirement plan.

For Shelley, on the other hand, the scales tip too heavily in favor of *career and financial security.* She is so intent on being responsible in the work and financial arenas that her gift is withering away, like a tender seedling that's not strong enough to push through concrete. She has focused on external needs so strongly that her artistic inner self feels lost and valueless. In order to give her writer's gifts room to grow, she must find a way to *balance her lifeline career with a deeper and more focused creative commitment.*

The Value of Life Balance

Balance is a key element in many philosophies, religions, and world views. The two great twentieth-century Western thinkers on human personality, Freud and Jung, both expressed the importance of balancing competing or opposing elements in the psyche. Current self-help and psychology writers also work extensively with the concept of balance. Dr. Stan Katz's book *The Success Trap*, for example, demonstrates convincingly that true success—which involves inner satisfaction, not just outward acknowledgment—is closely correlated with a balanced lifestyle. Truly successful individuals, he asserts, understand the importance family, friends, avocation, and service hold in life, rather than focusing solely on work or relying only on status and money as indicators of achievement. According to Katz, an integrated lifestyle will always be more gratifying than one in which there is an obsessive focus on work of any kind.

Balanced people—people who honor their emotional, spiritual, creative, *and* financial lives—are the ones we know of as "well rounded." They have many areas of interest from which to draw success; because they are reliant on no single identity or activity to validate them, they are less vulnerable than others to feelings of unworthiness or despair. For the same reason, they are able to understand criticism or rejection as specific to a given area of their life and not as a generalized personal failure.

Balanced people are able to see setbacks as a natural part of growth; be generous and genuine in their support of others, rather than competing with them; enjoy a general sense of confidence and optimism; understand frustration or anger merely as signals that something needs changing rather than as signs of unworthiness; enlist the help of others to achieve their goals; and avoid feeling totally devastated when they fail at something.

I suspect you can already see why these qualities of balanced people might be helpful to you as you make your way through the unpredictable and often difficult world of the arts (a world I'll be discussing in more detail later). What you may be less aware of is how necessary these same qualities—confidence, adaptability, optimism, resourcefulness—will be in the turbulent workplace of the twenty-first century. In other words, a good balance between the creative and financial needs in your life is essential in your art, your income-producing professional work, and your personal life as well.

But if balance is such a familiar concept—and it certainly does seem like an obvious and logical goal—why is *imbalance* so prevalent in the lives of creative people? Why do smart, disciplined, hard-working folks like David and Shelley so easily find themselves polarized at one end of the spectrum or the other?

Life in the Arts: The Harsh Realities

In our culture, imbalances like David's and Shelley's are not just common but almost inevitable. *Virtually every artist faces these types of balance issues or some variation of them.* The reason is that the creative and performing arts are fraught with enormous instability, far more than that which faces professionals in other fields. Consider the following facts—the four fundamental realities of life in the arts.

- **Reality #1: Competition is fierce.** It's been estimated that almost 50 percent of Americans want to write a book. Perhaps 10 percent of those actually complete a manuscript. The average large publisher actually accepts at most 10 percent of those finished submissions, often significantly less. Only a tiny percentage of those books go on to become financially successful. The odds are similarly stacked against the creator in the visual arts, theater, film, and music. Only 1.5 percent of the U.S. labor force is actually *employed* in artistic work. In other words, far fewer individuals "make it" in terms of either recognition or financial success in the arts than in most other fields.

- **Reality #2: Salaries are low,** *especially relative to fields that demand similarly high levels of expertise and talent.* A writer I know sold her first book to a major publisher—a tremendous and exciting success. But when she divided her total book payment by the number of hours (years, really!) she had taken to write the manuscript, she confided that she had earned far less per hour than the minimum wage. This is the rule, rather than the exception, in the arts. For every one artist who makes it big, there are ten more who just manage to make a living and hundreds more who struggle with no financial reward at all.

- **Reality #3: Objective standards for evaluating artistic competence don't exist.** A lawyer's excellence can be measured by objective standards at every point in her career: first by her grades in law school, then by how quickly she passes the bar, still later by how successful she is in winning at trial. Thanks to these kinds of measurements, there is a clear correlation between excellence and success in most fields; the better you perform, the better you'll do. In the arts, no such quantitative measures exist. Works by Rembrandt and Mark Rothko couldn't be more different in look or style, but both men are considered great artists. A play wins high praise from one magazine and withering scorn from the next. A film is roundly panned by critics, but becomes a popular success. A sculptor sells few sculptures during her lifetime, but becomes a huge phenomenon ten years after her death, when popular culture has changed in a way that facilitates a new understanding of her vision. Not excellence but trends, changing social concerns, personal and popular taste—that is, forces over which an artist has absolutely no control—define peer and public responses to any work. In other words, in the arts, excellence may or may not be rewarded. Thus, working in the arts can involve not only fierce competition and low salaries, but also a bewildering lack of positive results and feedback.

- **Reality #4: Success is difficult to sustain.** Even top artists in a field—the Oscar, Obie, and Pulitzer Prize winners, the bestsellers, the pianists who make it to Carnegie Hall, the painters who earn hundreds of thousands per painting—are frequently unable to utilize high praise and recognition to *sustain* success. Each time a show closes, a movie wraps, or a book draft is completed, they must start afresh again; being "on top" one moment never protects them from hitting the depths the next. If anything, great success can increase the pressure and "up the ante" on future work. At times, the roller-coaster quality of this existence can feel exhilarating; more often it is exhausting and anxiety producing.

The impact of these realities on the lives of creative people is profound and far-reaching. A person who aspires to be, say, a veterinarian need only train for and work at one field. In contrast, almost all artists must make room in their lives for *both* their creative commitment *and* a career that will provide or at least supplement their income. Even in the rare cases that an artist could just concentrate on expressing his or her vision—thanks to a spouse with a stable job, inherited wealth, a lottery win—it may be an unwise choice, thanks to Realities #3 and #4. To put 100 percent of your energy and effort into a field where your excellence may not be consistently recognized is to court anxiety, insecurity, and even despair. It is wiser, not just for the wallet but for the soul, to have another field of effort as well—a field where your capabilities will more surely gain you praise, advancement, and other tangible rewards.

Meeting the Challenge, Finding the Balance

For your artistic gift to flourish, I believe that you must face the afore-mentioned realities squarely and take responsibility for meeting the challenge they create. You must make the time and freedom you need to express your artistic vision—a vision which may or may not ever pay off in significant dollars and cents—and, *at the same time*, commit to a practical path that will keep a roof over your head, food on your table, some savings in the bank, and some semblance of sanity in your life! *In other words, you must find ways to balance your creative commitment with a lifeline career.*

Before I go on, let me emphasize that the terms "creative commitment" and "lifeline career"—terms you'll hear me use again and again in this book—can (and should) mean different things to different people. Each artist must define them for himself or herself.

For you, a creative commitment may mean making an hour a day to work on your screenplay; for someone else, it may mean keeping her entire schedule flexible to allow for auditions.

For you, a lifetime career may mean a private practice tutoring or word processing—in other words, a job that is not hugely ambitious or lucrative, but which serves your basic needs. For someone else, it may mean a highly demanding and well-compensated position as a lawyer—a concept I describe more thoroughly below.

How you define "creative commitment" and "lifeline career," then, will differ for every individual. What matters is not how you define them but how well you learn to *balance* these parts of your life—how effectively you are able to nurture *both* your artistic vision and your practical needs. Here again, finding a comfortable balance is a very personal matter. Some artists thrive when they live at least a little on the edge; some flourish only when their lives are extremely secure. Again, what's important is finding the particular balance that feels right for you.

This balance needs thought and care to achieve. But it's not impossible. Consider the ends of David's and Shelley's stories.

> *David came to my office at the recommendation of an actor friend, as a last effort to make his acting work. As I do with all my clients, I helped David assess his own personal strengths and interests and evaluate how they matched up to potential opportunities within the world of work. David came to see that the same talents that fed his acting—above-average intelligence, a fascination for world culture, a flair for language, empathy for human problems and struggles—could also make him marketable in the workplace.*

Among the many job paths he might have chosen, becoming a teacher of English as a Second Language (ESL) appealed to him most. He now works for a large tutoring organization. "My students are incredibly diverse—I'm never bored. And my company is used to employees who juggle their work with other pursuits, so they're willing to work with me when an acting job affects my schedule. I'm sure not affluent and probably never will be, but I can pay my bills on time these days, and I'm even building a savings account. Actually, though, the most incredible benefit is creative, not financial. Now that I don't have all of my eggs in the acting 'basket,' I'm more successful as an actor than I've ever been before! I know that I have work I really like doing whether or not I get a certain part, so I'm much more relaxed about the whole process. I'm convinced my confidence comes across."

•

As we worked together, Shelley began to realize that her options weren't as limited as they seemed. I encouraged her to avoid black-and-white, all-or-nothing thinking and to use her analytical skills to explore a middle ground. How much money did her family really need from her job? About how many hours a week would that take? What about working part-time or opening her own business in order to get more flexible hours? As Shelley examined the possibilities with a more open mind, she discovered to her surprise that she could work as little as twenty hours a week and still bring in sufficient income to keep her family's lifestyle stable. Armed with that knowledge and her skill with numbers, she created a detailed proposal that showed her firm the benefits of allowing her to transition to a part-time position. Today, she works twenty hours a week except during the crunch of tax time; the remainder of the "work week" is free to use for writing. Eventually, she hopes to shift her work still more away from straight accountancy, possibly setting up her own small business to help creative people do business planning! Meanwhile, "I'm a quarter of the way through the first draft of my novel already," she says. "Sometimes it's hard to tear myself away from the book in order to handle my work, but that small struggle is nothing compared to what I've gained. I'm at peace for the first time in almost fifteen years. Even my kids have noticed how much less 'mad' Mommy is. Maybe my book will never even get published, though I'm hopeful. What I do know for sure is that I feel so much better about myself now that I'm at least giving it a try."

Striking a Better Balance: Your Action Plan

I think you'll agree that both David and Shelley are dramatically better off these days—in real-life terms, *and* as artists. This improvement does not depend on pie-in-the-sky, fairy-tale happy endings. These are results that any creative person can achieve. They do not take incredible brilliance, incredible luck, or incredible will. They only require you to take five achievable steps.

1. You must understand how important it is to balance your creative and career commitments and how to identify the signs that this balance is not working in your life. I hope this chapter will inspire new thoughts about both of these issues.

2. You must reassess yourself; explore the reasons your creative and practical lives are out of balance, the barriers that make you reluctant to change, and the assets (skills, values, interests, experience) you have to work with.

3. You must explore the world of work to find a new field and/or work structure that can remedy the imbalance in your life and bring your creative pursuit and a lifeline career into a new and more equal proportion. The field could be a wholly new one, or one related to business skills you have already used in your work. The structure will be flexible and could be a full-time job for some, a part-time job for others, and a small-business or freelance arrangement for still others.

4. You must obtain the type of work you want in the new field and structure you choose. Whether you end up working for a single employer or for many freelance clients, you need to expand your network of contacts, develop a powerful resume and "commercial" (a term I'll explain later), and understand how to use the interview and marketing processes effectively to sell yourself or your small business.

5. Finally, as you make your way through each step of this process, you must always envision your creative/financial balance as a means of *thriving,* not surviving.

Thriving, Not Surviving: The Lifeline Philosophy

Thriving means that you have a win/win arrangement in your life. You are no longer afflicted by a survival mentality. You no longer believe that you must sacrifice either your art or your financial stability to make your life work. You expect to be nurtured by your income-producing work *and* by your artistic work, and you take the steps necessary to make that expectation reality.

As an artist, I'm certain that you know instinctively what it means to be nurtured by your creative work. That's why I have spent little time on that specific issue in this book. Given the time and freedom to do so, you will know how to structure your creative life!

But whether you're like David or like Shelley—that is, whether you have invested too little or too much effort into creating financial stability—you may *not* know what it means to be nurtured, as a creative person, by your income-producing work. This is where the concept of lifeline work comes in—work that is *neither* a pure "survival" job like David's nor a driven career like Shelley's.

A Survival Job...	Lifeline Work...	A Driven Career...
• Is a fairly or completely stagnant position. A waiter does not typically evolve into a restauranteur over time, nor a temp into an executive.	• Allows you to shape it in such a way that it evolves, changes, and grows over time, giving you opportunities to take on more responsibility, make more money, etc.	• Virtually demands increasing success, promotion, or sales; exists in a "publish or perish," "move forward or die," "make partner or get fired" atmosphere.
• Provides little challenge to your skills and talents.	• Stretches your potential.	• Overwhelms your potential, leaving little energy for pursuits outside the job.
• Has a short learning curve.	• Has a moderate to long learning curve.	• Has a moderate to long learning curve.
• Feels meaningless and adds little value to your life or the world.	• Relates to your values and fulfills a need, for yourself and others.	• Takes all of your energy and potential without adding meaning to your life.
• Represents a non-choice based on the assumption that it is the best that you can do without jeopardizing your creative goals.	• Represents a conscious choice, made after reflection and deliberation, about what is right for you as a whole person.	• Often reflects a choice based on appearances ("keeping up with the Joneses") or on gaining the approval of others, i.e., parents.

A Survival Job...	Lifeline Work...	A Driven Career...
• Assumes you have to sacrifice financial security for your art.	• Assumes that with careful thought and hard work you can achieve both artistic goals and financial stability.	• Assumes you have to sacrifice your artistic self for financial security.
• Exists merely to pay the bills.	• Pays the bills, but also offers satisfaction.	• Enables a comfortable or even opulent lifestyle, but feels empty.

In practice, lifeline work most often reflects one of three options:

- A salaried position in a field not related to your art but with sufficient flexibility to allow you a satisfying level of time and energy for your creative pursuits

- A teaching position in your area of artistic expertise

- Self-employment in the form of freelancing or a small business that may or may not be related to your art but which is, again, flexible enough to accommodate it

As all of this implies, a lifeline career does involve some sacrifice. It may not offer either maximum income or maximum time for creativity. But to the extent that it does involve elements of sacrifice, it does so in a balanced way. It is a compromise that allows all sides of you to flourish. It gives you both a stable financial foundation for your life *and* room for your artistic needs and goals, as the following playful exercise may help to remind you.

The Lifeline Exercise

1. Draw a line across a piece of paper. The beginning represents your birth; the end represents death. Mark an *x* at the point approximately reflecting your current age.

2. From birth to your current age, the line you've drawn represents your life, including good and bad times alike. Take a moment to mark along the line the places some of those experiences occurred. Note items that celebrate your accomplishments and successes and mourn losses as well.

---

3. From the *x* to the end of the line is the life you have left to live. Between these two points, draw a house. Be as creative as you can be, even if your skills in the visual arts are minimal!

4. Your house holds your dreams, goals, desires, and longings. How do you want to live from now on? What do you want to contribute? What has been missing from your life thus far that you would like to include in your life house? What new kinds of balance can you envision, even if the picture is vague? Note them all in and around your house.

5. The line underneath the house is your lifeline, your foundation. It is the stable ground that enables you to live out your dreams. You can't have a satisfying life unless you build both your lifeline and your dream house!

The Payoffs of a Good Creative and Career Balance

If you follow the steps in this book and create a better life balance, I can promise you that the results will be transformative.

- **You will become more confident**—because you will have proven that you can function well in both the artistic and everyday worlds. You will feel better, and your confidence may even improve your success in all areas of your life. In the words of Ellyn, a dancer, "Having steady work as a personal fitness trainer has made a big difference. I no longer seem desperate at auditions. As soon as that changed, people began to perceive me differently. In fact, my dancing roles have increased, not decreased, since I built a lifeline career."

- **You will experience more pride in yourself.** None of us enjoy merely surviving, whether that survival involves financial strain or, conversely, a life that makes us money but does not fit our values. When we spend our lives doing work that is either too menial or too divorced from our creative passions, our self-esteem invariably suffers. As Mario, an actor, put it, "I was at a point where I just couldn't wait on tables anymore. I was always angry at myself and almost contemptuous of the people I served. I wasn't able to shed those feelings until I 'took the high road' and began to use my skills and assets in a more beneficial way, to add sources of meaning and reward other than acting to my life. Now I feel a sense of pride in my own choices again."

- **You will feel more relaxed, yet infinitely more in control.** Ann, an office executive who is now on her way to her first photography exhibition, commented to me, "I had always imagined that spending more time with my camera would jeopardize my paying job. I kept on working doggedly, but inside I was seething that I "couldn't" pursue my artistic goals. In truth, I just wasn't looking for better solutions. Six months ago, I used your suggestions to propose a new part-time arrangement to my boss. He agreed immediately, commenting that he'd much rather have me stay on in a limited role than quit entirely. Finally, I'm feeling in charge of my life and choices again."

- **You will feel more free to take artistic risks,** now that you will have a strong lifeline career to fall back on. When a play closes, an exhibition ends, or a film wraps, you will always have other challenges waiting in the wings. Your identity is not wrapped up in every artistic success or failure. Conversely, you'll feel more at peace with the inevitable elements of routine in your lifeline career, since you'll always have the excitement of creative production to balance it.

- **You will feel more whole** once the artistic and career sides of your life mesh with, rather than compete against, one another.

- **You will find yourself better able to live in the present.** You won't be forever worrying about some future day when your financial house of cards will topple; you won't be forever dreaming of some future life that will allow you time for creativity. Your life will satisfy you *now*.

- **Your art may well become more powerful.** Once you're not drained by an unfulfilling job or a precarious existence, you'll free up energy for your gift.

As you can see, these changes are not just financial or practical but also spiritual and creative. In other words, this is a journey that will enhance every aspect of your life. I'm glad you are taking it with me. It's time to begin!

The Warning Signs of Creative/Career Imbalance

If you are reading this book, you probably have at least an intuitive sense that your creative commitment and your lifeline career are not in balance. After reading David's or Shelley's story, that hunch may have intensified.

Still, it's difficult to solve a problem until you've pinned it down quite clearly.

The checklist below allows you to evaluate the balance between the creative and financial/practical sides of your own life. Simply check any statements that apply. Answer with an honest response, not the one that seems most acceptable, comfortable, or admirable!

The Balance Inventory

____1. I feel fit and healthy.

____2. I feel that I have not spent enough time developing my creative potential.

____3. I may get angry or disappointed when I am rejected, but in some way these expectations motivate me to prove myself the next time.

____4. I feel that I am making as much progress as I need to in my art.

____5. I have many family members, friends, and professional contacts that I can count on for advice.

____6. I'm waiting for the day I can do what I want to do.

____7. I feel confident about who I am and where I'm going.

____8. I always said I'd be able to excel in my art once I proved myself at a "real" job, but I'm still immersed in that job rather than in my creative work even though I have succeeded.

____9. I'm a good friend to others. I tend not to be jealous, but rather supportive and generous with praise.

____10. If I'm truly honest with myself, I have to admit that I feel as though I've been waiting for my "big break" in my art for a very long time.

____11. I make time for outside hobbies and interests.

____12. I would describe myself, and others would describe me, as a driven person.

____13. I would have to say that at this point in my life, I'm not satisfied with my accomplishments.

____14. I organize my life around a strong sense of purpose. I am more a "doer" than a dreamer.

____15. I don't plan regular vacations, or if I do, I can't relax and enjoy myself.

____16. Before I take action, I think of several alternatives and the ramifications of each.

____17. I tend to be a loner and don't have many close friends.

____18. I know myself well: my strengths, weaknesses, needs, feelings, and tendencies.

____19. When I am rejected or criticized, I tend to blame others or "the system" to protect myself from hurt feelings.

____20. I consider myself a person who can achieve anything I set out to
do.

____21. I am often in debt or close to it.

____22. I am optimistic, despite occasional setbacks.

____23. I tend to make up my mind very quickly and jump into things I'm
excited about.

____24. I seem to bounce back from adversity. I'm not overly depressed for
long periods of time.

Score questions 1 through 12 at one point for every odd number checked. Score questions 13 through 24 at one point for every even number checked. A score under 3 indicates substantial life imbalance; a score from 4 to 6 indicates moderate imbalance. Scores from 7 to 9 reflect a moderate level of balance; a score above 10 suggests that your life is in healthy balance between creative and career commitments.

If your score indicates any level of imbalance, the following chapter will help you understand why it exists and how to begin the process of change.

A Word of Reassurance

You may think that changing the balance between your creative work and lifeline career will be a lot of hard work. Indeed, striking a new balance will require courage, flexibility, a willingness to consider new options, and a commitment of time and energy.

Yet as an artistic person, you also have significant advantages as you make this new transition. You are, by definition, creative—a person who is able to investigate, explore, and initiate new things. You are likely to be imaginative and good at assimilating new information. You may well be multitalented. For all these reasons, your potential for reaching a new and more satisfying balance in your life is high. You need only be willing to break through the barriers to change so that you can explore the *full* range of your abilities . . . possibly for the very first time.

Chapter Two

Overcoming the Barriers to Change

For all the sad words
of tongue and pen
The saddest are these:
It might have been!

—John Greenleaf Whittier

Art is a jealous mistress.

—Ralph Waldo Emerson

If I repeat "My will be done" with the necessary degree of faith
and persistency, the chances are that sooner or later and somehow
or other, I shall get what I want.

—Aldous Huxley

By now, you will probably have a clearer sense of the creative/practical imbalance that affects your own life. In subsequent chapters, I'll guide you through the actual, real-world steps necessary to correct that particular type of imbalance. Before we begin the *tangible* part of that process, however, it's important to acknowledge the *intangible* roadblocks that may be standing in our way.

The problem, of course, is not that you experience a *temporary* imbalance between your career and creative needs. There are times in every person's life when such short-term imbalances arise. An actor might put her freelance image-consulting practice on hold for six months while touring in a play, for example. Conversely, a novelist in between books might focus almost exclusively on her well-paying editing business for a few months until an idea for a new novel takes hold. As these examples suggest, conscious choices to privilege one aspect of your life over another for a specific period of time can be both healthy and productive.

Instead, the trouble in most creative individuals' lives arises when imbalances become *long-term*—extending over years or even decades—or *unconscious*—arising from blocks or mistaken assumptions rather than from a free range of thoughtful choices. When long-term, unconsciously motivated imbalances grip you, you find that you're essentially paralyzed—totally "stuck." You can't make even achievable changes. In fact, you can't even envision the possibility of any other status quo. This is the situation that both David and Shelley were in at the start of their stories in chapter 1.

Getting, Staying, and Living "Stuck"

In his book *Getting Unstuck*, Sidney Simon summarizes this frustrating experience with great insight. Applying his analysis to the out-of-balance life situations of creative people, one might describe the experience of being stuck as follows:

1. **Being stuck is setting goals and making plans but always putting off the first step until next week, next year, or some time when conditions will be better.** Many creative people find themselves in this scenario. The reason? Procrastination protects you from fear. Dreams and plans can't be measured and evaluated. They have no competition, face no obstacles, and are always successful! If you never act, you can't be judged a failure.

2. **Being stuck is allowing fear, disappointment, rejection, or loss to keep you from taking the risks you'd really like to take.** This behavior, also very common in creative people (who tend to be sensitive and perfectionistic by nature), rests on the assumption that failures and mistakes reflect your own lack of personal worth, rather than on the more correct belief that errors, disappointments, problems, false starts, and all sorts of "bumps in the road" are inevitable parts of art and life. In contrast, those who move ahead into new endeavors confidently without allowing themselves to get stuck tend to see setbacks as signs of growth and ambition, rather than of failure.

3. **Being stuck is allowing fear *of success* to hold you back from making a full effort or holding a high ambition.** You get a great audition opportunity . . . but you somehow don't get enough sleep the night before to be fresh, energetic, or rested. A peer gives you a great contact in a regional dance company . . . but you somehow don't find the time to follow through. Fear of success manifests itself at times when things are going well. And, illogical as it may seem, as many people secretly fear success as those who fear failure. Indeed, it can be uncomfortable to feel that you have surpassed your parents, spouse, friends, or peers, to make a claim that you and your creative work are valuable, to become a "star." To avoid that discomfort, you may find that you stay stuck by limiting or sabotaging yourself, often subconsciously.

4. **Being stuck is feeling that you cannot take a new direction because you've committed so much to your previous one.** This is the same thinking a gambler is trapped into when he or she is losing. Somehow, that next roll of the dice must redeem all of the previous losses! Sadly, this strategy doesn't work any better in life than it does in gambling. Past a certain point, sticking to a path that isn't working for you is unlikely to improve your life. In fact, no level or length of investment is a valid reason not to take the steps necessary to remove yourself from counterproductive circumstances.

5. **Being stuck is prioritizing others' opinions of your change above your own inner beliefs or needs.** If you value the opinions or judgments of other people over your own needs or hopes, you're actually demonstrating a lack of trust in them, as well as in yourself. You're assuming that they will judge or criticize you, rather than support or encourage your growth. Certainly, those around you may become uncomfortable when you change. Yet many of them (in fact, all of them who are truly worth your time and energy!) may ultimately support and help you.

6. **Being stuck is not seeing your options.** It's not that you don't act on other alternatives . . . it's that you genuinely don't see them. All choices but the one you've made seem impossibly flawed, inappropriate, or unacceptable. This kind of tunnel vision tends to become stronger over time, as you unintentionally reinforce it with each new life choice. Joseph, for example, was a lawyer who had always yearned to develop his acting skills but chose not to do so in favor of a more practical career. Over the years, the idea of acting seemed more and more

impossible and unlikely. Not surprising, considering that Joseph's intense focus on his legal career exposed him almost exclusively to lawyers and other white-collar professionals like himself, rather than to more diverse role models. Luckily for him, a client chanced to invite him to a theater-company benefit one evening. For the first time in years, Joseph met individuals who combined careers and creativity, often in very imaginative ways. Some worked good jobs but were committed volunteers. Some used their vacations doing summer stock. One joined business and creativity by acting as administrative director for the theater company. "I realized how narrow my vision of my options had become that night," Joseph says. "Suddenly I recognized that there were many different ways to bring my love of acting back into my life, involving many different levels of investment, intensity, and commitment. I'd simply closed my eyes to them."

7. **Being stuck is secretly or not so secretly believing that you're not smart enough, talented enough, practical enough to "have it all."** Like most manifestations of being stuck, this one is an issue of self-esteem. Rather than visualizing a win/win situation in which you can succeed both creatively and in a lifeline career, you believe that you just don't have what it takes to accomplish one or the other.

8. **Finally, being stuck is coming up with endless, perfectly good reasons not to change.** Change almost always feels threatening, since it brings you into unknown territory. Rather than face it, you may find that you're secretly looking for reasons *not* to change! In truth, though none of your options may be perfect or risk free, some will be good enough to create a positive change.

Are *You* Stuck?

Do you recognize any of those feelings or beliefs in yourself? If you're not sure, try answering the questions below, which may help you personalize the experience of feeling stuck in a career/creative balance that is less than satisfying.

"Am I Stuck?" Checklist

____I'm afraid to admit that my career has fallen short of my expectations.

____I'm afraid that if I change directions, I'll be letting my family down.

____In truth, I believe my current work is all that I can do.

____I suspect I could probably use some of my talents in another field, but I don't even know what my alternatives are.

____I sometimes feel that my best artistic days are behind me—that I've reached a dead end and have developed creatively as far as I can.

____I tend to get overwhelmed or sidetracked before I can begin to take effective steps to change my situation.

____I'd secretly be relieved if I were suddenly offered meaningful work in another field.

____I'd like to change my situation, but I'm afraid of what others will think.

____Basically, I'm afraid to try something new at this point.

____I tend to feel that exploring other fields, pursuits, or careers would mean that I'm a failure in what I'm doing now.

These questions provide a good litmus test. If you answer yes to even one, you're probably stuck in some kind of career/creative imbalance. If you answer yes to more than one, you may be severely stuck.

A New Readiness for Change: Turning Points

The experience of being stuck in a career/creative imbalance is an uncomfortable one. But even if you're not sure yet how to correct it, the fact that you're reading this book probably means that you're ready for a change—ready to open up new possibilities for either greater career stability or greater creative expression in your life. (I refer to the moment when a creative person begins to be ready for a better life balance as a turning point.) Over the years that I've worked with clients, I've learned that such turning points typically occur during one of six different moments in an individual's life.

The "Is This All There Is?" Turning Point

Like the "nonturning-point turning point" described below, this is a subtle change that builds over time. It becomes evident when you find yourself feeling that your life is without true meaning—somehow flat. Out of this sense of emptiness, a new motivation to take the risk of change arises.

"I found myself haunted by the feeling that I was wasting my life. Or maybe that I wasn't even living my own true life at all," says Jacques, a doctor who had demonstrated exceptional talent in the visual arts as a child and young man. "The funny thing is that, to the people around me,

I looked like a hero. After all, I made people well. But the longer I worked in medicine, the *less* unique or significant it felt to me. At the time I started feeling this, I hadn't spent time on my painting in years. Still, I realize that art was what was missing. I knew then that I had to make some changes and let some of my own creativity back into my life."

For Melissa, a poet, the question "Is this all there is?" arose at a moment of artistic success. "I won three awards in one year, and one of them was really a prestigious one," she explains. "I thought it would be thrilling. Instead, though I'm grateful to have been recognized, my private reaction was to ask myself, 'So what?' I still didn't have health insurance, a retirement plan, a car, a nice apartment, or enough money to travel the way I dreamed of doing. I still had to struggle through each day as a temp, the career I'd chosen to make time for poetry. It was as though blinders had been taken off. I began researching other options and within six months was writing newsletters for two large businesses. The newsletter work was steadier and more lucrative and used very different writing skills—a really good balance for my poems."

The Rock-Bottom Turning Point

Laura, a fashion designer and stylist, admits that she habitually lacked focus and was highly scattered in her life and in her arts career. "Then, one day, I had to write a check to the utility company for which I knew I had no funds. A day or two later, I had to ask my parents for a handout to get me through the month's other bills. Coming so close together, these problems made me feel incredibly low and incompetent. I realized that my refusal to organize my life and plan in a thoughtful, careful way was having a negative impact not just on me but on those who loved me. It wasn't creativity; it was just chaos. I finally found myself really motivated to change." Now in the exploratory phase of her career research, Laura is finally ready to take control of her career and life planning.

The Mortality Turning Point

A first experience with true physical vulnerability makes many of us more willing to consider new options, address old problems, and adjust the balance of our lives. For Shimeika, a real-estate agent who had always dreamed of singing, this wake-up call took the form of a bout with cancer. Suddenly, she realized that the time to make her life more balanced was *now*. "The first thing I did once my treatment was completed was set up a meeting with a career counselor," she says. "It was clear that I needed to address aspects of my life other than financial security."

The Milestone Turning Point

Whether it's thirty, forty, fifty, or older, milestone years and birthdays are a loud wake-up call for many. "Turning forty was a real eye-opener," says Jerry, a professional bass player. "I guess I'd always seen myself as young, hip, loose. But suddenly, I couldn't think of myself as a kid anymore. I visualized myself at fifty or sixty and recognized how foolish and deluded I'd look if I didn't grow, expand my options. I realized that if I wanted a home and family, now was the time. I had to do something . . . anything! I'm exploring teaching and physical therapy programs, since both careers would give me enough freedom to keep playing on weekend nights. I plan to volunteer before making a final decision. I don't have any tangible results to show yet, but I feel much better having taken these small steps."

The same kind of chronological turning point can affect someone who's invested *too* heavily in a lifeline career. For Joseph, the lawyer introduced earlier in this chapter, the eye-opening experience of seeing new creative options came just weeks after his fiftieth birthday. "I was already excited by a new sense of possibility, but having this chronological milestone shortly thereafter really underscored the point. It told me that there was no time to waste."

The Nonturning-Point Turning Point

Sometimes it's what *doesn't* happen that sounds the alarm. *Not* starring on Broadway, *not* writing a bestseller, *not* getting representation by a major gallery, *not* becoming first violin for the Philharmonic can precipitate change just as surely as actual life happenings.

Career counselor Nancy Schlossberg, Ph.D., has aptly labeled such perceived lack of success as a "nonevent." In her view, though the realization that one has not reached original career goals is painful, the payoff can be dramatic. Once you accept and reinterpret all that you did accomplish, she says, the energy arising from what initially feels like disappointment can be transformed into a powerful action plan for the future.

"I had what you might call a major 'Aha!' moment one day as I looked at my resume," says Carol, a potter and ceramic artist. "I realized that in the course of almost twelve years of dedicating my whole life to my art, I just hadn't moved forward much in terms of visibility, price, prestige of the galleries that sell me, or any other kind of external recognition. It's hard to explain how I felt at that moment. It wasn't that I gave up on my ceramics. In fact, I dedicate just as much time to artwork as ever. I just accepted the fact that some great breakthrough to art superstardom might not be in the cards for me, even if I devoted another decade entirely to my art. It sounds depressing, but it didn't feel like that. In fact, I felt relieved and even excited. I was suddenly free to look for career recognition in other areas."

The "Been There, Done That" Turning Point

Over the years, behavior that previously felt comfortable and even enjoyable can begin to feel frustrating through sheer repetition and familiarity. Harvey, who has a good sales job, explains. "In the early years, sales was a real challenge. It was so different from the world of photography, which is where I always thought I'd be. It was exciting. But now I've met the challenges it has to offer, and frankly, I'm bored. I landed a big account the other day, and it just meant nothing. What *would* mean something, I realized, was taking pictures seriously again. I'm not yet sure whether I'm going to move out of sales entirely or whether I'll try to negotiate a more flexible schedule with my current employers. But I suddenly know that something has to change."

The Bad News . . . and the Good News

Turning points tend to be painful, or at least bittersweet. They involve a shedding of comfortable habits and assumptions and, as the stories above attest, often some difficult self-realizations as well. The good news is that out of these moments of discomfort comes a new power to change and grow. In each of the kinds of situations described above, creative individuals gained a sudden new awareness of dissatisfaction with some element of their creative/practical imbalance, along with a stronger motivation than before to make a change. Identifying with one or more of these situations is almost certainly a sign that you, too, are feeling the strain of a disproportionate relationship between your creativity and your lifeline work, *but are ready to begin changing.* You may *feel* stuck, but in truth you are ready to explore new possibilities in your life! It's time for the big question: How can you break through the barriers that got you stuck in the first place?

For the answer, turn back for a moment to chapter 1 and the early part of the stories of David and Shelley. As you can tell, they are intelligent people, each highly competent in his or her field and each quite perceptive. The unhappiness, imbalance, and sense of being stuck each felt when their story opened were not the result of stupidity, carelessness, or simple ignorance.

Instead, David and Shelley's difficulty keeping their creative and practical lives in balance had its roots in their deepest vision of themselves.

David stayed stuck in his dead-end jobs because his whole identity was wrapped up in being an artist. Even though his instinct told him that his devotion to his art was not working well in his life, he couldn't bring himself to do what seemed tantamount to admitting failure and giving up. Shelley, on the other hand, was affected—perhaps even afflicted—by an overidentification with the persona of wage earner, a vision handed to her from someone else—in this case, her parents. At the start of her story, their immigrant anxiety still shaped her fears, making her privilege the need for security over every other goal and desire. To give up even the smallest element of the career that gave her material rewards felt dangerous to her, even though she and her family could in fact have afforded some reduction in her income. If David was like a starving man who can't reach for food, Shelley was like a satiated woman who hoards unneeded and unwanted provisions.

As both stories suggest, being stuck has an addictive quality over time. "Starving-artist" types like David become addicted to the cycle of fear and hope that accompanies each new audition or opportunity, along with the sense of drama that this cycle brings into their lives. Even when paying opportunities to pursue their art don't present themselves, they may use classes, workshops, and artists' groups to bolster this sense of excitement and creative accomplishment. "Closet creatives" like Shelley seem less overtly addictive, yet they too are so habituated to the status quo—in their case, stability and security—that they cannot change. In their case, material possessions often become a means of satisfying the emptiness of unfulfilling, uncreative careers. In each case, as you'll see, breaking through the limiting vision involves taking a less black-and-white approach to life. David's life became more secure without requiring him to give up creative excitement. Shelley's situation became more free and expressive, yet left her with much of her original sense of stability.

Do you have beliefs similar to either David's or Shelley's that may be holding you back from a complete and creative exploration of your options? Before you review the more detailed examination in this chapter, take a moment to jot down your thoughts. Don't try to be too analytical or precise at this stage. Just note what your intuition tells you. You can look again at these notes after reviewing the section on limiting visions, which will help focus your insights.

Beliefs That Limit My Thinking about Career Issues and/or Keep Me Stuck	
1.	
2.	
3.	
4.	

Your Limiting Visions

David and Shelley at first stayed stuck in unhappy, unfulfilling creative/career imbalances less because of any actual barrier than because they defined themselves in limiting ways. In their different ways, the deepest visions they had of themselves prevented them from thinking more flexibly, exploring more openly, fulfilling themselves more richly, and discovering new and more rewarding lifestyles more quickly. In this, they are like most of us. It is often our innermost picture of ourselves that is our biggest enemy. Once we can redraw that mental self-portrait, the supposed "reasons" we "can't change" come toppling down with miraculous ease.

The following are the most common limiting visions shared by creative people—the inner personas that keep them trapped in less-than-effective balances between creative and career imperatives. These limiting personas may overstate what you feel to be your own traits. (I've deliberately made each persona a bit exaggerated just to make the point.) Or, you may see parts of your beliefs in more than one persona. As you'll see, each one can manifest itself in several different ways. But over the years, virtually every one of my clients has seen himself or herself in at least one of these limiting visions.

You'll notice as you review the list that although each limiting vision is ultimately unproductive, each tends to have powerful short-term benefits. You may recognize yourself not just in what a specific limited vision loses you but also in what you believe you gain.

Along with each limiting vision, I've provided at least one initial barrier-breaking action. Each is a small step that responds to specific aspects of that vision. Use these steps in conjunction with the broader barrier-breaking strategies that begin later in the chapter.

Limiting Vision #1: Defending Your Artistic Vision (At All Costs)

Defending your artistic vision at all costs can involve you in taking on one of several roles. You are probably defending your artistic vision too strenuously if you feel like:

- **The Anointed One.** You feel almost as though your creativity is an unstoppable drive that is virtually forced upon you by some unknown god, force, or demon. For you, your creativity is transcendent—a force that lifts you beyond ordinary experience. Musician Peter Townsend summed up this feeling of calling and even ecstasy when he commented, "When I'm on stage, I feel this incredible almost spiritual experience, lost in a naturally induced high." This type of vision does help you make a passionate commitment to your creativity and to keep on working at it even when the rewards seem to be few. It infuses your days with color and drama, making existence feel purposeful, reassuring you that you are not one of the ordinary "drones" who will pass through life without meaning. But to turn your mind to mundane practical matters feels like a betrayal of your calling. Instead, you feel you must defend your gift from petty concerns and distractions, even when those involve effectively managing the practical sides of your life.

- **The Wild Child.** You're the original "rebel without a cause," a born contrarian, a natural "bad boy" (or girl). Just on principle you're against most commonly held beliefs and anything ordinary, conventional, predictable, or accepted. You may be a drinker, smoker, taker of controlled substances, eater of unhealthy foods, misser of deadlines, thrower of tantrums, and/or frequent quitter of jobs—and if you're not, you secretly long to be! Your heroes are resisters, dropouts, burnouts, nose-thumbers, nose-piercers, mad geniuses, and all other creatures of extremes. Many of the greatest creators in history viewed their gift this way. The gifted writer William Faulkner put it differently: "An artist is a creature driven by demons. He doesn't know why they chose him, and he's usually too busy to wonder why. He is completely amoral in that he will rob, borrow, beg, or steal from anybody to get the work done." Janis Joplin, the poet Rimbaud, and many others were Wild Child types. The positive side of this wildness is that it encourages unpredictable and original thinking, but the negative side is obvious: partial or total self-destruction.

- **The Purist.** Purist types are less dramatic than Wild Children or Anointed, but they have the same need to defend their artistic identity—or, as they might put it, their artistic integrity—no matter what the consequences. You're a Purist if you tend to be focused on one option, one art, one subject, one form to the exclusion of all others. Your art form is likely to be "high art"—sonnets rather than limericks, portraits rather than cartoons, chamber music rather than Top Twenty. You feel a bit sorry for those who diversify and, in your mind, "dabble." You feel outright anger at those who "sell out" to commercial or popular art. You know that you would never stoop that low, even if it means you'll never be widely recognized or successful as an artist. Your Purist tendencies help you by allowing you to complete difficult projects, to ignore the many distractions and temptations that pull you away from your goal, to focus on a single artistic vision, and to trust your deepest instincts about your destiny. History is full of creative people (like Emily Dickinson and Vincent van Gogh) who were Purists—people who became successful only because they were so focused on a single artistic vision that they pursued it long after others would have found a more comfortable and achievable objective. On the other hand, history is also full of less celebrated Purists whose single-mindedness led to neither artistic fame nor life satisfaction.

How it unbalances your life: When your limiting vision is to defend your artistic identity, you may actually be *more* comfortable when your life is risky, insecure, or frustrating, as that can feel like the badge of the true artist. This is the most pervasive barrier because it gives you reasons to stick with what's familiar, even though it leaves you dissatisfied. As I've mentioned before, even a familiarity that seems superficially dangerous or daring is less threatening than growth or change. Believing that you are better off as someone who does not balance intense creativity and originality with duller, more practical considerations seems risky, but it's actually a risk-reduction strategy, since it helps protect you from the discomfort of exploring new ways of being.

As you'll also note, none of the above roles offer you flexibility. You become so locked into your vision—be it of grand destiny, rebellious marginality, or aesthetic purity—that you can't shift gears or capitalize effectively on the practical opportunities that present themselves. The early part of the film *Tootsie* illustrates this problem with hilarious accuracy. Michael Dorsey is a Purist type who is so focused on his ideals of great acting that he remains poor and in constant conflict despite considerable intelligence and talent. He cannot even succeed in a television commercial, because he can't adjust his focus to the mundane realities of advertising.

Start breaking the barrier by: allowing yourself to ask if you are defending your familiar vision too much. Ask yourself if you really want to remain *exactly* as you are now and if your current situation feels completely satisfying. Could you make some changes, try some things differently, while leaving other aspects of your life as is?

- Make a list of reasons *not* to change and then pair each reason with a good reason *to* change. You'll likely find that the good reasons to change are fairly easy to find. As you consider them, you may find that you're ready to move closer to the fuller, more balanced life you deserve.

- Consider new models. For each great artist who was a Purist, a Wild Child, or an Anointed One, there is another who balanced creativity with career quite effectively. The brilliant poet Wallace Stevens worked in insurance; another great twentieth-century literary figure, William Carlos Williams, had a lifetime career as a doctor. Similar examples of those who balanced an artistic commitment with more practical considerations abound. Being aware of these models can help you break out of a limiting vision that puts any consideration of self-protection, profit, or comfort at war with your artistic identity.

Limiting Vision #2: Fear of Success

Limiting Vision #2 typically manifests itself in one of two ways:

- **The Almost But Not Quite type** sabotages him- or herself just a moment short of reaching a goal. You get a personal introduction to a gallery owner—but you don't have time to send your slides to her immediately, and by the time a few months pass you're too embarrassed to do so at all. You have a callback for an audition— but you stay out late the night before and don't perform at your best. Your actions don't look dramatic or self-destructive like those of the Wild Child. In fact, few people but yourself even know that you have done something subtly self-defeating at just those moments when your dreams might be realized. You yourself may not acknowledge that your own actions (or lack of them) are stopping you. Some variation on the thought "they wouldn't have wanted me anyway" is the way Almost But Not Quite types tend to view these situations, placing responsibility for their lack of success on others rather than admitting that they themselves did not "go for it" fully.

- **The Human Sacrifice** is you if you work for someone or something other than—and in your eyes more important than—yourself. Maybe you keep on toiling away at a boring and unfulfilling lifeline career because your kids deserve to go to Harvard rather than the state university. Maybe you don't take that good corporate training job because if you didn't have the time to sell tickets, usher the audience, print up the playbills, and do just about everything else, the wonderful local theater company would give up the ghost. There are always a million reasons you "can't" let go, ease up, and let someone else do some of the work that prevents you from reaching your dream. Sure, there are options other than sacrificing yourself, but all of the trade-offs are always unacceptable—you just *have* to go on, even though it seems like other people keep urging you to relax.

  Like all of the other modes I describe in this section, the Almost But Not Quite and Human Sacrifice roles have their benefits. Most importantly, both tend to keep your existing relationships and their power balances intact. If you were more achievement-oriented or surpassed your current level of success, you believe, others might become resentful or angry; in contrast, sacrifice leaves your "approval level" high. "Of course I want success," you seem to say. "But it just doesn't work out." Or, "But I can't—my kids [or whatever] are just too important." Moreover, sacrificing your own needs for your art or your lifeline career lets you avoid the additional risks or responsibilities you may associate with life at the top. As long as you're giving success up for someone or something else, you don't have to worry if you can sustain it!

How it unbalances your life: The unbalancing effects of fear of success are obvious. If you're not letting yourself succeed at either your lifeline career or your artistic goals, your life is *de facto* out of balance. Those with a fear of success also tend to build powerful resentment over time as they watch others go unapologetically after what *they* want. Resentment, like all negative emotions, is not an effective emotional place from which to explore your art, build a career, or improve your life.

Start breaking the barrier by: adjusting your focus from what others will feel if you surpass your current achievement level (or even theirs) to what you want, need, believe, and feel. Obviously, this is a complex process that may require many different steps. A key to breaking the barrier is to realize that you deserve, and don't need to protect others from, your success.

- Use your creativity to visualize yourself as a true success—the person you would be if you did not "have to" give up what you want for others or other causes. What is your lifestyle like? Who are the people sharing your life with you? What pleases you? What troubles you?

- Visualize three steps you have already taken to move forward into the more balanced life you desire . . . and then three more steps you can take now. They need not be big ones; allow yourself to feel comfortable with them and avoid feeling that you must transform your life overnight.

- Fantasize about the worst thing(s) that could happen to you if you take the risk of succeeding in a balanced life. Would you lose anything essential? What? Who? What other losses would you face? What could you do to avoid them? How could you "sell" people on your plans, and what would you want them to know that would help them better understand your new goals?

Limiting Vision #3: Fear of Failure

The common manifestation of a fear of failure is a kind of false contentment. As a **Contented One**, one of your biggest points of pride is that your goals for your life and your art are modest. You're never the one that demands much from people, life, or creativity. Statements like, "I don't need much to make me happy," "My life is just fine," "No, of course I don't mind sacrificing financial stability for my art" (or vice-versa), and "I love my tiny apartment/boring job/etc." feel comfortable to you. Statements like "No way—I need much more than that" or "Of course I need both financial security and the chance to express my creative vision" seem almost unthinkable. You can also recognize a fear of failure in yourself if you find yourself thinking that you don't deserve more than what you have or if you are avoiding experiences that could expose you to significant rejection, failure, or even disappointment. This type of feeling typically comes from overly critical or unrealistic judgments early in life, most often from parents.

Within reason, realistic expectations are a wonderful gift, and making goals attainable quite often results in success. After all, you probably *won't* win an Oscar, a Pulitzer, or a Nobel Prize! So, you figure, if you avoid lofty or ambitious goals and have low expectations, you avoid the pain of disappointment. The problem is that you don't set more achievable, compromise-goals that stretch you, either.

How it unbalances your life: If you suffer from a fear of failure, you may well be *too* realistic; you'll demand much *less* than either your art, their lifeline career, or both can give. This type of "faux" contentment—a sense that you will be unacceptable if you demand more from life—puts you in an emotional and creative straitjacket. It is also a self-fulfilling prophecy. If you set overly low standards for yourself, you may find yourself on a downward spiral of never getting ahead, of never succeeding in the loftier goals that remain half-hidden at the back of your mind.

Begin breaking the barrier by: allowing yourself to widen your outlets for satisfaction and learning to set gradual, achievable goals.

- Make a list of ten positive attributes about yourself. You're looking for ten significant positives, not trivialities! Then, list five personal accomplishments from any area of your life—career, school, social life, and so on.

- Review the skills you already have. (See chapter 3.) You will probably be surprised by how many latent areas of accomplishment and validation you have to call on.

- Give yourself permission to clarify what you want and need. After years of denying your hopes and dreams, you may not have a clear idea of either. Inside, however, you *do* know what you want! Start with the most obvious: happiness, money, success, and love. Write them down, making them as clear and quantifiable as possible. Instead of "money," for example, be specific: "I need *x* dollars a year to live without fear and be free to paint" or "I want a supportive partner with his/her own interests and a good sense of humor." Once your list is written down, own these goals. Take responsibility for them, making a list of the smallest achievable steps you can take *now* to begin reaching them. You can't guarantee you'll be on the stage of a major opera company tomorrow, but you can commit to showing up at two auditions a month. You can't immediately change your life from that of a nine-to-five attorney to a successful writer, but you can commit to signing up for a writing workshop and writing three mornings a week. As you take even these small steps, you'll begin to feel more powerful in your own life.

- Set more than one goal at a time. Leaving all of your eggs in one basket will only exacerbate your fear of failure because every rejection becomes very significant. People who succeed (and succeed comfortably, without undue stress) are often those with diversified lives, interests, and pursuits. They are less troubled by setbacks, obstacles, or rejections in one life or goal area because there is always some forward movement or reason for optimism in another.

Limiting Vision #4: Perfectionism

Perfectionists wait for ideal conditions in which to produce their art, get a lifeline career, or make the move from a lifeline career into their creativity. If you're a Perfectionist, you are frustrated when circumstance or limitation prevents such perfection. It's an all or nothing approach. You may be a successful professional in a lifeline field who won't write/paint/compose/act at all until you have a wonderful studio and eight hours a day free; alternatively, you may be a struggling creative type who won't even look for a full-time job until your novel/play/part is absolutely finished. Your expectations can become so high that you become paralyzed and unable to work at all. Conversely, you may begin so many different projects, in so many different art forms or styles, that you can never finish any of them—and hence never have to face judgment.

Perfectionism guarantees that you will always work toward excellence. In this sense, some element of the Perfectionist resides in every artist. But perfectionism out of control ultimately destroys both artistic production and life balance.

How it unbalances your life: Perfectionism is obsessive; like all obsessions, it crowds out all other concerns and creates imbalance almost by definition. It is also a type of fear of rejection. As a Perfectionist, it's hard for you to accept what virtually all successful artists and business people understand—that in the real world, there are always flaws, limitations, weaknesses, and frustrations, but the work must go on anyway! You tend to feel that because you can't achieve your impossibly high standards, there's no point in trying at all.

Begin breaking the barrier by: adjusting your expectations to doing your personal best, not achieving perfection. Perfection is in your mind, but your personal best can exist in reality.

- Review those whom you admire. Whom would you use as role models? Carefully observe their patterns of behavior. If they are people you know, talk to them about their goals and standards of achievement. If they are well-known figures, present or past, take another look at their life stories, paying attention to their levels of actual and perceived success. You'll begin to note that most of them had significant ups and downs in terms of both artistic and life achievement, including outcomes that did not live up to their own or others' expectations.

- Realize that your personal best is actually a compromise position. It's based on striving for excellence, which leads to action, rather than for perfection, which leads to paralysis. First, write down your dream goal as specifically as possible. Then, write down the lowest possible accomplishment. For example, the first might read "write insightful, highly original, and beautifully crafted screenplay acclaimed by all critics and made into a major motion picture with Dame Judy Dench, leading to a Best Original Screenplay Oscar"; the second might be "finish a screenplay, any screenplay, at any point." Then identify a reasonable compromise position—one that stretches you beyond past accomplishments or limitations but doesn't demand the moon. That would sound more like "within one year, finish first draft of screenplay, polished to a level where I can get feedback from fellow writers I respect."

- Remember that achievement is always a series of goals, not the one monumental, monolithic act or task Perfectionists sometimes envision it as. No single step is or must be perfect; it must only provide a foundation for the next. The writer of the personal-best screenplay goal, for example, would then move on to future goals, such as "revise screenplay according to feedback and submit to agent."

Limiting Vision #5: Going It Alone

Those whose limiting vision is that they must go it alone at all costs play the role of **Loner/Stoic**. If this is you, you believe you must accomplish your goals without recourse to "crutches" and therefore fail to ask for help even when it is readily available. You were probably "trained" early on to be self-sufficient and perhaps to be a winner at all costs. Though you may have the same number of family and personal relationships as anyone else, you don't put much effort into finding and using mentors, teachers, or networks and tend to be surprised when others do. Instead, you are proud of your total independence and even the pain you suffer as a result of it. You tend to think that complaining or asking for help is childish or weak. It may even feel dangerous, as you'll tend to view others more in the light of potential adversaries or competition than as potential aids.

Many creative people share at least some of the Loner/Stoic's leanings toward total autonomy, partly because they cherish their unique vision and partly because their inner creative world is more compelling than many real-world relationships. Walt Disney commented ruefully that "I love Mickey Mouse more than any woman I've ever known." Being a Loner/Stoic and taking responsibility is admirable and useful—but only up to a point.

How it unbalances your life: As a Loner/Stoic type, you tend to be even more isolated than the usual artist—and that's saying something! Whether they are starving-artist or closet-creative types, Stoics/Loners tend to waste time "reinventing the wheel" and to stay stuck in whatever imbalance they find themselves because they do not avail themselves of the human resources necessary to change, get feedback, and shift directions. In truth, going it alone and/or competing at all times is exhausting. It takes valuable energy—energy that could actually be better used striving for life balance.

Begin breaking the barrier by: becoming aware of available sources of support in your life and the world around you. Even if it's uncomfortable to actually utilize these resources at first, it's helpful to grow more conscious of the mere fact that they exist! What friends, peers, or family members do you have who might help you with one or another of your needs, goals, or dreams? What classes, books, Web sites, clubs, or organizations address your artistic goals or life situation? This list might include an almost infinite variety of assistance: a spouse who has offered numerous times to watch the kids during your night "off" to write, a boss who would actually be perfectly okay with allowing you to skip lunch hours to take off early once a week for a photography class, a friend with an "in" at the local theater, or a support group of artists struggling to balance their art with their jobs.

Use this book itself as a resource. You'll note that it is full of strategies that involve meeting your goals through hearing others' stories and making use of outside knowledge, whether it be through networking, research, or simply use of the materials in the Resources section.

Adding Shades of Gray to Black-and-White Visions

A common theme in all of the above personalities is their tendency to engage in black-and-white, all-or-nothing thinking. For the Perfectionist, the only options seem to be utter perfection or humiliating failure. For the Loner, there is only total solitude or total dependence. For the Purist, creative effort is either totally pure with lofty ideals or a disgusting, slavish pandering to the masses.

To the extent that you share traits with one or more of these personas (and almost all of us do!), you are subconsciously allowing catastrophic thinking to keep you stuck in one place. When the perceived alternative is so dire, how can you change?

In fact, reality is simply not starkly black and white. Middle grounds not only exist but also occupy most of the available space in life. You can usually find a compromise position that fulfills you and doesn't lead straight to disaster—*if* you look for it! The problem with all of these personas is that they prevent you from looking for it—or, even worse, from even believing that more flexible solutions exist. To get out of the all-or-nothing trap, you simply need to broaden—*un*limit!—your vision of what you can and should do and to trust that disaster will not strike. As an Anointed One, for example, you can reimagine yourself as capable in—and called to—fields beyond the arts. This kind of broader vocational sense is reflected in such affirmations as "I am deeply committed to my art, *and* I am a highly competent person in the world." It can be acted on by ensuring that your personal goals encompass all areas of your life, not just your art, and by acting on them appropriately. As a Purist, you can recognize that integrity and adaptability can in fact be compatible. Though the history of the arts is full of Purists, it is also full of creatives like Dickens and Titian—artists who were greatly gifted in art despite the fact that they shaped their work to be highly successful in the world.

As you can see, these are changes in attitude—quite literally, re-visionings. Though the changes in attitude involve no outward action, you'll be pleasantly surprised at how much simply understanding your own limiting visions does to open you up to change in your life. Your expanded, more complex, less defensive image of yourself prepares the ground for the real-life actions you must now take, which can be summed up in three broad barrier-breaking strategies that apply to all of the limiting visions previously described.

Three Action Steps to Breaking Your Barriers
Barrier-Breaking Strategy #1: Understand Your Past, and Recast It Positively

This first step in breaking the barriers to change involves first analyzing what brought you to this turning point. Some may find the step difficult;

for others, it is empowering.

Carole Hyatt and Linda Gottlieb's book *When Smart People Fail: Rebuilding Yourself for Success,* a book I recommend for anyone experiencing a turning point or desiring more balance in their creative and career lives, outlines a process of reinventing oneself after not meeting personal goals or expectations. The first step is to understand why you did not reach your goals. Many of the reasons probably have little to do with your level of talent—they are related to externals such as bad luck or lack of connections, or are tied in with other elements of your personality, such as lack of commitment, self-destructive or limiting behavior, and so on. Either way, they do not represent the totality of who you are or who you can be. Understanding the reasons you did not experience the career you expected, the authors state, allows you to learn from them rather than to repeat the same pattern in a new undertaking.

Their second step is to recast the events in a positive manner. Hyatt and Gottlieb believe—and I heartily agree—that highlighting past flaws or negatives, as many creative people do, only guarantees that you will remain stuck. Instead, they suggest you rebuild confidence by examining your career with a focus on your achievements, even if those achievements did not come in the form you'd hoped for. Refocusing on the future is part of this step, too. "I began to see myself as an individual on a new exploration, not as a failed bass player," says Jerry, the musician we met earlier. "It made a huge difference."

What are the positives, the strengths, the achievements in *your* past? Include each of the professional, the personal, and the creative spheres in your list. Make that list as rich, as complete as possible—a task that often means probing or pushing yourself to remember things you usually take for granted. Remember, too, that your true accomplishments may include things that are intangible or overlooked by the outside world. Don't let any lack of external validation cause you to slight them. Making a full commitment to your acting (even if you haven't gotten prominent roles yet), successfully moving from a small town to a major city in order to pursue your art (even if your life there now feels insecure and marginal), doing good and useful work in your day job (even if your heart isn't in it)—these are all valid, useful, and very positive accomplishments, whether or not they look like it on the outside.

Essentially, this step is a process of making peace with your past. It's impossible to move into a new, more balanced life if you are stuck in regret, shame, or self-criticism, feeling that you have "done it all wrong" or "wasted your life." As one of my clients once put it, you can't stride forward if you're standing in a ten-foot-deep hole! In contrast, once you have made peace with your past and understood its many positive and successful elements, you'll be able to build on strength rather than on disappointment.

Barrier-Breaking Strategy #2: Set Concrete Goals

Hyatt and Gottlieb also suggest that you expand your options. Once you have stopped seeing yourself as a victim and perceive new possibilities, you can begin to take the small, positive steps that give you confidence to make bigger changes.

These steps become your goals, and therefore setting effective goals is the second step of your barrier-breaking strategy. As Stephen Covey writes in his highly acclaimed book, *The Seven Habits of Highly Effective People*, defining your goals creates the source from which productive behaviors flow. If you do not know where you are going, you cannot define the steps that will take you there or avoid the detours that will lead you off track. Without goals, you have no action, only dreams.

Many creative people feel uncomfortable with conscious goal-setting, preferring to let their lives flow intuitively. Unfortunately, that approach often results in choices made in reaction to circumstances or others' goals, rather than in response to our own needs and visions. For that reason, I encourage you to begin the process of setting actual goals now.

Recognize from the start that your goals will change. You have only begun to equalize your focus on creativity and a lifeline career. You may not yet have any concrete idea of exactly where you are going—and that's fine. Therefore, goals set now are provisional, not carved in stone. It doesn't matter if they change; what matters is that they exist. It's as though you're beginning a walking tour: You can't take a step until you face yourself in *some* direction. Even if your direction alters dramatically over time, having defined goals gets you started on your journey. In a later chapter, you'll read the full story of Dawn, a playwright who started a new lifeline career in Web site design. Dawn's goals changed dramatically as she experienced the reality of her new business. She regrets some of the choices she made along the way, but she doesn't regret her original goals. "They weren't *perfection,* but they also weren't *stagnation,*" she says. "That's what mattered to me. Even going on the detours I did, I'm still much further along the road than I would have been if I'd never set myself new tasks."

It is also important, as you begin the goal-setting process, to set a full range of goals and experience all of them as part of the meaning of your life. By definition, balance is about wholeness and integration. You cannot move toward a more balanced existence by ignoring huge parts of your life! Instead, you must rediscover and reintegrate the aspects of yourself you've underplayed or denied. As singer Carla puts it, "When I discovered computer programming—a much more challenging and better-compensated lifeline career than the word processing I was doing—I realized that what I was searching for was another part of *me!*"

Your goals should therefore encompass your creative life, your practical life, *and* the personal sphere. By the latter category, I mean matters like health, relationships, leisure, family, pastimes, and so on. I include such issues even though they are technically outside the scope of this book because they too have an integral relation to life balance. Often, in fact, a creative/professional goal cannot be achieved without a corresponding personal goal. Without goals such as "Eliminate all caffeine except morning cup of coffee" or "Limit alcohol to weekends," you may not be able to achieve goals having to do with interviewing effectively or increasing your creative production. Your goal to "Make doctor's appointment to correct migraine headaches" or "Spend 30 minutes each day just playing!" may provide exactly the healing, rest, or re-centering you need to make new creative or lifeline career changes possible.

Finally, note that some of your goals can include a commitment to reverse negative action or deliberate inaction. Powerful goals can include such items as "Turn down all freelance graphic assignments under $100 in order to focus on larger, more stable clients," or "Work no overtime at the company in order to get home at 6:00 each weeknight to paint."

With all this in mind, begin to define your goals. Once you have a rough draft of your goal list (not too many goals, by the way; four to ten are ideal) use the following questions to ensure that each is as powerful as possible.

- **Is this what *I* want?** It will be difficult if not impossible to meet your goals if they are defined in response to the expectations or needs of someone else or the world in general. Accomplishment does not arise from "shoulds," but from authentic passions, needs, and drives. Think about each goal carefully to ensure that it flows from your own needs and choices. If the true reason behind a goal is to look sensible or successful to the outside world, strike it from your list.

- **Is it consistent with my true values?** Does this goal reflect your beliefs and fit well within the other areas and pursuits of your life? Is the accomplishment you're targeting truly important to you? Don't make writing a literary novel your goal if the kind of writing you enjoy best is mass-market thrillers; don't make breaking into film work your goal if your true love is theater.

- **Is it realistic?** Effective goals are challenging but achievable. They make you feel stimulated and optimistic, not overwhelmed. Note that "realistic" does not mean "easy," "immediate," or "guaranteed." Effective goals may require persistence or real effort. But they don't require superhuman performance, genius-level talent, or incredible luck.

- **Is it concrete?** Most goals fail because they are too big and too vague. In contrast, an effective goal is stated in specific, concrete language and involves relatively small, measurable steps. It is worded so that you will know when you have achieved it and so that achieving it is possible within a limited time frame (see more on time frames below, as discussed in Strategy #3). Consider the following goals:

Weak, vague goal: I will leave my job in the finance department of the state government to work as a computer consultant and paint.

Strong, concrete goals: Before I quit my job, I will secure three computer-consulting clients and develop two more potential prospects. I will print business cards and organize my home office so that it is ready for business. I will mail announcements of my new business to 100 personal and professional contacts.

I'm sure you can see the powerful difference between these two goals. The ultimate aim of the second is no less ambitious than that of the first, but the individual steps that lead to it are specific and achievable, and therefore empowering.

Cooking provides the perfect analogy to the process of setting concrete goals. Recipes are the breakdown of a complex result into small, specific steps. For example, it's very difficult to make a perfect soufflé. Paradoxically, it is very *easy* to accomplish most of the individual actions taken in the course of making the soufflé, especially those that occur near the beginning of the process. A good soufflé recipe makes a challenging project feasible by correctly defining and ordering the necessary actions.

Webb, whose creative commitment is glassmaking, attests to the power of concrete steps. "I start each week by recasting my goals. In each list I always include at least one item at which I absolutely *know* I can succeed—something that involves a small or single step. Often, it's one component of a larger, longer-term goal: ordering brochures and application forms from two schools a week so that I can apply to several art-appraisal programs next year, gathering bank statements and checkbook records into a file so that I can balance my checkbook next week—something like that. It sounds silly, I know. But you wouldn't believe the sense of momentum created by actually accomplishing even the smallest individual goals—or how painless progress becomes if you can only make each step small enough! My entire life is easier, more streamlined, and more effective since I began planning this way."

- **Is it framed in a manner that leaves it up to me?** Right from the start, accomplishing a goal must be understood as *your* responsibility. If you are counting on others to do the work for you, the result will no longer be in your control, and your ability to accomplish what you want will be entirely in someone else's hands. "Meet with Marsha to get information on the personal trainer business" or "Ask Jim for advice about literary agents" are perfectly acceptable—as long as you're clear that if these strategies do not get you want you want, it remains up to you to develop other ways to meet your goal.

Barrier-Breaking Strategy #3: Set Target Dates

Until you have a time limit for your goal, all you have is an idea. Good, concrete goals are always accompanied by time frames. Specific deadlines, taken seriously, help create both accountability and urgency. Deadlines are always motivators. They may also help you ensure that you've broken your individual action steps down into sufficiently manageable units. "Enroll in one computer class by the end of the month" and "send for catalogs of computer-graphics schools by April 15" are goals that prompt and permit effective action; "become computer literate within two years" is not.

Amy is an office manager who wanted to balance her life with a stronger commitment to art photography. Her goal was to have her first photography exhibition within one year. In order to accomplish this, she set preliminary goals of spending three hours each weekend taking photographs and, in addition, using the fourth weekend of each month to review her collection of images, shaping them over time into a coherent group for exhibition. After six months, she added another interim goal: to send out one portfolio and query to a gallery each week. Demonstrating the point about flexibility I made earlier, Amy found that despite sticking to her interim goals, she did not have a show lined up at the end of the first year. She assessed what she had been doing, decided that it still made sense, extended her final goal another year . . . and had her first exhibition eighteen months after she began her goal-setting process. "Sure, it took longer than I originally expected," she comments. "But if I hadn't set a time frame in the first place, I'll still be aimlessly puttering around without a gallery!"

In Summary

To continue the cooking comparison I began above, let's consider this book to be a recipe for a better-balanced life. In each of the chapters that follow, I will outline specific, *do-able* steps that will help you progress toward a better balance between creativity and lifeline career, from understanding the world of work, to deciding between employment and entrepreneurship, right through marketing yourself well. Before we begin that process, however, it is helpful for you to summarize your own situation, blocks, desires, and intended action. Complete the questions in the form below to do so. Your answers will give you a clearer sense of where you are and want to be. You should revise your list as you work your way through the exercises in this book, adjusting or adding specific action steps and time frames as necessary. The purpose of completing this form now, right at the start of your exploration, is simply to help you better understand yourself in light of your various *current* needs, desires and stumbling blocks and to provide a baseline against which you can measure your growth.

Goal-Setting Summary as of _____ (Date)			
Desired Outcome	**Artistic**	**Practical**	**Personal**
What are the advantages in my current situation?			
What are the disadvantages of staying there?			
What do I want to achieve overall? (Create a specific overview.)			
What are the advantages of reaching that outcome?			
What are the disadvantages of reaching that outcome?			
What blocks are stopping me from meeting my goal?			
• Do I need more information? What kind?			
• More/different training? What kind?			
• New skills? What kind?			
• More support? —Emotional? —Social? —Logistical? —Financial?			

Desired Outcome	Artistic	Practical	Personal
How can I use my *assets and strengths* to overcome my barriers and blocks?			
What must I do to achieve my outcome? (List actions *and* time frames in each of the three spheres. These action steps should include action to remove the blocks and limitations you just identified.)			
Step #1:			
Step #2:			
Step #3:			
Step #4:			
Step #5:			
Step #6:			
Step #7:			
(Add as many steps as you need.)			

Chapter Three

Reassessing Your Values, Skills, Motivations, and Decision-Making Style

Looking at yourself in the mirror isn't exactly a study of life.
—Lauren Bacall

There is only one corner of the universe you can be certain of improving. And that's your own self.
—Aldous Huxley

My one regret in life is that I am not someone else.
—Woody Allen

As the previous chapters suggest, you can't develop a new and more successful lifeline career without learning to look at yourself in a whole new light. You will need to examine your basic values more consciously than ever before in order to adjust your working situation to a balance that reflects what matters most to you. Then, you'll need to reassess your values, skills, motivations, and decision-making style to see how they can be used to help create a life and career situation that supports such balance.

This career-related self-assessment sounds daunting at first, since even those of us who have been working in the world of "day jobs" rarely think about such issues consciously. Yet the process of reassessment is also an empowering one. Most of my clients tell me that they found it both fun and reassuring. They are surprised at how clear their values turn out to be and delighted at how many valuable skills they actually have. By the end of their personal reassessment, even though they have yet not yet taken action, they feel that they are already well down the road to finding a lifeline career that will be both pleasant and profitable.

One client, an actress named Jenny, summed it up well. "As a performing artist," she told me, "I took for granted the fact that I couldn't handle most office, business, or corporate tasks. When I did my personal reassessment, I found that assumption to be dead wrong. I actually had lots of skills that could be used very successfully in business. The thing holding me back was a sense of inadequacy, not a lack of skill! I started to feel more confident than ever before as my whole vision of myself changed from one of *incapacity* to one of *capacity.*"

Shawna, an aspiring potter who was working in a large retail chain, agrees. "I was always afraid that I wasn't creative enough to make it worthwhile to spend time working on my ceramics. That sense of inadequacy, of being less 'artistic' or creative than a true artist should be, was one of the reasons I held back from investing any real energy in my art. As I did the reassessment exercises, though, I discovered that creative and artistic interests and skills were very prominent in my personality and life! With that reassurance in mind, I'm finally taking some strides to make pottery a more significant part of my life."

Capacity in Creative People

Creative or gifted people often grow up with a sense of being different—a feeling that they are the odd one out, the misfit, the oddball, the proverbial square peg trying to fit into a round hole. Hurt by peer pressure or parental misunderstanding in their formative years, many of them tend to perceive their difference as a flaw: an inadequacy, an inability, a lack.

Is this true of you? Do you simply assume that because you aren't naturally drawn to the business or professional world, you don't have the talents to succeed there? Do you see your difference from those in the "normal" world as a negative, rather than a positive? Do you feel this even if you are a "closet creative," who actually *does* work in the world of nine-to-five jobs, but does not feel truly comfortable there?

Nothing could be further from the truth than such assumptions. As Jenny's comment suggests, I believe that creative people tend to be capable people, people who are multitalented and have a wider than usual range of capacities. I'm sure you remember the Hans Christian Andersen tale of the ugly duckling. Just as the duckling's difference was not a flaw but rather its beauty as a swan, your inability to just follow the pack into the average nine-to-five job is as likely to arise from an abundance of imagination, originality, drive, or sensitivity as from any lack.

In fact, in more than a decade of working with people in the arts, I have never met a single creative person who could not succeed in at least one, if not several, lifeline careers. All of them, without exception, had the capacity to make a strong and meaningful contribution to the world, both within and *beyond* the arts.

It will help you tremendously if you can begin your process of personal reassessment and career transition with an attitude of capacity rather than inadequacy. Come to the tasks that follow with an attitude of discovery, not defensiveness. Assume that you have many previously unexplored gifts and capabilities, and it will be all the easier to find them. Don't think in terms of "I can't compete in the world of business." Think in terms of "I haven't yet chosen to explore my capabilities fully, but now that I *have* chosen to do so, I will discover new talents and strengths in myself that will enable me to succeed."

To help build your confidence, let me generalize for a moment about the typical qualities and needs of creative people. In my experience, creative people are generally:

- Original thinkers
- Good problem solvers
- People who perform well under pressure
- Hard workers who enjoy challenge
- Willing to give their all, to push themselves to their limits
- Willing to take risks
- Excellent at inspiring and motivating people
- Enthusiastic about what they do
- People who believe in themselves and their convictions
- Inspired by, and inspiring about, projects they believe in
- Good team players and collaborators, yet also people who work well alone
- People who enjoy learning and new experience
- Capable of practical tasks and considerations when motivated to do so!

As you can immediately see, these are not "oddball" traits but qualities which are highly valued in the modern workplace. In fact, the creative person is the prototypical worker for the new millennium!

"I was always the rebel, from grade school onward," says Sharlene, a painter who also works for a Web site design company. "I made up my own stories and characters rather than just reading boring old books; I never colored in the lines or thought inside the box. Even at my ostensibly free and creative art school, my work was considered too 'pop,' too wild, too playful, too diverse in subject and style. Then one day, more or less by accident, I got involved in Web site design. Bingo! Suddenly all of the things that drove people crazy before—my creativity, my playfulness, my love of pop culture, my tendency to take risks and go for wild effects, my ability to work in all sorts of different styles—are exactly what make me successful. It's as though I've suddenly come into my own."

As Sharlene has discovered firsthand, the fast-paced, international, ever-changing nature of modern business is altering the type of worker that is most valuable to employers. Though Web site design and certain other technology-related fields represent an extreme, the basic American business model is no longer the conservative, conformist, obedient, blue-suited IBM worker but the young, wildly creative and iconoclastic Web entrepreneur. Knowledge—and the ability to acquire it quickly and without preconceptions—is the key asset of the "new professional." Qualities such as initiative, problem-solving skills, independent thinking, creativity and vision, flexibility and adaptability, love of learning new subjects and skills, sensitivity to diversity, and strong communication skills are newly valued assets. Breadth of ability—the capacity to do a number of jobs in a number of areas—is increasingly crucial as well. *Creative people tend to be strong in all of these areas.* In addition, the twenty-first-century workplace will put a high premium on knowledge of foreign languages (increasingly valuable in the new "global village"), analytic skills, ability to work both independently and as a team player, and of course, computer literacy. Creative people who have or can add these capabilities to their resumes will be highly valued in the changing world of business.

To take this one step further: in general, creative people *like work which:*

- Enables them to create new ideas, services, and solutions
- Is fun, challenging, and varied
- Reflects their personal beliefs and values
- Creates opportunities for others
- Lets them learn new skills and meet new people
- Is flexible in format and schedule
- Is done within a cooperative environment

Here again, these job characteristics can be found in many fields—and the number will grow as modern technology continues to create more flexible, less rigid business structures. The trend is toward hiring consultants, part-time employees, and temporary workers in a variety of high-level positions, not merely in the clerical roles that were traditionally the province of the "temp." Thus, creative people have new opportunities for lifeline careers that provide flexibility for creative pursuits. This is a boon both for the "closet creative" who wants to transition from full-time to more flexible employment in order to make more time for artistic efforts and for the creative professional who wants to balance artistic pursuits with highly flexible (i.e., temporary or part-time) lifeline work.

Colin, a performance artist, illustrates this point. "In the old days," she says, "I had two choices: a full-day temp job or nothing. But lately it is getting easier and easier to make more flexible arrangements. The PR firm I work for now let their full-time receptionist go. I work there part-time, in the afternoons only, when they're most busy. They save a lot of money because they're no longer paying a full-time salary. I get a steady salary but keep my mornings free for creating my pieces. It's the perfect deal. I'd encourage all artists to consider arrangements like this. They're definitely out there if you look."

The same flexibility is true in terms of location. Computer networks, e-mail, laptop terminals, pagers, cell phones, teleconferencing, overnight mail, and faxes have permanently altered the way we work. As a result, geography has become less of a factor in determining employment. We are already seeing increasing numbers of arrangements in which workers "telecommute" from one city to corporate headquarters in another town, or in which employees work in the office only a few days a month, operating from home the remainder of the time. Such flexible, off-site working agreements will become even more common as this new century unfolds. Because they eliminate commuting time and permit you to work for far-flung organizations, such situations will help facilitate your life as a creative person.

In sum, as you begin your reassessment process, you should feel every confidence that your transition to a more balanced life will succeed.

Naturally, of course, you are not just any "creative person." You are yourself, with your own unique set of values, skills, and interests, and these individual traits will shape your new career choices. The self-assessment tools that follow help you identify your personal values, skills/interests, and motivations. With this information in hand, you will be much better equipped to identify an appropriate lifeline career.

Defining Your Values

Your values are your beliefs about what is important to you personally and in the world. I believe that understanding your own values is the cornerstone of successful career planning, or restructuring, for several reasons.

First and foremost, *if you do not believe—i.e., find value—in the lifeline career you choose, your work will feel meaningless no matter how successful you are, and your lifeline career will drain rather than energize you.*

A corollary is equally important: *If you do not find value in the lifeline career you choose, you will probably not be successful—or at least not as successful as you could be.* Commitment and passion are just as important in lifeline careers as they are in artistic fields. John Lennon once said, "If being an egomaniac means I believe in what I do . . . you can call me that . . . I believe in what I do, and I'll say it." Even if it isn't your primary passion, a good lifeline career should be work you feel exactly that way about—work you put your name to proudly.

Scott, a poet, demonstrates the risks of planning a lifeline career without considering all of your job-related values first. He has all the talents it takes to be an excellent paralegal: intelligence, excellent attention to detail, and the ability to comprehend complex issues quickly. Yet he hates his paralegal position, despite its stability and excellent compensation, and has not received the raises and recognition other, less competent peers have enjoyed.

"I took this job because working for a large firm offered the best pay and benefits. But the truth is that I despise fancy, loophole-exploiting lawyers and the huge corporations that are their clients," he admits. "I don't really believe I'm contributing anything of worth to the world with my paralegal work, and that bothers me. No matter how hard I try to conceal it, those feelings probably show." The problem? Scott's position matches his talents, but contradicts one of his most basic job-related values: the desire to be useful in the world. In the course of career counseling, Scott realized that he needs to look for a paralegal position in an organization that more closely reflects—or, at the very least, does not directly contradict—this value. Once there is congruence between his fundamental beliefs and his work, he'll enjoy his job far more—and probably be better rewarded for his talents, too.

Glenda, in contrast, is a writer who enjoys and succeeds at her lifeline career because it *does* reflect her core career-related values. She funds her more literary and esoteric projects by writing mystery novels under a pen name. "Flexibility, independence, recognition, and variety are among my most important career values, and writing mystery novels gives me all of them. Most writers I know look down on genre writing. They think I'm just in it for the money, but they're wrong."

Ellyn, the dancer and fitness trainer we met earlier, feels the same. "Bodily health, flexibility, and expressiveness have always been very important to me. For that reason, I don't see personal training as a trivial occupation. I see myself as a healer and teacher who provides a crucial service, since I genuinely believe that I'm helping my clients as I teach them how to become stronger and more limber."

In order to identify your own core values, review the following list, which you'll use for the exercises that follow. It summarizes the potential values a given job might reflect.

The Values Checklist

____**Friendship** (developing close relationships, which may extend into the personal sphere, with people from work)

____**Community** (working among those who share your interests and values, whether or not you become personally close to them)

____**Creativity** (expressing yourself; using your full artistic and intellectual capacity)

____**Earnings Potential** (attaining financial purchasing power through strong and rising income)

____**Security** (ensuring that your job and salary are stable)

____**Benefits** (receiving health and unemployment insurance, paid vacation, a pension fund, etc.)

____**Advancement** (enjoying frequent or rapid opportunities for growth or promotion)

____**Social Usefulness** (contributing to the betterment of the world)

____**Public Contact** (being in frequent or ongoing dialogue with colleagues and the public)

____**Status** (enjoying prestige through your lifeline job)

____**Teamwork** (collaborating with others)

____**Autonomy** (being self-employed or working with minimal direction from others)

Variety (changing tasks or responsibilities frequently)

____**Task Predictability** (knowing in advance what responsibilities you'll handle each day)

____**Time Predictability** (maintaining the same daily schedule)

____**Flexibility** (retaining the freedom to shape your tasks, schedule, or work format)

___Travel (traveling frequently, i.e., at least 20 percent of your working time)

___Time Freedom (retaining free time in your work schedule)

___Power and Authority (exercising control and commanding respect)

___Recognition or Fame (becoming known to professional peers or the public for your capability/success in your field)

___Personal Challenge (testing your abilities against those of others)

___Intellectual Challenge (testing your abilities against set goals; stimulating your mind)

___Influence (guiding or changing the opinions of others)

___Assistance (directly helping individuals or small groups of people)

___Aesthetics (working in an appealing or attractive environment)

___Excitement (experiencing risk or adventure in your work)

___Idealism (contributing to ideals, issues, or causes that are important to you)

___Other (if necessary, insert alternative values that express your core needs and beliefs)

Using this checklist, complete the following brief exercises.

Values exercise #1: Your Core Values

Begin by choosing the five values that are most important to you in a lifeline job. (Remember that you are exploring values in the context of a lifeline career, not in the context of your creative pursuit.) Try to keep the list to five items by sticking to those things that feel truly important, and not merely preferable, to you. If you still have too many, try turning each of your "short-list" values into its opposite: "Community" into "Isolation," "Idealism" into "Cynicism," "Security" into "Insecurity." Which negative values would feel the hardest or most painful? Those are the values whose positive sides are likely to be highly important to you.

As you complete the exercise, try not to judge or second-guess yourself too much. The goal here is to help you move toward a job which works *with* your personal "grain," and that requires honesty.

Values Exercise #2: Values Restatement

Take five minutes or so to craft these values into a short, concise statement about yourself and your lifeline job needs. Pretend that you are answering a question about what you want most in a job. Don't be perfectionistic about the writing; it is not a public statement, and you're simply looking for something that accurately sums up your career-related values. Feel free to rephrase each value to match your personal beliefs or situation, and, if necessary, prioritize among the five values. Save your values restatement when you've completed it. You'll want to use it as a values "yardstick" against which to measure potential careers.

Here are some examples of value restatements. Notice how different each of them is and how clearly it directs its writer *toward* or *away from* certain types of work. The final restatement, for example, is from Scott, the paralegal we met earlier. Had he done this values assessment before choosing his lifeline career, he might still have ended up as a paralegal (a job that fulfills four out of his five values), but he would not have chosen to work for a firm that violates his humanistic beliefs.

> "*Variety* is my single most important value in a lifeline job—I get bored easily, and I could never stand to do the same thing over and over! I want to balance the solitude of my painting with a position that involves *Friendship* and *Teamwork*, and even in the context of a lifeline job *Creativity* is important to me. *Earning Potential* is my final value, although I wouldn't take a high-paying job unless it reflected my other four values as well."

> "*Security* is my first and foremost career value. The whole point of a lifeline job, for me, is to gain the stability I need so that I can invest my creative energy into my music. If I have to think too much about keeping or changing jobs, that won't happen. For the same reason, I want both *Task Predictability* and *Time Predictability*, too. My fourth value is *Autonomy*—having a boss looking over my shoulder doesn't appeal at all. Finally, I want a job that fulfills my *Aesthetic* value. I spend so much of my time as a performing musician in dark, smoky bars that I'd like to work in a pleasant environment the rest of the time."

> "*Benefits* for myself and my child are key, since they are the single thing I can't affordably provide in my artistic career as a self-employed painter. *Social Usefulness* is a close second on the list—I am drawn to humanistic and charitable causes, and I would feel uncomfortable and ambivalent if the work I was doing were negative or destructive in any way. *Intellectual Challenge* and *Influence* are important because they would make the position more fun for me. I would also like *Time Predictability*, which would facilitate my life both as a painter and a parent."

Values Exercise #3: Existing Values

Using the full values checklist, identify the five values most reflective of your current working situation. Your purpose here is to compare your values identification with your current reality, including your day job or career.

Values Exercise #4: Missing Values

Again returning to the full values checklist, select the five items that are most noticeably or painfully missing from your current situation. This exercise tends to bring to life any disparity between what is important to you and your actual, real-life situation. My clients often find this exercise somewhat painful. However, knowing for sure just how big a gap there is between their current reality and their true values is a powerful first step toward change.

Values Exercise #5: Past and Future Values

Take a moment or two to extend your exploration of values into both the past and the future. Are the five career-related values you've chosen now the same ones you held five or ten years ago? Do you think they will be the same ones you'll make a priority five or ten years from now? This exercise is a way of reminding yourself that it is natural for your values to change somewhat over time, especially at turning points. In fact, a change of values is one of the most powerful signals of a major turning point or transition in your life. A thirty-five-year-old dancer might experience this kind of change as he realizes that he does value financial comfort and security and no longer wants to live a life that does not provide it; a thirty-five-year-old corporate executive might undergo a similar values shift in the opposite direction, recognizing that her financial assets no longer feel very meaningful without more opportunities for sustained self-expression.

If you can already see such changes coming, you may want to build them into your lifeline career planning from the start. I also suggest that you do a values assessment every few years to see if your new lifeline career needs any adjustment.

Values Exercise #6: Brainstorming

Looking at your values restatement, "brainstorm" to see if any occupations that fit these values occur to you. Don't be too serious or intellectual at this stage—just see what arises naturally. If no ideas come up, don't worry; it may be that you are simply not familiar enough with what I call "the world of work" to see possibilities. Later chapters will yield more than enough ideas. If one or more potential occupations do occur to you, however, keep them in mind as you begin exploring the world of work. It may be that your instinct is telling you something.

Reassessing Your Skills

Now that you know what *values* are important to you as you transition to a new lifeline career, you need to evaluate what *skills* will get you—

and serve you—there. The skill assessment process is helpful in two different ways. *Identifying* your skills builds confidence and gives you a sense of career directions you might take. *Labeling* your skills—fitting them into a name or category—helps you market yourself more effectively to employers.

Whether or not you have ever worked seriously in the world beyond the arts, you already have job skills. To identify them accurately, use the following checklist, which my colleague Judy Kelso developed, to complete the exercises below.

Skill Check List

Communication

___Writing: creative writing, prose, poetry, expository writing, essays, reports, copy writing for sales

___Editing newspaper articles, magazine pieces, manuscripts

___Interviewing: evaluating people orally for a specific purpose, obtaining information from others

___Speaking publicly to an audience, individually to many people, on radio or TV

___Selling ideas, products, policies, to others

___Listening to extended conversations between others or from one person in order to help him or her

___Motivating others for peak physical performances, others for psychological efforts, helping them to overcome their inertia

___Explaining: justifying one's action to others, making complex ideas clear to others

___Proposal writing for government funding, for revising organizational operations

___Fund-raising on a person-to-person basis, such as door-to-door collecting for charity; from large foundations or organizations; for political candidates; through sales of products and services; through advertising

___Persuading: influencing others to see your point of view, persuading others to help you

___Reading large amounts of material quickly, reading written materials with great care

___Corresponding: answering inquiries by mail, initiating letters with others, soliciting information by direct mail

Information Management

___Auditing: assessing the financial status of an organization or program

---

____Record keeping: orderly keeping of numerical data records, keeping log of sequential information, creating and maintaining files, creating and maintaining clear and accurate financial records

____Measuring: obtaining accurate scientific measurements

____Calculating: performing mathematical computations, assessing the risks of an activity

____Updating: keeping a file of information up to date, completing records, acquiring new information on an old topic

____Budgeting: outlining the costs of a project, assuring that money will not be spent that exceeds available funds, using money efficiently

____Working with precision with numerical data, in a time and space situation calling for little error

____Computer skills: knowledge of computer applications (word processing, spreadsheet, etc.), programming knowledge

Manual/Physical

____Assembling technical apparatus or equipment

____Using instruments of a scientific nature, or a medical nature, related to motion, related to transportation

____Repairing mechanical devices, equipment, furniture, etc.

____Using manual dexterity to manipulate objects

____Constructing mechanical apparatus, physical objects

____Operating scientific equipment, mechanical devices, vehicles, electronic data equipment, etc.

____Moving with dexterity: being able to move athletically, with speed and grace

____Using strength and stamina: able to stand, lift, carry, or climb for long periods

Personal Attributes

____Ability to work independently with minimal supervision

____Desire to help people

____Ability to work under pressure

____Ability to relate well to all sectors of the population

____Ability to consistently exhibit patience and compassion

____Ability to be tactful and understanding

____Desire to deliver services to the sick

____Ability to help others cope with problems

____Possess sense of humor

____Good physical health

___Ability to work well with a team

___Resourceful

___Calm under stress

___Ability to persevere

___Exhibit good judgment

Human Services

___Recruiting: attempting to acquire the services or support of other people

___Serving: providing a service to an individual, serving a product to individuals

___Advising: giving counsel to others

___Coaching: guiding the activities of an athletic team, tutoring

___Negotiating between individuals or groups in conflict

___Committee working: attaining objectives through committee processes, creating and implementing committee structures

___Counseling: helping people with personal/emotional concerns, life development concerns, family matters, etc.

___Confronting: obtaining decisions from reluctant others, giving bad news to others, resolving personal conflicts with others

___Group facilitating: facilitating the positive interactions of members of a group, specific facilitation involving therapy

___Handling complaints from customers, from citizens to government agencies, from parents of students, etc.

___Teaching in lower school or college classrooms, to individuals who perform certain tasks, or in a tutoring environment

___Rehabilitating: helping people to resume use of physical limbs; working with disabled people through nonphysical media, such as art and music

___Meeting the public: acting as receptionist, giving tours, greeting, being a public representative of an organization, selling products in a public place, polling the public

___Mediating: being a peacemaker between conflicting parties, acting as a liason between competing interests

Managerial

___Administering a specific project, activity, or test

___Deciding: making decisions about the use of money, making decisions involving others, making decisions about alternative courses of action

___Organizing time so that many tasks are completed in an efficient manner

___Delegating: distributing tasks to others, giving responsibility to others on a work team

___Supervising: directly overseeing the work of others, overseeing building management, supervising the leasing of apartments

___ Managing: being responsible for the work of others, having responsibility for the processing of information or data, guiding the activities of a team

___Coordinating: numerous events involving different people, great quantities of information, activities in different locations

___Problem-solving: identifying possibilities and alternatives, developing answers or solutions

___Organizing: bringing people together for certain tasks, gathering information and arranging it in clear, interpretable form, arranging political activity, rousing the public to action

Analytical

___Inspecting: physical objects to meet standards, people to determine criteria or detect information

___Appraising: evaluating programs or services, judging the value of something, evaluating performance of individuals

___Classifying: sorting information into categories, deciding about placement of people into programs

___Researching: extracting information from library, people, physical observations

___Analyzing: quantitative data, physical or scientific data, human/social situations

___Investigating: seeking information that individuals may attempt to keep secret, seeking the underlying causes for a problem

___Interpreting other languages, obscure phrases or passages in English, meaning associated with statistical data

___Compiling: gathering numerical and statistical data, accumulating facts in a given topic area

___Reviewing: reassessing the effects of a program, the performance of an individual; evaluating a play, book, movie

___Finding information from obscure, remote, or varied sources; finding people who can be helpful to you or others

Design-Planning

___Abstracting/conceptualizing parts of a system into a whole, ideas from surface events

___Imagining: new ways of dealing with old problems, artistic ideas or perspectives

___Anticipating: staying one step ahead of moods of the public, being able to sense what will be popular in consumer goods, anticipating a problem before it develops

___Handling detail work: doing numerous small tasks within a short period of time, making sure small details are not left undone

___Initiating new ideas, ways of doing things, new approaches, personal contacts with strangers

___Making layouts for printed media, newspapers, public displays, posters

___Sketching pictures, people, diagrams, designs

___Predicting: forecasting physical phenomena, the outcomes of social interactions, the outcomes of contests

___Creating: new ideas, new ways of solving mechanical problems

___Designing interiors of rooms, buildings—plans involving processing of information

___Planning: anticipating future needs of an organization, scheduling a sequence of events, arranging an itinerary

Skills Exercise #1: Transferable Skills

Moving down the checklist, mark each and every interest area/skill you have demonstrated to your own satisfaction. Do not include items you merely feel you *might* do well; the skills you check should be things you have actually done. However, don't fail to mark items just because you haven't demonstrated those skills in a paid job. If you're the person friends call when their electricity goes out or their table legs wobble, you are entitled to check the "Repair" skill in the Manual/Physical section of the checklist, whether or not you have ever been paid for doing so.

Your finished list comprises what career counselors call "transferable skills"—*existing* talents and capabilities that can be transported into *new* or *arising* employment.

Ellyn, the dancer introduced earlier in this chapter, says that identifying her transferable skills was the key to beginning her rewarding career as a personal trainer. "As I worked through the skills assessment, I found that I was very strong in both the Manual/Physical and Services areas. It occurred to me almost immediately that the role of fitness trainer would let me use both my understanding of fitness and physiology and my strengths in 'people' skills, such as serving, advising, and coaching. When I realized that training was a career that fit my values list, too, it seemed perfect—and it is!"

Jenny, an actress who has also become a successful corporate trainer, makes the same point even more emphatically. "As an actor, I listen to a producer or director's needs, prepare and, if necessary, research my role, and ultimately speak before an audience. I have to think on my feet, remain energetic, and bring the same program to life numerous times. Once I began to identify those skills, it was obvious that corporate training was a totally logical career choice for an actor, and for me specifically. If you want my opinion, in fact, there is no difference between the skills that make a good actor and those that make a good trainer. Only the venue and the content are different, not the basic talents I use."

Skills Exercise #2: Favorite and Not So Favorite Skills

Not all the skills you have are skills you'll want to spend your life using. Work your way through the items you've marked and underline those you truly enjoy. Obviously, these skills should be at the center of whatever lifeline career you choose.

Now, to assess the strength of your distaste or discomfort with each item, take a look at the items you marked off but didn't underline. Which are skills you feel neutral about or are only slightly reluctant to make part of your job? Though you wouldn't want to focus solely on such skills for a job, they may be worth highlighting during your job search, as diversity of skills helps make you more marketable. Fitness trainer Ellyn, for example, has strong selling and persuasive skills. She does not especially enjoy these roles and would not feel at home in a job that placed great emphasis on them. However, she *is* comfortable using them to market herself as a personal trainer.

Which, in contrast, are things you do well, but do not enjoy *at all*—skills that would seriously diminish your career satisfaction if using them frequently were a requirement? If you feel strongly enough, it may be appropriate to downplay these skills, or even eliminate mentions of them from your resume. Remember that all self-knowledge, even what looks ostensibly like negative information, is important in career decision-making. The fact that you are a good waiter, telemarketer, or clerical worker, for example, does not mean that these roles are right for you!

Glenda, the writer discussed previously, has powerful organizational and record-keeping skills. Though she has used these talents in various jobs, she finds them deeply unsatisfying. She says, "During the time I was struggling to build up a lifeline career as a mystery writer, it was tempting to keep my administrative jobs and accomplishments on my resume as a kind of failsafe. More and more, though, I found that I just hated that kind of work. Eventually, I had to face the fact that as long as I kept those skills on my resume, I would continue to get those kind of jobs. One day, I took the plunge and eradicated administrative references completely from my resume and 'personal commercial.' It felt scary, and in fact I had to scramble for a couple of months, but it was one of the best decisions I ever made. These days, people know me and refer me to others as what I want to be: a writer and editor."

Skills Exercise #3: Developing Skills

New interests arise and develop at various points in our lives, requiring us to learn new skills in order to fulfill or explore them. This is a normal, and indeed healthy, part of personal growth. Shifts in interests and the skills that relate to them, like the changes in values discussed earlier, often arise at or near turning points.

Review the skills checklist one final time. Mark five skills you'd like to develop. They may be avenues you've tried before and wish to experience or learn more fully; skills that now seem valuable, interesting or enjoyable to you even if they didn't in the past; or talents such as computer graphics, which you believe would make you more marketable in a new lifeline career. Often, they are skills or capabilities that you identified earlier in your goal-setting action plan.

Skills Exercise #4: Brainstorming

Just as you did with your values statement, try some brainstorming to imagine occupations that use your strongest and most enjoyable skills—the items on the checklist you both checked and underlined. What is your dream job with regard to your skills? How do any ideas you come up with match your values?

Reviewing Your Motivators

Many career counselors and vocational psychologists believe that personal motivations are important determinants of career satisfaction. In other words, enjoying and succeeding at your job involves understanding not only *what* you like to do, but *why* you like to do it, *when* you do it best, and *how* your beliefs push you toward success or failure.

Motivators—both the ones we are conscious of and those that operate unconsciously—are as unique to an individual as skills and values. One person may be pushed into peak performance by competitive situations, while someone else might actually feel unwilling to "beat" others. One person may feel paralyzed by situations that involve risk or danger, while another may feel energized and stimulated by them. For some, the potential for fame acts as a strong driving force; for others, it provides little motivation or even acts as a deterrent. In each case, both responses to a given motivator are perfectly acceptable. What is important is to understand what forces motivate you in particular and to learn to use those forces effectively.

Subconscious motivators, which operate automatically in response to past or childhood experience, are so huge and complex that it is impossible to cover effectively here. The Resources section at the end of this book includes several excellent volumes that touch on this subject, however, and your local bookstore or library is likely to have many more. Within the scope of this book, I can only urge you to be as aware as you can of the patterns of your professional and creative lives, especially the negative ones. Behavior that is consistently self-limiting, self-sabotaging, or self-destructive is often a tip-off to the existence of unhelpful unconscious motivators.

Conscious motivators—the identifiable present-day forces that drive you toward success or failure—are easier to work with. They can involve both positive and negative forces—the desire to *gain* something (approval, recognition, fame) and the desire to *avoid* something (failure, danger, disapproval). Clearly acknowledged and managed effectively, both positive and negative conscious motivators can help you to excel. Weaver Sarah, for example, is highly motivated by tight deadlines, even though most people find deadlines paralyzing or difficult. "I find it very hard to work well on projects that have no clear or imminent time frame. In fact, I used to do virtually all of my work at the last minute—sometimes mere hours before a piece was due at a gallery or a client's shop! I've finally broken that pattern, which created too much stress. But I'm still aware that looming deadlines motivate me to do some of my best work and free up some of my most original ideas. I schedule my activities around them quite consciously, in both my art and in my lifeline career of consulting." By understanding that deadlines are one of her key motivators, Sarah has found a way to turn them from a negative into a positive force.

The checklist below summarizes the most common personal motivators. Use it to complete the following exercises. You'll notice that some of the items on this list are also seen on the values checklist you worked with earlier. If service (i.e., Social Usefulness), is one of your strong *values,* it may be a strong *motivator* for you as well. Conversely, if tangible rewards such as earnings, status, authority, and so on are not among your values, it is unlikely that they will motivate you strongly.

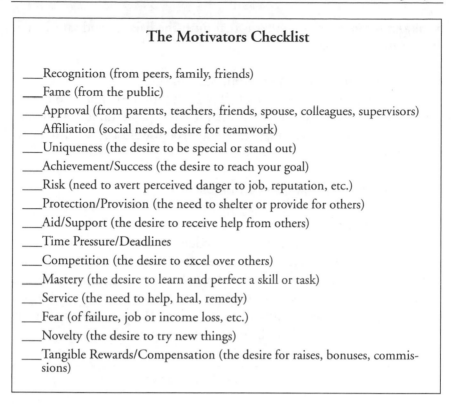

The Motivators Checklist

___Recognition (from peers, family, friends)

___Fame (from the public)

___Approval (from parents, teachers, friends, spouse, colleagues, supervisors)

___Affiliation (social needs, desire for teamwork)

___Uniqueness (the desire to be special or stand out)

___Achievement/Success (the desire to reach your goal)

___Risk (need to avert perceived danger to job, reputation, etc.)

___Protection/Provision (the need to shelter or provide for others)

___Aid/Support (the desire to receive help from others)

___Time Pressure/Deadlines

___Competition (the desire to excel over others)

___Mastery (the desire to learn and perfect a skill or task)

___Service (the need to help, heal, remedy)

___Fear (of failure, job or income loss, etc.)

___Novelty (the desire to try new things)

___Tangible Rewards/Compensation (the desire for raises, bonuses, commissions)

It's helpful to note that motivators can work for us in a variety of areas in our lives. Susan Walden, a Broadway singer and actress turned TV and radio baseball announcer, is a wonderful role model in this regard. Success was a powerful motivator for Susan, who always felt that she could succeed at anything she put her mind to. This motivation first powered her to endure the isolation and snubs she encountered as she began her career as a radio sports personality. Ultimately, she succeeded well in this field, and was even rewarded with a position as a network's national TV commentator for the New York Yankees. Soon afterward, however, Susan was diagnosed with breast cancer. The same drive for success that had helped her in her career also assisted her now and fueled her ability to appear at each of the season's games despite grueling chemotherapy. "At that point, it was more than just about me," she has said. "I was fighting for all women who wanted to break into the male world of televised sports."

We all wish we had motivators as positive and strong as Susan's. Unfortunately, our early conditioning often passes on more mixed messages. As you grow to understand your own motivators better, however, you can break out of unconscious patterns that limit the balance and satisfaction of your life and career.

Motivators Exercise #1: Motivation Summary

Work through the checklist quickly. Without too much conscious deliberation, mark those motivators that feel like powerful forces for you. These instinctive responses may help guide you toward or away from particular fields.

Motivators Exercise #2: Success Summaries

If you do not have a strong response to any of the items on the motivators checklist, the easiest way to understand what motivates you is to analyze instances in which you succeeded. Use the format below to explore five different instances of success from any area of your life (not necessarily just creative or professional ones). Try to break down *in detail* what your specific success was, what it was that pleased and drove you most strongly, and what skills you used. The following are two of the Success Summaries of Ellyn, the dancer turned personal trainer.

Ellyn's Success Summaries

My success #1 was: Using knowledge gained from a series of yoga courses, I volunteered to lead mid-day yoga breaks for my dance company, then sold the service to a local theater company as well.

What motivated me was: mastery (the desire to use skills learned in class), novelty (the desire to expand my capabilities into the new area of yoga), recognition (the desire to exhibit my physical skills), and competition (the desire to stand out from my fellow dance-company members).

I used the following skills: moving with dexterity, strength and stamina, selling, persuasiveness, teaching.

My success #2 was: I took up kayaking and completed an eight-hour skills course at the top of my class.

What motivated me was: novelty (the desire to try out a new hobby), mastery (the desire to become good at this new pastime), competition (the desire to do better than my fellow kayakers), and approval (the desire to please the kayak instructor).

I used the following skills: manual dexterity, moving with dexterity, strength and stamina, operating skills, resourcefulness, good health.

In only two Success Summaries, Ellyn has already identified several motivational "themes" that are particularly powerful for her, including competition, novelty, and mastery. This information pointed her toward jobs which involve specific disciplines and tasks to master, allow for new experiences and challenges, and involve measurable work that can be compared to that of others—all qualities that her chosen lifeline career, personal fitness training, offers.

Motivators Exercise #3: Your Ideal Work

Using all of the new self-knowledge you've gained through your values, skills, and motivators exercises, create a picture of your ideal job or freelance situation. While I have included a space for the type of work you'd do (that is, the field or profession) don't worry about that too much at this point. Instead, focus on the other qualities of your dream work—ideals you should now be able to envision much more clearly than before.

My Dream Work

Location (town, state): _____

Location (office or facility): _____

Type of organization (purpose and format, such as *corporation, nonprofit, government agency*) OR type of business format: _____

Size and type of staff OR type of clients:_____

Hours and days of work/schedule: _____

Intensity level: _____

Values used: _____

Skills used: _____

Interests used: _____

Motivators drawn on: _____

Things to be avoided: _____

Compensation (including benefits, bonuses, etc.): _____

Other features: _____

Keep your ideal work form as you move on to the more specific tasks of evaluating the world of work, researching careers, and finding the right position or freelance business. Whether or not the lifeline work you ultimately choose reflects all of these ideal qualities (and most real-world jobs involve some trade-offs), this information will help provide a touchstone for guiding you toward what you truly want.

A Final Area of Reassessment: Your Decision-Making Style

Now that you're explored your values, skills, and motivations, your reassessment process is almost completed. There's only one more area to review: your personal decision-making style and the degree to which it's working for you.

Decision-making is a crucial element of finding a better balance between a lifeline career and a creative commitment. Without a good decision-making style, you'll tend to sabotage even the best research, thought, and networking.

Is your existing decision-making style working well for you? Together, these seven questions provide an effective way to check. Before you ask yourself them, note that none of them concerns the *outcome* of your decision(s). Because you can't control the world around you and because circumstances change over time, sometimes a less-than-optimal result can arise from even a well-considered choice. The fact that you are no longer satisfied with your career as a business manager at thirty-eight, for example, does not mean that your decision to go into business was not a good one at twenty-six; similarly, the fact that your first novel does not sell immediately does not mean the choice to write it was a bad one. In answering these questions, then, consider only the way you made the decision itself, rather than whether or not the results validated the choice you made.

The Decision-Making Quiz

____1. Have I made careful and appropriate decisions in the past? (Include in your consideration decisions made in both the professional and personal spheres, including choices about such significant issues as education, serious relationships, and career.)

____2. Do I take full responsibility for the decisions I make?

____3. Am I patient, i.e., do I devote the appropriate amount of time (a month or even longer for major choices) to researching, considering, and finally making important decisions?

____4. Have I been willing to take some risks to make sound decisions that involve change?

___5. Do I get all the information necessary to make a good decision?

___6. Do I evaluate the results of each significant decision and then make another one if necessary?

___7. Are my decisions based on my own needs and beliefs rather than fear of or concern for others' opinions?

If you answered "yes" to all of the above questions, congratulations! Your decision-making style is effective and will function well for you as you use this book to build a better balance between your lifeline career and your creative commitment.

For most of us, however, the answer to at least one of the seven questions is "no." If you answered "no" to one or more of the questions, take a moment to review the following decision-making styles to see which styles your "no" answers best fit into.

Decision-Making Style #1: Impulsive

This is your style if you tend to make decisions quickly or on the spur of the moment, with the goal of changing your current situation as painlessly and rapidly as possible. It is one of the most common decision-making styles. Most of us want the easiest and quickest possible route out of our discomfort, especially when we're at a difficult turning point. I see this often as I work with clients. Lawyers, accountants, and businesspeople come to me for help after enduring long periods in a dissatisfying career; artists arrive when they are in considerable debt or facing other similarly dramatic life crises. Driven by an urgent sense that their life is not working for them, these clients are highly motivated to change, which is very positive; the problem comes when they seek instant solutions to problems that have taken years, even decades, to create. I hear things like "What's the fastest class I can take to make more money?," "I can't stand my job any more. I'm quitting, and I don't care what the consequences are," or "My friend has offered me a job. No, it's not necessarily what I had in mind, but it's there, and I'm taking it."

In response, I give them the same guidance I'll give you if impulsivity or speed characterizes your decision-making style. Good career and life choices arise from what is *right*, not just from what is fast. Dull as it sounds, they tend to take some research, some legwork, and some thought. In contrast, hasty or reactive choices rarely yield truly satisfying results. Don't shortchange yourself! Have enough patience, and enough faith in yourself, to give yourself at least a bit of time, especially if the decision involved has long-term consequences or involves a sizable commitment of your time or money.

"I always knew that the scripts I was writing wouldn't pay my bills for years to come, if ever," says Dawn, a playwright. "I also knew I wanted a better 'day job' than the temp word processing I was doing. When people started to talk about Web site design, I thought I'd found my niche. It seemed perfect for me. I've always loved computers and was the first person I know to get on the Internet. I've surfed the net enough to be familiar with lots of sites. I'm highly creative and very visual. The choice seemed so clear. What could possibly go wrong?

"Lots, as it turns out," she continues ruefully. "I hadn't really faced how much training time I'd need to devote to software and technical issues before I would truly be up to speed. I hadn't realized how many people had already jumped on the Web-design bandwagon or how competitive the field would be. I hadn't thought about the fact that many of my competitors were already graphic designers with great portfolios and art-school degrees to their credit—credentials I just couldn't fight against, at least not while still charging a reasonable fee. Six months into my new 'career,' I was still nowhere.

"I'm not saying that Web design isn't a great option for lots of people," she adds. "In fact, it might have worked for me if I'd been realistic from the beginning—for example, if I'd done enough research to understand that I'd have to invest an entire year just in training and marketing myself before I could expect to make any income. But I let myself be fooled by the glamour of it without exploring the realities. If there's one thing I'd say to another creative person in my position, it's to look before you leap. Don't invest lots of time or money planning on a career until you understand its pros and its cons inside out. Make sure your decision is truly realistic before you commit yourself."

If appropriate or necessary, consider interim, temporary, or short-term options to buy you the time to make a sound long-term decision. If you're a businessperson who can't stand your dull, noncreative job one more moment, for example, you might decide to take a vacation, enroll in a night class in your artistic discipline, or commit yourself to spending Saturdays working on your art for a specified period—say, two months. During the same period, you could also work on a proposal to your employer changing your job to a consulting or part-time arrangement. Through this strategy, you'll avoid paying the high price of a longer-term impulsive decision.

Decision-Making Style #2: Dependent

If this is your style, you tend to let others make decisions for you, or at least follow their guidance a bit (or a lot) too much. You'll find yourself asking for advice frequently and/or tending to do what others expect of you. This latter tendency is particularly common among closet creatives who have decided upon a "sensible" job in response to their parents' or peers' expectations.

When clients ask me what their decision should be, or when they report to me the opinion of someone else as a compelling factor in their thinking, I work to help them open up their options by brainstorming a number of alternatives. As you consider your positive and negative responses to a whole group of possibilities, you will often find it easier to decide for yourself.

Another way to overcome an overly dependent decision-making style is to list the expectations, needs, or opinions of others before beginning to make your choice. Once you have consciously acknowledged what others want, you can then decide which of the items listed seems valid *to you*. As a final step, you might ask yourself what other ways there are of achieving similar goals or results different from what has been suggested to you—options that will feel more consistent with your own values or needs.

"My parents really wanted me to get a law or business degree so that I'd have true financial security," says Dale, whose real love is printmaking. "My friends at college also urged me in that direction—they were mostly heading for pretty lucrative careers. I felt very torn, since I really wanted to take some time off to work on my printmaking. I was very tempted to just do what seemed sensible to everyone else."

Then Dale did the listing and exploration exercise just described. "Writing down everybody else's expectations confirmed that even if it was essential to people around me, making lots of money wasn't important to me. But some basic financial stability was," he reported. "With that in mind, I brainstormed to come up with less black-and-white alternatives—options other than spending years in a graduate program I'd hate *or* throwing any chance of a secure future away for my creative work. My eventual choice was to enter a two-year arts administration program whose graduates typically go on to become managers of cultural organizations. It will keep me in the world of the arts and give me more flexibility than a traditional business career. I'm really glad I explored other options rather than just caving in to others' realities."

Decision-Making Style #3: Fatalistic

Fatalistic decision-makers let circumstances or chance determine what they will do; they often remain passive or do not act even when some choice or action is required. If your style is fatalistic, you'll react to situations as they present themselves rather than making proactive choices on your own behalf. For example, you might interpret a gallery showing, an audition, or a callback as a "sign" that you should stay solely in the arts or a raise as a sign that you should stay in business—even though your existing situation is very unsatisfying. Explanations of your choices that begin with, "I couldn't . . . " or "It just happened that . . . " are also tip-offs to a fatalistic style.

The antidote to this problematic style is simply to recognize that you *do* have the power to shape your own future—and that if you don't choose to do so, some other person, group, or force will almost surely do it for you. Which will create a better life for you: your own decisions, or random chance?

Decision-Making Style #4: Delaying

If this style is yours, you'll find that you tend to put decisions off, hoping perhaps that circumstances will intervene and you won't have to choose after all. You may fail to gather the necessary information to make a good decision; alternatively, you may gather so much information you become anxious, overwhelmed, and unable to take action.

This style is usually related to the barriers of perfectionism or fear of failure, as described in chapter 2. Use the strategies in that chapter to begin to overcome these blocks. Recognizing that even small decisions will tend to break your sense of paralysis can also help.

Decision-Making Style #5: Intuitive

Intuitive decision-makers make the choice that "just feels right." In other words, they think some nonspecific emotion leads to a more or less magical arrival at a decision.

Like impulsive decision-making, this is very common. At times, particularly when practiced by intelligent, creative, and sensitive people, it can lead to satisfying results—but only at times! Equally often, vague and unanalyzed feelings can lead you astray. This is especially true when you are embarking on a whole new life path. Certain options, behaviors, or situations may make you "feel" uneasy, for example. Therefore you may conclude that they are not for you, when in reality your discomfort stems simply from the fact that they are untested and unfamiliar. Thus, while emotional messages should always be *part* of your decision-making, they should always be backed up by information as well.

A New, Balanced Decision-Making Style

Whatever style or styles you've used to make decisions in your past, it is a *balanced* style that will serve you best as you shape and restructure your more balanced future. A balanced decision-making style brings both factual *and* emotional considerations into the task of choice. Methodical planning, objective information gathering, and thorough follow-through are combined with reflection about inner well-being and personal preferences. Emotional realities and reactions are not discounted, but neither are they allowed to take control.

The balanced style involves researching alternatives, weighing pros and cons, choosing the most desirable option, and then developing a plan of action. Regardless of your past styles, you can incorporate these steps into your current career exploration. I'm confident that they will help you make the most effective, appropriate decisions possible.

Step 1: Research Your Alternatives

Exploration is the most time-consuming, but also one of the most important, steps in the process. It can be long, but it can also be exciting as you meet new people, develop new ideas, and perhaps realize that the range of possibilities open to you is much less limited than you may have thought. Dale's story, told previously in this chapter, is an example of the sense of freedom and satisfaction that can come simply from researching *all* of your alternatives.

Keep in mind that your information needs to be complete and unbiased. Don't rely on the information of only one person, source, or group. Jody, for example, was a blues singer who wanted to supplement her income and explore careers that were more satisfying than that of waitress, her then current means of earning a living.

She was fluent in French and loved the language, so teaching college French was one possibility. Another was to explore teaching English as a second language (ESL). Tutoring in French and working in a travel agency were other, though initially less appealing, options. As part of her preliminary research process, she sent away for applications to Ph.D. programs that would certify her to teach at the college level and made an appointment with a French professor at a nearby college. She also read a book on ESL, spoke with one ESL teacher each at a community college and language center, and studied the required certification materials. This range of sources was an excellent foundation for her decision-making.

Step 2: Identify at Least Two Serious Options

Selecting at least two options to consider seriously is extremely valuable. It keeps you from getting so invested in any one possibility that you become biased and helps you feel confident once you've made your choice, since you'll know that you explored potential options fully. Having more than one choice open to you can also help you identify priorities or values that one option alone may not uncover.

Jody, for example, notes, "As I mulled over the research I had done, I found that ESL teaching would offer me a variety of working arrangements, a wide range of locations in which I could work, a steady income, and a relatively brief training period. It was not as lucrative as college teaching would be in the long run, nor was it as impressive sounding. But those were relatively minor negatives compared to the very long and expensive schoolwork involved in getting a Ph.D. I hadn't really thought much about that issue when I initially chose teaching French as one of my alternatives. But the minute I began looking at the course catalogs, I realized that I simply wasn't willing to put either my singing or my income on hold for years while I earned an advanced degree. Comparing the two choices really helped bring that to my consciousness."

Step 3: Outline the Advantages and Disadvantages of Each Alternative, Evaluating Them Carefully

What are the probable outcomes of each of your alternatives? Is each consistent with your values and skills? What are each option's three major advantages and three major disadvantages? Use your imagination and creativity to project yourself into the future and to feel, as well as analyze, how each choice might resonate.

Bill, a musician who considered the lifeline careers of social worker and piano teacher, identified the following pros and cons. The lifeline career of social work had an excellent job outlook and offered lucrative hourly fees and flexible hours, but required long and expensive training. The career of piano teacher also offered good hourly rates and excellent flexibility. There was no training requirement—a real plus. But the income resulting from it would be much less steady than that from a social-worker position—a negative. As both Jody's and Bill's lists show, no choice is perfect. What's important is deciding which advantages are most attractive and which disadvantages are least troubling for *you*.

Step 4: Choose One Alternative and Develop a Plan of Action

This is the same process described in the goal setting described in chapter 2. It involves turning a preliminary idea into a concrete plan of achievable steps.

As musician Bill considered his two options, he realized that he, like Jody, was not ready to commit to the time and expense involved in getting an advanced degree. This understanding enabled him to proceed wholeheartedly with a plan to start teaching piano. He had already gone through Step 1 of the decision-making process, so he had a good knowledge of local piano teachers, prices, and other relevant facts. The first step of his plan was to create business cards and a flyer; the second step was to distribute the flyer as widely as possible in local music stores, libraries, schools, churches, and other places that potential students or their parents frequented.

Step 5: As You Take Action, Evaluate the Results

If the initial steps in your action plan reveal unforeseen obstacles or problems with the alternative you have chosen, you can repeat the steps above with other alternatives as many times as possible, until your choices are fully narrowed down and a final commitment is made. Often, however, you'll find that having gone through the careful process above, your decision is a sound one which will stand the test of time and form the basis for a strong course of action toward a new and more balanced life.

Section II

Exploring and Expanding
Your Work Options

Chapter Four

Employment versus Self-Employment: Which Is For You?

I should never have made my success in life had I not bestowed upon the least thing I have ever undertaken the same attention and care that I bestowed upon the greatest.
—Charles Dickens

When people agree with me I always feel I must be wrong.
—Oscar Wilde

The man who is employed for wages is as much a businessman as his employer.
—William Jennings Bryan

The most important choice affecting your rebalanced life is what field you'll enter. But the second most important choice is whether you'll pursue your chosen field through employment or self-employment. Most careers chosen by creative people (and increasingly, most careers in general) can be structured through either employment or self-employment arrangements. Each format has its own advantages and disadvantages. The one that is right for you will depend on your personality traits, situation, and preferences.

The choice between employment and self-employment is even more important for the creative individual than it is for the "ordinary" person. For the average working person, an overly confining job or a draining small business is a headache but not necessarily a disaster. As a creative person, however, you'll find that the wrong working arrangement may make the pursuit of artistic work virtually impossible. There just won't be enough "left" in you at the end of the day, week, or month if you have to work against your own personal grain as either an employee or free agent. You will thus want to make this choice very carefully, based on a free, yet thorough and realistic, exploration.

Before moving on to some exercises and information that will help you decide which working arrangement is best for you, let me take a moment for some definitions. For the purposes of this book, the terms "self-employment," "entrepreneurship," "small business," and "freelancing" are interchangeable. Technically, there are shades of difference—for example, "entrepreneur" carries a connotation of risk and the requirement of capital, whereas "small business" is often used to describe operations that require a physical setting such as storefront or office, as well as employees—but they do not affect the basic mindset, personality traits, or work issues involved.

Entrepreneur or Employee: Different Needs, Different Visions

As you consider whether to pursue a salaried job or freelance work, I think it is important to recognize that one is not better than the other. Our culture tends to glorify entrepreneurship these days, but productive, meaningful, and even visionary work can be done within traditional corporate or institutional structures as well as in small businesses. There is nothing wrong with valuing teamwork, predictability, and structure! Focus on your true needs—on what will create the best and most satisfying life balance for *you*—not on glamorized images projected in popular myths.

Remember, as well, that as a creative person you don't need to prove to the world that you are an entrepreneur or a risk taker; you are already one in your art! Your art demands personal vision, risk, challenge, unpredictability, self-marketing, hard work, and all of the other key elements of small business in a highly competitive field. Keep this firmly in mind as you consider your working options. Some artists find that they simply don't want more risk or unpredictability than they already have in their art. Others prefer to extend the self-directed vision of their art into their business life. Either choice is completely valid, and either can work very effectively to create a balanced life.

Finally, bear in mind that the choice between employment and self-employment does not have to be a permanent one. You may find that your personal needs and even traits change somewhat over time. "I liked the predictability of my salaried job when I graduated from college," says JoBeth, a journalist who is working on a novel. "The sense of building a bank account and having a life structure was satisfying. But these days I'm feeling more ready to make my own personal mark and more able to weather the uncertainty of freelancing. Moving into freelance journalism feels like an exciting challenge!"

Conversely, the needs of David, the actor I introduced in chapter 1, have shifted in the opposite direction. "I've had enough excitement and unpredictability to last me a lifetime. At this point, a regular schedule and income feel just right." As these perspectives show, it's not necessary to make a lifetime commitment to either employment or entrepreneurship at this time. (If you're not ready for self-employment now but like the idea as a future possibility, see the exercise at the end of this chapter.)

The Entrepreneur Inventory

To see if entrepreneurship or employment is better for you, begin by taking the personal inventory below. I'll discuss many of the specific issues it covers in more detail later on in this chapter; for now, your goal is simply to see which traits or beliefs match yours most closely. Mark each statement either True or False.

The Entrepreneur Inventory

____I am often called a self-starter. I'll be able to work productively and complete projects on time even without external motivators such as supervisors or company deadlines.

____I have a strong social support circle and don't need to depend on work for companionship.

____I am decisive. I don't mind making important decisions without much discussion or backup from peers, and I don't care if people disagree with my choices.

____I tend to be innovative and don't mind that the things I try are considered offbeat or odd.

____My personal records, finances, and taxes are quite organized, and I'll bring the same order to my business.

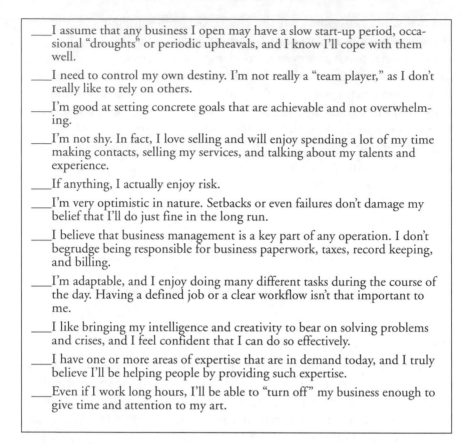

____I assume that any business I open may have a slow start-up period, occasional "droughts" or periodic upheavals, and I know I'll cope with them well.

____I need to control my own destiny. I'm not really a "team player," as I don't really like to rely on others.

____I'm good at setting concrete goals that are achievable and not overwhelming.

____I'm not shy. In fact, I love selling and will enjoy spending a lot of my time making contacts, selling my services, and talking about my talents and experience.

____If anything, I actually enjoy risk.

____I'm very optimistic in nature. Setbacks or even failures don't damage my belief that I'll do just fine in the long run.

____I believe that business management is a key part of any operation. I don't begrudge being responsible for business paperwork, taxes, record keeping, and billing.

____I'm adaptable, and I enjoy doing many different tasks during the course of the day. Having a defined job or a clear workflow isn't that important to me.

____I like bringing my intelligence and creativity to bear on solving problems and crises, and I feel confident that I can do so effectively.

____I have one or more areas of expertise that are in demand today, and I truly believe I'll be helping people by providing such expertise.

____Even if I work long hours, I'll be able to "turn off" my business enough to give time and attention to my art.

Every "true" answer is worth one point. If you score 12 or more, you'll probably be very happy in business for yourself. If your score is 7 or less, your nature is probably better suited to traditional employment. If your score is between 8 and 11, review your answers carefully. Are they scrupulously honest, even if you wish you were different? If this reassessment still leaves you in this range, you are a balanced type who can succeed either as an employee or a small businessperson.

The Eight Contrasts
The eight contrasts below, each expressed as a polarity, a juxtaposition of two opposing perspectives, can help you clarify whether you are more suited to employment or self-employment. Review them to see which end of each polarity sounds more appealing and appropriate to you. Remember, as you do, that your choices will not reveal *who you are* so much as *where you are right now.* Your personality may lean to one end of each

issue, but, as stated earlier, over the years your life may encompass periods when you need stability and the support of others *and* periods when the risks of uncertainty and the responsibility of taking initiative feel tolerable or even welcome. Note, too, that there are many shades of gray between these polarities. Salaried positions may offer varying levels of personal initiative, lone decision-making, and uncertainty; self-employed situations can be structured to feature some appreciable measure of teamwork and consensus. I've highlighted the distinct, contrasting ends of each spectrum simply to throw the issues into sharper relief.

These contrasts reaffirm what I mentioned earlier: Neither entrepreneurship nor employment is better, and neither situation can be said to be perfect. A self-starter is not a better worker than a team player; a person who takes the initiative does not work harder than one who can maintain an operation smoothly. Indeed, each perspective can contribute to success. If you are tempted to believe that independence is somehow more noble than working with others, remember that freelancers face the challenge of finding balance in terms of social interaction. The question is what feels most comfortable for you right now.

Contrast #1: Self-Starting versus Teamworking

If you are drawn toward self-employment, you probably feel driven by a personal mission, important purpose, or compelling goal. It is this inner vision that continually motivates you to produce. You may feel that existing organizations do not provide exactly what only *you* can do or provide. Your purposefulness (some might say your stubbornness!) about your own vision propels you forward without prodding by a boss or superior. Instead, you're your own boss, able and willing to start, manage, and complete projects on your own.

Roger, who worked in investment banking for over ten years, finally left his high-pressure job to open a business as a financial planner. His new business gives him more time to write—he's working on his first novel—but it also satisfies his personal vision better than corporate life ever did. "It sounds corny, but I have a vision of how financial planning should be done. It may not be right, but I believe in it very strongly. It doesn't trouble me that thousands of others do the same job, and I find it satisfying to be able to control exactly how my services are offered rather than having to temper my ideas to suit colleagues or supervisors. That's an added benefit of having my own business I didn't anticipate."

In contrast, if you are more suited to employment, you may feel that the individual mission and vision required of you as a creative or performing artist supplies sufficient purpose in your life. You have drive and motivation in your lifeline work, but you're comfortable as a part of a team of colleagues and supervisors, which provides mutual support and completes projects together.

Contrast #2: Lone Decision-Making versus Reaching Consensus

This issue is related to the first, because it extends from a highly personal sense of vision or mission. People who function well as entrepreneurs often love to make decisions alone, control all aspects of their choices, and be totally in charge. Others may call them impatient or opinionated. If this is you, you prefer taking the leader role when you work with others. You like being responsible for the final decision and getting the credit, but you're also willing to take responsibility for unsuccessful outcomes and mistakes.

If you function better as an employee right now, you are probably more comfortable with finding consensus with others than with having sole control. You may feel "burned out" by the solitary choices of your creative pursuit. The processes of dialogue, brainstorming, and negotiation present no problem for you, and you're comfortable moving ahead with a project even if the choices involved are not all yours. You probably enjoy playing a number of roles, from leader in some tasks to peer or subordinate in others.

Contrast #3: Tolerance of Ambiguity versus Need for Clarity

The freelance life is an ambiguous and unpredictable one. You probably will not have a regular paycheck, a predictable working day, an assurance of future income, or a guarantee of who your clients will be. On an intangible level, you'll get no clear performance reviews and no bonuses, raises, or awards that tell you you're doing well. Some people will want your services, others won't, and it won't always be clear why. If you're suited to entrepreneurship at this time in your life, you won't mind any of this ambiguity very much.

Creative people generally handle ambiguity well, since their artistic life is full of it. However, you may be at a point in your life where creative ambiguity is enough all by itself. The balance that employment provides—the sense of clarity about what role you play, what your income and schedule will be, what your expectations are and how well you're performing—may offer a welcome relief.

A fascinating case in point emerged from a recent *New York Times* article about Johnny Staats, a superb mandolin player who works as a United Parcel Service driver in bluegrass country. Staats's music has earned him a record contract, but he is keeping his job with UPS. "The music business is shaky. One minute you're living on steak, the next minute you're living on beans," he is quoted as saying. He does, however, practice the mandolin on his lunch break! Staats is a wonderful example of the way some creative people actually thrive in the clarity of structured employment.

The need for clarity and predictability often affects the creative person especially strongly during the period when he or she is building a family. At this stage of life, contributing to the stability of the family unit takes more precedence, and creative people may be more strongly drawn to steady employment under these circumstances than at any other time.

Contrast #4: Taking the Initiative versus Maintaining Operations

Entrepreneurs tend to like starting something new and thrive on change. They enjoy problem solving, such as repositioning a product or service based on new trends or information. They love custom tailoring services to fit unexpected needs and reshaping their business plans over time. "If it ain't broke, don't fix it" isn't a credo that works for them. Instead, they are often exploring, altering, or just tinkering with what they do.

"Back in the days when I was employed I instinctively tended to take on positions involving the start-up of something new or the redesign of something that hadn't worked. I felt energized by the challenge, but I got bored once things were running smoothly. When I'd quit, people would never understand; to them, the job was just getting good! Self-employment is perfect for me. Each day's challenge is new and fresh." The person who made these comments, Cheryl, is now a freelance book writer and ghostwriter. Each new book represents anew the start-up opportunity she relishes.

Employment, in contrast, often features maintenance of existing systems, services, or tasks. While part of your role as a staff member or manager may involve launches, explorations, and new challenges, it's likely that some or most of it will require you to travel routes already laid down—routes which may need some refinement, but not radical restructuring. You can often use aspects of your creativity, but your ideas and creations are not the whole of what is produced. This is especially true in larger, longstanding companies; in small or start-up organizations work may feel more like entrepreneurship. As with the ambiguity/clarity issue above, this trait of employment can offer a welcome balance to the constant reinvention of artistic creation;

working as a company employee can be a healthy way of bringing predictability into your life.

Luis, a drummer, agrees. "I have two young kids and a jazz band I love. That's enough surprise and challenge for me! I really like going to my job at the county offices and knowing that almost everything I do will feel familiar. I've fixed my desk, my files, and my systems so that they all work well, so each task fits in perfectly. I simply keep our systems going. It's a no-brainer, and I like it that way."

Contrast #5: Driven To Do It All versus Willing To Do Your Part

The ability to *follow through* on new ideas and plans is the essence of this issue. As a small businessperson, you need to thrive on the hard work involved in making your vision reality, with all the myriad tasks and details that involves. *You* plan the free seminar for potential clients. . . . *You* get the flyer designed. . . . *You* proof the flyer. . . . *You* put it up. . . . And you don't mind! You understand that, in the amusing words of one of my clients, "Inspiration without implementation is hallucination," and you enjoy that challenge.

Those drawn to employment are often highly accomplished and equally hard working. But they're not driven to do it all themselves. They're happy to have others help with the myriad aspects of getting the work done, from the senior vice president who defines the annual work plan down to the mailroom worker who stamps the envelopes and the purchasing agent who makes sure the toner for the copier has been ordered.

Janie, a writer whose lifeline was once freelance writing, says, "I had so many ideas. I only wished someone else could carry them out! By the time I sold each idea to the right publication, I was exhausted, and the idea had lost its appeal. I certainly had no desire to work on my novel." With that in mind, Janie gave up her business as a freelance article writer and became a staff writer for a magazine. "My assignments are given to me now, and therefore my day feels nicely structured. This gives me more energy to do my own creative writing."

Contrast #6: Business-Minded versus Project-Minded

All creative people are multitalented and multi-interested. They are naturally curious and tend to be adept at a variety of things. However, many creative people are not what I'll call "business-minded." The aspects of work involving records, paperwork, and behind-the-scenes processes do not appeal to them at all.

If you're an employee, you can often avoid some or all of this type of work. Unless it is very small, your organization will likely have a book-keeper, some assistants, a MIS (Management Information Systems) department, a payroll system, janitorial support, and other in-house services. With those in place, you can focus on your job without having to cope with the kinds of details you find least pleasant.

In contrast, being business-minded—having an interest in and a willingness to handle business issues, budgets, sales, and paperwork—is essential for the freelancer. At least in the early days, typically no one but you will file the taxes, send the invoices, make the deposits, or maintain the records. You need not *like* these tasks or even be innately good at them, but you must be resourceful enough to either do them adequately yourself or find appropriate supports.

Jeff is a fine artist with a longstanding ability to cook at a gourmet level. He now plans to become the chef in a bed-and-breakfast business operated with his friend Steve, a retired ad executive who owns a house on the coast of Maine that the two will renovate for the purpose. Jeff will run the restaurant and provide artworks for the B&B's walls, but he will also keep the books for the enterprise. "Business management and accounting is very important in making something like this successful," relates Jeff. "I actually like that aspect of things, and I take that part of my role as seriously as I do the cooking. In fact, I know that if I don't do the accounting right, I won't have any ingredients to cook with! I'm even looking ahead to when the inn expands. I've identified my friend Mary, an experienced hotel manager, as a great possible source of more business management expertise." Jeff's attitude is exactly that necessary for a successful entrepreneur.

Contrast #7: Sales-Oriented versus Non-Sales-Oriented

"When you have a job, you have to sell yourself once every few years at most. When you freelance, you have to sell yourself ten, twenty, two hundred times a year . . . and let me emphasize that no matter what your service or product is, as a small businessperson, you are always selling *yourself*. If you don't feel comfortable selling yourself, don't freelance!" So says Cheryl, the writer mentioned earlier, and she's right. Confidence, energy, self-assurance, and an eagerness to sell your expertise are essential for your small business to succeed. You need to be at a point in your life and career where you know you have expertise in your field and can comfortably convince others that they will benefit from your knowledge, delivered through your service or product.

Many highly accomplished individuals choose to remain employed so that they can receive equitable pay, flexible schedules, and other advantages without having to sell themselves anew each day, week, and month. Fitness trainers who choose to be affiliated with a gym rather than maintain a private practice; lawyers who work within a partnership; computer experts who work for a firm's MIS department rather than consult for individual clients—examples of this type of choice are all around you. You yourself may be drawn to employment rather than self-employment if you are naturally shy or uncomfortable putting yourself forward or perhaps your goal at this time is to *build* your expertise and confidence rather than market it. Many future entrepreneurs first take salaried jobs in their chosen industry to hone their skills and to develop contacts.

Other people who stay on as salaried employees have found a satisfying situation and are content not to market themselves again. "I'm always toying with the idea of opening my own private practice. I could make more money per session that way," comments Ellyn, the fitness trainer. "But my current situation at a day spa—which gives me a lot of freedom in scheduling and lets me work at a great facility—is really good, too good to make it appealing to get back into marketing myself and all the hassles that entails. I wasn't really good at it, anyway."

For fashion designer Kuniko, on the other hand, selling herself and her art are an integral part of her vision. After many exhausting years at a major fashion house she became a consultant to fashion designers looking to launch new lines. To meet her is to know why these designers immediately feel they need her help. She exudes confidence and the assurance that she can lead them to further success. While marketing and promoting herself constitute extra work, these responsibilities also let her shape the way she works with her clients. Her business and her art have become one.

Contrast #8: Optimistic verses Perfectionistic

Psychologist and professor Martin Seligman, Ph.D., has spent most of his working life researching the attribute of optimism. Though optimists may be generally lively and upbeat, they are not necessarily always sunny. They may worry and experience sadness just like anyone else. The difference is that they don't take setbacks, problems, failures, or criticism as personally as others might. They see difficulties as a normal part of life, not as exceptions that indicate failure or inadequacy. Optimists tend to view negative events as temporary rather than permanent ("It takes time to get clients" versus "I've gone two weeks without a new account. I'll never get anyone to pay for what I do") and as specific rather than global ("Today's presentation wasn't my best. Next time, I'll give myself a full half-hour to center and focus myself before I speak" versus "I'm no good at sales"). They feel good about themselves and the world around them and therefore are comfortable taking educated risks.

It's easy to see that optimism, as Seligman defines it, is essential if you are to feel comfortable having your own business. If you tend instead to be a perfectionist—worrying over small flaws rather than celebrating the big picture, taking failure or criticism personally, tensing up when you must take risks, believing that setbacks signify lack of worth—the ambiguity and variety of the entrepreneur's life may be overwhelming. If you're not naturally optimistic, you may be heartened to learn that Seligman's research shows that optimism can be learned. For the creative person who would like to escape perfectionism, traditional employment can be an excellent teacher. Within the stable structure of working assignments, support, and supervision, you can often learn to be optimistic about your skills over time.

Summarizing Your Employment "Mentality"

Use the chart below, which summarizes the inventory presented earlier, to identify some of the traits and preferences that will tend to make you more comfortable in one setting or the other.

You'll Like Self-Employment If....	You'll Like Employment If....
You tolerate ambiguity well and can handle an up-and-down, feast-or-famine existence. If anything, unpredictability spurs you on and feeds the energy of your art.	You function best in the world *and* in your art when your work life is predictable and your performance is defined by clear standards.
Your current circumstances allow you to take considerable risk.	You're at a point in your life where a steady salary and benefits are necessary for your own or your family's well being.
You don't mind working alone some or most of the time; in fact, you prefer it that way.	You appreciate having a support network and enjoy frequent and varied interactions with colleagues, supervisors, and mentors.

You'll Like Self-Employment If....	You'll Like Employment If....
You have strong feelings of confidence in your expertise.	You wish to develop or hone your skills and expertise in your current field or a new one.
You enjoy starting new things and are motivated by the excitement of starting from scratch.	You are willing to sacrifice some chances for creativity in exchange for certainty.
You have a sense of inner purpose or mission from which productivity naturally flows.	You prefer getting directives and deadlines to motivate you in a work situation.
You strongly desire to be in charge and like control and decision-making.	You're just not as concerned with decision-making as you are with stability.
You prefer idea generation to detailed follow-through.	You thrive on hard work and like to follow through, even when that involves you in lots of small, seemingly petty details.
You are very organized and self-disciplined whether or not anyone else is motivating you.	You're willing to work hard, but you'd prefer keeping as much energy as possible for your art rather than draining yourself totally at work.
You have a wide range of both practical and creative skills and enjoy using them.	You work best with external motivators and supervisors.
You love (or at least accept) the challenge of always selling yourself.	You're not attracted to business details such as record keeping, budgeting, and accounting.
You are optimistic and believe that everything will work out well.	You're not comfortable with sales or self-promotion.
You like the risk of being an artist and want to extend that sense of adventure and challenge into all areas of your life.	You don't like the risk of being an artist; you want to do truly excellent work and may focus on flaws or improvements.
You're glad to sacrifice the "cushions" that a job offers for the fun of having a business all your own.	You don't like the risk of being an artist and you don't want to make your life even more unpredictable; you'd rather have lifeline work that balances the uncertainty of your creative goals.
	Medical and pension benefits, paid vacation and sick days, and a regular income are very important to you.

Self-Employment Options

Chapter 7, "Popular Lifeline Careers for Creative People," as well as chapters 5 and 6, will help you identify potentially suitable fields of work, whatever your chosen employment format. To help trigger your imagination, I've provided a list of some careers that are often done on a freelance or self-employed basis. The list is neither exhaustive nor complete; it is simply intended to show you how many businesses, both traditional and more offbeat, are open to you if you choose self-employment. What appeals to you?

Common Entrepreneurial Ventures

SAT/Test preparation tutor	Accountant
Financial advisor	Editor
Resume Preparer/consultant	Nutritionist
Attorney	Calligrapher
Tailor/fashion designer	Bookkeeper
Public speaking coach	Transcriptionist
Makeup, style, or image consultant	Furniture or craft maker
Self-defense instructor	Retirement planner
Jewelry designer	Holistic healer
Brochure or marketing writer/editor	Genealogist
Repairperson	Photographer
Pet grooming	Caricaturist
Relocation consultant	Handwriting analyst
Massage therapist	Weight loss consultant
Personal trainer	Researcher/fact finder
Wedding consultant	CPR/First aid instructor
Midwife	Swimming teacher
Cooking teacher	Organizational consultant
Bed and breakfast owner	Storage space designer
Personal shopper	Personal development coach
Yoga teacher	Instructional video maker
Computer setup or tutor	Party/events planner
Caterer or private cook	Architect
Gardener/landscape designer	Parenting workshop teacher
Grant writer	Dance or music instructor
Tutor	Travel consultant
Public relations specialist	Graphics/web site designer
Speech pathologist	Corporate trainer
ESL teacher	Elocution coach
Writer/ghostwriter	Interior decorator

The Entrepreneur in Your Future

I often work with clients who prefer stable salaried employment now but are attracted to the idea of eventually going into business for themselves. I encourage them to keep a file of the ideas and opportunities that present themselves over time, even if they have no immediate intention of acting on them. You might also try doing the following exercise, adapted from Laurie E. Rozakis's *The Complete Idiot's Guide to Making Money Freelancing*, every so often, perhaps every year or so. It will prompt you to consider all aspects of your life as possible inspirations for small businesses. The fun part is that since you're not intending to actually set up shop any time soon, you can brainstorm freely, without worrying that your ideas are silly or impractical. You might be surprised to discover, some day, that a concept or business that seemed quite offbeat or impossible when you dreamed it up is now of genuine interest.

"I got a lot of teasing from both my creative friends and my colleagues at work about how organized I am," commented C.J., a writer who once worked in marketing. "People commented all the time on my filing system, notebooks, and the other organizational tools I developed. I never took it seriously until I began thinking that I'd like to leave full-time work in order to make more time for my writing. A painter friend jokingly suggested that I go into business helping artists organize themselves and their workplaces, and a few months later, I did the small business brainstorming exercise. Bingo, my freelance organizing business was born! I now work three days a week doing just that and I'm booked weeks in advance. I feel that I provide genuine value by helping talented people function better at their art and lives, and the work is challenging without being draining . . . a perfect balance to my own writing." C.J.'s unique niche business demonstrates how even the smallest elements in your life can provide a wonderful foundation for a future small business.

With that in mind, the exercise consists of identifying the elements of eight key areas of your life, then brainstorming small business opportunities for any that you can. Again, be free and fluid as you do so. No one need even see this form but you!

These two exercises show how different life themes and elements can be "spun" into new business ideas. They also demonstrate the different ways the exercise can be used. Scott laughingly admits that with four kids to raise and a fairly satisfying job, he's not going to make the leap into freelancing any time soon. Instead, he'll probably negotiate with his employer for a more flexible schedule to make a bit more painting time possible.

Scott Sills' Small Business Brainstorming Ideas

As Of June 23, 2000

LIFE ELEMENTS	FREELANCE OPPORTUNITIES
Actual Work Situation: Information Technology Vice President	Computer consultant to businessesand individuals
Educational Background: B.S., Computer Science	Computer setup, repair, networks, web design
Additional Training: Web design, MCSE networking	Same as above
Life Experience: Husband, father of two sets of twins, extensive traveler, athletic experience, college tennis team	"Raising Twins" seminars
Personal Contacts: Computer Technology Association, past President of PTA, Rotary Club, Country Club	
Hobbies and Interests: Daily fitness workouts, golf, tennis, family activities	Tennis afterschool program Tennis/golf lessons
Artistic Pursuit: Painting	"Art for Executives" seminars
Three Greatest Strengths: Technological/technical, social, athletic	

Judy, on the other hand, was galvanized into action by completing her latest brainstorming chart. "I could see how many satisfying freelance options were open to me and that motivated me to make a definite plan to quit full-time teaching by 2002. I'm researching faux finishing and greeting card production as my two main small-business ideas, though I'm sure I'll uncover others as well if neither seems viable after more exploration. I'm really excited by this new sense of openness in my life."

Judy Denver's Small Business Brainstorming Ideas
As Of December 1, 1999

LIFE ELEMENTS	FREELANCE OPPORTUNITIES
Actual Work Situation: Elementary school art teacher	Private art lessons for kids and adults
Educational Background: B.A., Art Education	something, anything with art!
Additional Training: Faux finishing, computer graphics	Faux and decorative painter, computer graphics and design
Life Experience: Raised in France until age 13	French tutor; guide on vacations featuring art museums and cultural sites in France
Personal Contacts: Friends in France and America, members of art associations	
Hobbies and Interests: French language, travel, museums	Freelance translator of art books and articles in French; guide (see above)
Artistic Pursuit: Printmaking	Greeting cards and small prints to be sold at art fairs
Three Greatest Strengths: Creative, linguistic, interpersonal	

Chapter Five

Understanding the World of Work

We work not only to produce but to give value to time.
—Eugene Delacroix

One of the dangers of the American artist is that he finds himself almost exclusively thrown in with persons more or less in the arts. He lives among them, eats among them, quarrels with them, marries them.
—Thornton Wilder

I do not like work, even when someone else does it.
—Mark Twain

The self-assessment process in chapter 3 should have given you a clearer idea of the qualities you search for in work. You have a better sense of your abilities outside your particular artistic field, the values you bring to a job, and the needs you bring to the workplace. Building upon this information, chapter 4 has given you a new sense of whether your needs will best be suited by employment or self-employment.

Now, your needs and preferences must be matched with actual work. How you go about the evaluation process involved depends on your current level of comfort with the world of work and lifeline career fields. In this regard, you'll find yourself part of one of three groups:

- **Group 1: Some creative people who have subordinated their artistic dreams to a career may feel very comfortable with the world of work and where they will fit into it.** If this is you, you may wish to move ahead to the chapters which deal specifically with finding new salaried employment or forming a freelance business.

- **Group 2: Others who have privileged career stability over creativity find that they want to move into a whole new field in order to create a lifeline career that is more satisfying and a life that is more balanced.** If this is you, the exercises in this chapter may help you reacquaint yourself with skills, interests, and areas of work beyond those you use in your current area of business.

- **Group 3: Creative people who have invested time and energy mostly or only in their artistic work—even highly intelligent and capable ones—may find figuring out a career path a difficult step.** The sheer variety of jobs in the modern marketplace feels daunting. The possibility of breaking into, much less succeeding in, any of these fields feels remote. It feels easier to stay where you are and settle for whatever work just happens to come your way. If this feels true for you, be reassured. It's a natural response. Artistic people often work in isolation from other members of the labor force, as writer Thornton Wilder put it so well in the words at the opening of this chapter. Needless to say, this tendency to bond closely with other creative people has its advantages. It can provide a sense of community, of shared values and missions, that is reassuring and supportive. But it can also limit the ideas and information creative people get about careers beyond the world of the arts. As a result, it may feel difficult to even begin to link your skills, interests, and needs to lifeline careers. This chapter is meant to help you begin that process comfortably.

An Introduction for Group Three: Putting Your Toe in the Water

If you are a "starving artist" type, one way to make the task of building a lifeline career feel less daunting is to gradually widen your acquaintance with the world of work and business. Read the business section of your local paper, noting any trends or careers that pique your interest. Speak with noncreative professionals about their field and the path that led them into it whenever you have the chance. Make a practice of noting the lifeline careers of the artists you meet and of considering whether any of those careers might be right for you.

Sometimes, this kind of openness to career information can help you fall straight into a lifeline job. An example is the career of Ellen, an actress who performs in many regional theaters. By being open to the many opportunities in the world of business, several years ago she happened upon a job as personal assistant to a sports psychologist. By the time she left his employment for a theater company in Seattle, she had not only learned to make his appointments and type transcripts of his sessions but had also organized the material for his first book. Next, she did similar work for a marriage counselor in Washington State. Now, wherever Ellen is acting, she contacts local college and university psychology departments and promotes her services as a personal assistant prior to her arrival. Her next employer is a money-management expert in Saint Louis. "I might have 'fallen into' the first job, but I made the rest of them happen," she notes. "It's wonderful work—very varied, and always flexible enough to leave time for my show-business career. It's increasingly profitable, too. With every new job, I raise my fee!"

More often, the right lifeline career for you won't arise this easily. Don't push it at this stage. Don't attempt to do actual career research yet, and don't put pressure on yourself to find an "instant" career. Look at this part of the process as simply dipping a toe into the deep water of the working world.

Understanding the Big Picture: Career Centers

In addition to cultivating an openness to information about non-arts careers, most of my clients also find it helpful to have an overview of the world of work—a kind of "big picture" vision that can help them find their niche most easily. A broad perspective can be useful whether you are searching for a new lifeline field after many years in the working world or considering lifeline work for the first time.

Career development researchers have broken down the world of work into related groups of jobs, or career clusters, using a number of criteria. I have found that the most helpful clustering system for creative people seeking a new lifeline career is a breakdown that categorizes fields by worker traits: by the skills and interests of the people engaged in these occupations, rather than by the activities of the occupations themselves. This kind of cluster lets you more easily match up the personal traits you've identified in your self-assessment with actual careers. Many, though not all, of the types of work listed in such clusters can be adapted to both standard employment and self-employment.

Below, you'll find information relating to the six career clusters developed by vocational psychologist John Holland. Review them once or twice to discover which three clusters seem the most interesting or likely to you.

For obvious reasons, the artistic cluster will probably be one of your first choices. Unfortunately, many careers in this cluster are not realistic options to balance your existing creative work, since they suffer from the same instability, unpredictability, and low compensation that your field of art does. While there are exceptions (some of which are reflected in the case histories throughout the book), they are relatively few. It's important, therefore, to identify at least one, or preferably two, non-artistic clusters that suit your traits and interests. You may then be able to choose a non-artistic career that complements your creative work or one that blends artistic components with qualities from other clusters. (For a list of such "combination careers," see the end of this chapter.)

As you do this, try to think "outside the box," moving beyond those personal traits that are already familiar to you to focus on the broader sense of yourself and your capabilities that you developed during your self-assessment process. Don't worry if you don't seem to fit exclusively into any one cluster—most of us have a range of capacities, which is all to the good when it comes to hunting for a job.

Cluster 1: Realistic

The people: Realistic people find mechanical things and processes fascinating. They feel rewarded by working on projects. You may be a Realistic type if you have good manual or physical coordination, like to repair or build things, or like to work outdoors.

The jobs: Carpenter or cabinetmaker, forest ranger, construction worker, mechanic, police officer, air-traffic controller, dental technician, pilot, appliance repairperson, wine maker, cable repairperson, engraver, farmer, jeweler, fitness trainer.

The balance they offer: The jobs in this cluster can balance your creative work—which probably involves much thought and imagination and which can be measured by no truly objective standards—with the pleasure of working on something concrete and tangible . . . something which, unlike a work of art, has a definite end point or result. A number of my clients have mentioned that Realistic work, such as repairing something, building something, and so on, lets them relax their creative mind. "The word processing I used to do to make a living left me way too drained to write. The carpentry work I started doing last year is actually much *more* demanding—I do customized cabinets that require lots of precision—but it uses totally different skills than my writing does," says Paul, a poet. "I come back to my manuscript refreshed and eager to write. If anything, my lifeline career now helps me bring energy and freshness to my art, rather than competing with it."

Cluster 2: Investigative

The people: Investigative types like to observe and analyze situations before they act. They enjoy both the careful investigation that precedes problem solving and the problem solving itself. They are curious about how things work and why they are the way they are, and they are willing to invest time to explore such questions fully. You may be an Investigative type if you were the kind of child who loved to pull apart alarm clocks or build detailed models, if you tend to research major purchases obsessively before you buy, or if you are attracted to detailed or complex projects.

The jobs: Engineer, x-ray or other medical technician, systems analyst, computer programmer, chemist, physician, tool designer, researcher, scientist (botanist, anthropologist, meterologist), archaeologist, chiropractor, veterinarian, pharmacist, dentist, psychologist, translator, audiologist, actuary, criminologist, market research analyst, mathematician.

The balance they offer: Like jobs in the arts, Investigative careers involve lots of exploration and inquiry. They allow you to use aspects of your creativity, such as curiousity and imagination. The difference is that they also involve detailed, often tangible, problem-solving work. Many Investigative jobs demand substantial time, dedication, and training, so they may not be ideal for those whose priority is energy and time for their art. Other Investigative jobs, however—translator, medical technician, and acupuncturist among them—offer sufficient flexibility to work well as lifeline careers.

Cluster 3: Social

The people: Social people are drawn toward working with other people in a helping or supportive role. They like to help others solve their problems or develop their potential. They tend to be concerned with the welfare of others, like being around other people, and may have a strong social conscience. You may well be a Social type if you have naturally been drawn to volunteer work for good causes; if you have found yourself taking on informal roles as tutor, mentor, or helper; if you are the type of person everyone turns to for guidance or reassurance; or if you find yourself arguing passionately about injustice, unfairness, or need.

The jobs: Social worker, teacher, nurse, dietician, housekeeper, employment interviewer, athletic coach, clinical psychologist, speech pathologist, librarian, fundraiser, community organization director, tutor, guidance counselor, financial-aid counselor, recreational therapist, sign-language interpreter.

The balance they offer: Social jobs bring creative people out of the narrow world of the arts, expose them to a wide variety of people and life situations, and allow them to make a visible difference in others' well being. Sheri, a ceramic artist, comments on this with a laugh. "Sometimes I can't believe the self-absorption of artists—myself included! We mean well, but the truth is that we can complain about our work, our woes, our poverty, and how unfair the world is for hours. My part-time position as fund-raiser for a local women's shelter helps me keep all that in perspective. I'm surrounded by those in real need, real crisis—women who are genuinely testing their survival skills and courage. Knowing that my work at the shelter makes a difference to these women and others like them feels great. It's built up my self-confidence tremendously."

Cluster 4: Enterprising

The people: People in this group are energetic and dynamic. They are naturally drawn to leadership roles and the stimulus of being in charge. While Conventional types (described next) don't mind working on small aspects of a task or business, Enterprising ones gravitate toward the bigger picture. Rather than shrinking from responsibility, they relish some measure of risk, whether it is the challenge of making decisions based on others' input or the effort to persuade people to buy things. They typically value wealth and will work hard to achieve it. You may be in this group if you ran for school offices, tend to end up as the head of committees you join, have gravitated toward entrepreneurial activities, find yourself bored by predictable or risk-free activities, or aspire to be a director, producer, or gallery owner, in your artistic life.

The jobs: Salesperson, buyer, wholesale or retail sales representative, real-estate broker, hotel manager, department head or supervisor, manager, superintendent, lawyer, producer, judge, collector, investigator, travel agent, columnist or commentator, newscaster, and newswriter.

The balance they offer: Enterprising jobs make use of the independent spirit common to almost all artists but apply this spirit to a wider and more public sphere. Whereas an artist's decision-making may affect only the form, content, and marketing of his or her artworks, the decisions of someone in an Enterprising job impact an entire organization, process, or segment of the public.

The boldness and flair required of Enterprising people will often appeal to creative people. Yet be aware that Enterprising jobs can be so dynamic and creative that they sometimes swallow up a creative commitment entirely. James, a classical musician who decided to go to law school, had this experience. "I can't say I liked law school much, but once I started practicing as a defense attorney I fell in love with the challenge of it. These days, I'm putting a huge amount of creativity into crafting good cases, writing good briefs and arguments, and outwitting the prosecutor in the courtroom. Because there's something real at stake, it's very exciting. Playing the violin feels like pretty small potatoes in comparison. I have no doubt that I'll return to writing my music, but for now, my creativity is pretty well occupied." This issue is one to consider if you choose an Enterprising career to balance your art.

Cluster 5: Conventional

The people: Conventional types enjoy well-ordered activities and well-designed tasks, including clerical ones. They feel most comfortable knowing what is expected of them, least comfortable in leadership roles and chaotic situations. Often, they have office or mathematical skills. Whereas the Enterprising type gets bored with predictability and structure, the Conventional person savors it.

The jobs: Clerk (file, tax, media), secretary, assistant (personal, library, administrative), bookkeeper, accountant, court reporter, data enterer/word processor, bank teller, hand worker (ornaments or small crafts), and cashier.

The balance they offer: Many artists find a lifeline career in Conventional jobs, mostly because they offer a stable balance to the unpredictability, riskiness, and open-ended nature of the arts. Conventional careers usually involve skill but not risk or huge challenges. Also, typical Conventional skills such as accounting, proofreading, and data entry are highly adaptable; that is, jobs in these fields are not limited to any one company or location. For all of these reasons, they are a common choice for those seeking creative balance.

The experience of Jamal, an aspiring screenwiter, bears this out. "My creative work involves writing scripts that have to do with racial issues and then trying agressively to sell those scripts in a very competitive marketplace. That's enough challenge, without adding in a risky or demanding day job. Being a proofreader doesn't sound very impressive, but it's perfect for me. It's varied enough to keep me interested, but not so demanding that it drains me. It's also a skill that will be in demand whether I stay here in New York or eventually move to L.A. to be closer to the movie market."

Cluster 6: Artistic

The people: Whether or not you are currently working in the arts, if you are reading this book this cluster probably needs little explanation for you! People in this category naturally use their imagination when dealing with any situation. Their solutions to tasks or problems are often innovative, distinctive, or creative. Self-expression is very important to them, and they are typically independent thinkers. They feel stifled in an environment that emphasizes only group work, bored by tasks that have no room for creativity, and frustrated in situations that require conformity.

The jobs: Singer, musician, composer, lyricist, model, actor, director, set or lighting designer, dancer, choreographer, painter, sculptor, ceramic artist, graphic designer, art director, photographer, art teacher, writer, humorist, stylist, clothing designer, fashion consultant, style or wedding consultant, make-up artist, video editor, audio-visual production specialist, or special-effects consultant.

The balance they offer: As I noted above, Artistic careers typically *don't* offer the balance you need as you look for a lifeline career to balance your creative commitment. They demand the same qualities—innovation, originality, imagination—as your art, and they are often compensated just as poorly (or, at the least, as unpredictably).

There are exceptions, however. Some Artistic jobs—such as graphic design, landscape architecture, interior design, or art teaching, among others—are commercial enough to let you use your artistic talents yet also give a measure of job stability not available in the "fine" or "high" arts, especially once you have established a career.

Similarly, the same art you pursue creatively may have commercial possibilities. I know an art photographer who photographs children to supplement her income, a writer who writes annual reports to support her work on a novel, and musicians who compose both serious work and commercial jingles. Their reports on their experience are mixed. "I just love photography, whether it's of kids or the landscapes I shoot for my own satisfaction. It doesn't matter—I just love taking pictures, and I'm glad to make my living from doing it," says Bridget, the art photographer.

In contrast, Jean, the novelist and business writer, finds this combination of creative pursuit and lifeline career frustrating. "I sort of fell into business writing, which seemed natural because of the writing interest and training I already had. But even though the money is good, I'm considering a change. After eight hours of sitting at a computer churning out a business newsletter or report, the last thing I want to do is sit back down at the computer again to work on my book. In fact, I've written almost none of my own work for over six months now. I think my life—and my writing—would feel better if I had the courage to try a job in a different field." If you do choose to balance your creative commitment with another Artistic career, it's wise to pay attention to the potential for burnout, as Jean demonstrates.

Combining the Clusters:
Blending Artistic and Other Elements in Your Work

As I mentioned earlier, the basic career clusters above can be combined to identify work that melds artistic and other components. The listing below identifies a number of possibilities. More details on such jobs can be found in *The Career Guide for Creative and Unconventional People* by Carol Eikenberry, Ph.D. (Full information on this and other career books can be found in the Resources section at the end of this book.) As you review this list, you'll note that some of the jobs have an overtly artistic element (for example, landscape architect or interior designer), while others do not. The role of clergyperson or minister, for example, may not seem to incorporate artistic components. But when you look closely at what it entails—writing sermons or talks and organizing the theme and drama of ceremonies or services, among other things—a distinct creative/artistic element is revealed.

Careers combining Investigative and Artistic components: art appraiser, acquisitions librarian, college professor, curator, architect, staff or journalistic writer, experimental pscyhologist, social psychologist, medical/scientific illustrator, art restorer, computer programmer, critic, editor, reviewer.

Careers combining Enterprising and Artistic components: public-relations representative, promotions and/or salesperson, publications editor, program director, fashion coordinator, wedding consultant, lawyer.

Careers combining Social and Artistic components: teacher (elementary through high school), counselor, dance therapist, music therapist, speech pathologist, drama coach, cantor, minister or clergyperson, fitness trainer, corporate speaker/trainer.

Careers combining Realistic and Artistic components: interior designer, landscape architect, bonsai cultivator, musical instrument maker or repairperson, model maker, miniature set designer, stage technician, window decorator, jewelry/crafts maker, chef.

Careers combining Conventional and Artistic components: handwriting analyst, social secretary, personal assistant, police artist. (Note that there are fewer careers in this combined-cluster category than in others. This is because the Artistic and Conventional clusters are opposite in nature and involve mutually exclusive tendencies.)

Applying the Cluster Concept

Now that you've reviewed the clusters and their combinations, it's time to apply them to your needs, preferences and situation.

Of the six original clusters (not the combined ones), what three are the most interesting or appropriate to you?

1. _____
2. _____
3. _____

Working from the clusters you've chosen and from the combinations that include those clusters, name six potential careers that are worth further consideration and research. Note briefly what appeals to you about the job.

1. _____Key qualities: _____
2. _____Key qualities: _____
3. _____Key qualities: _____
4. _____Key qualities: _____
5. _____Key qualities: _____
6. _____Key qualities: _____

Especially if you had trouble filling up the six slots above, consider your existing knowledge of work and careers. Are you aware of any additional or related careers that could be added to the list above? If so, list them here.

1. _____ 2. _____
3. _____ 4. _____

With this information in mind, you can now move on to researching work in your fields of potential interest. For more on the research process, simply move on to chapter 6.

Chapter Six

Discovering a New Career

The aim of the artist is just to investigate. That's all I want to do: investigate and present the results.
—David Bowie

Dancing is just discovery, discovery, discovery.
—Martha Graham

Committing to a new career is a big decision. Just as you wouldn't marry someone after a single look across a crowded room, you shouldn't choose a career path based on a handful of facts or a bit of intuition. The best way to make a reasonable and realistic choice is to gather additional, more specific information.

"Research" has a dull, nuts-and-bolts sound. Yet many of my clients find that they enjoy discovering all of their options. It feels quite similar in some ways to their creative pursuits, which are also filled with a certain kind of research. Actors research complex roles, while writers do background research on the era or themes of their novels. As the quotations at the front of this chapter suggest, you could say that the entire job of being an artist is one of research—research of the world, its meanings, its experiences. Similarly, exploring potential new lives and working identities and finding out about activities that were unfamiliar to you can be a wonderful and quite creative adventure.

The research process has tangible benefits as well. Good preparatory research will help you not only *choose* a wonderful lifeline career but actually *get* a wonderful lifeline position or business. The facts you learn, the industry concerns or buzzwords you become familiar with, the experience you get from interning or volunteering, and the personal contacts you make during your career research process are the same advantages that will help you land clients or a good employer when the time comes.

In addition, solid research—the kind that allows you to make a realistic assessment of a field—can save you lots of time and heartache. The story of Dawn, told in chapter 3, is an excellent case in point.

Research Resources: Getting Started

In this information age, resources that can help you in your investigation of jobs are so abundant they can be bewildering. Essentially, though, they all fall into one of four categories:

- Printed and Online Material
- Work Experience
- Training and Education
- Personal Contacts and Networking

These information sources are complementary, and each can give you a different kind of information. Printed material, for example, tells you about the *facts* of a career: the training required, the potential income, the industry's trends, and more. Work experience, in contrast, lets you get the *feeling* of it—a sense of whether or not you would actually enjoy doing the work. Basing a career decision on one without the other gives you only part of the picture.

As you get started, I'd encourage you to choose *three* potential careers to research, even if only one really stands out. You'll feel able to make a stronger judgment by having several options, each with its own pros and cons, to evaluate. You'll also feel more confident having one or two "fallback positions" if your first choice, like Dawn's, ends up seeming unrealistic.

Use the first source of career data, printed and online material, to explore all three possible choices. At the end of this part of the research process, you'll probably find that you have a single very strong preference. Then, use *all* of the four sources of information to explore this single lifeline career.

Printed and Online Material

Printed and computer-based material is the best place to start your research. There's an abundance of literature on virtually every career, and most of it is easily accessible through your computer's Internet connection, libraries, bookstores, college career centers, newspapers and magazines, and company reports and newsletters. The following are some of the best printed and online sources.

The Occupational Outlook Handbook (OOH). This is the "Bible" of career education and a wonderful place to start your research. The OOH describes each occupation, its education and training requirements, its earnings and advancement possibilities, and its employment outlook. It even lists related occupations you might explore and gives sources for further information about a given field.

Career Information Delivery Systems (CIDS). These computer-based systems—increasingly available at libraries, schools, government agencies, and private organizations—contain information about hundreds of occupations, along with data on related education and job training programs. CIDS can also link career options with personal characteristics such as interests and aptitudes. Information is displayed on the computer screen but can also be printed so that you can keep it with your career file.

Major newspapers. Most major newspapers publish frequent articles on local or even national business trends. Many also publish a yearly supplement that projects the effects of social, political, and economic changes on the labor market. *The New York Times* labor supplement, for example, is published each year, approximately in mid-October. It covers *all* regions of the country and is a superb summary of the most up-to-date employment outlook data. And don't forget *The Wall Street Journal,* a daily which often publishes features that give detailed glimpses of a wide array of careers, businesses, and trends.

As you check newspaper information, don't neglect the classified section! Even before you're actually looking for a position, classifieds can give you an overview of a particular local job market: what is in demand, what pays, what skills or experience are required, and which companies are hiring regularly.

General-interest and specialized magazines. Many general-interest magazines today offer columns or features about careers. *Time* and *Newsweek,* for example, often carry a feature or two about business news and trends. Though periodicals like *Forbes, Fortune, Business Week,* and *Barron's* specialize in finance, they are often a source of good overview material on business trends. Even a magazine as apparently far afield as *Cosmopolitan* often publishes a feature on a particular career! Check your library's *Guide to Periodicals* to see what's been recently printed on your potential careers.

Increasing numbers of magazines specialize entirely in some aspect of career, entrepreneurship, or job success. These publications not only can give you lots of specific information; they also can provide ideas. In today's diverse work world, there are lots of possibilities out there!

Spend an afternoon browsing through the periodicals section of your library or of a good bookstore that sells magazines. Check with a good reference librarian to make sure you haven't missed any good periodical sources, and review those that are most relevant to your particular potential careers.

Books. Thanks to the book industry's trend toward niche publishing, books on particular careers and small business, as well as job-hunting strategies, are more plentiful than ever before. A number of such books are listed in the Resources guide at the end of this book. You can probably find books with information on your specific potential careers in your local library. *Writer's Market,* for example, is updated annually and includes current fees for lifeline writing careers such as magazine writer, greeting card writer, business writer, and more, as well as listings of organizations who buy such writing.

There are several ways to check out available book resources. Review the current edition of *Books in Print,* which lists available books by author, title, and subject. (Your local library or bookstore will have a copy.) Scan the offerings of one of the Internet booksellers such as Amazon or Barnes and Noble. Or, you can browse through your library and local bookstore if your town has a sizable one; be sure to check not only the Career Information shelves but also the Business sections, as both may have relevant titles. With any book publication, of course, you'll have to check the copyright or publication date to ensure that specific information about trends and salaries is up-to-date.

Industry unions, clubs, and professional organizations. These highly specialized groups can be an excellent source of information about a given career. The National Writer's Union, for example, works to inform and advocate for writers, including journalists and technical writers; it may have useful information for you if you are considering a lifeline job in either field.

Internet/Web sites. The Internet is one of the most abundant sources of career information. Sites related to jobs, small business management, and careers are diverse and updated frequently. You can find both general-information and specific (i.e., company or organization, government agency) sites. Some of the best sites available at the time this book was written are listed in the Resources section at the back of this book. However, sites change and are added constantly. Search under keywords relevant to your specific career interests frequently, and check more general keywords as well.

Work Experience

Printed and online material gives you a factual overview of your potential careers. But actual work experience is an invaluable source of firsthand information. It can help you understand whether a given career would be comfortable or uncomfortable, challenging or dull. This kind of hands-on sense of what a job is like is crucial to making a sound choice about your lifeline career. It is also helpful (in fact, it may be downright necessary) in building a resume that will allow you to gain entry in a field that demands prior work experience.

If you're a creative person who has concentrated primarily on your art rather than on the development of your career, you are probably asking how you can get work experience when you don't yet have the skills or background to be hired. There are several excellent ways to do so. The following three work experience formats may also be useful to those who are transitioning from an overly demanding or unsatisfying lifeline job, since they provide hands-on experience in a new role, field, or career.

Volunteering

Volunteering is an ideal way to learn about a career firsthand. As I noted above, it is also an excellent means of getting relevant experience. Volunteer opportunities abound. Virtually every nonprofit organization has a volunteer program, and even the smallest may use the services of hundreds of volunteers. Often, however, the tasks that result from an organization's standard volunteer program—word processing donor appeals, manning a reception desk or gift shop, labeling newsletters, giving tours, and so on—will not give you the kind of experience or information you need.

Instead, be proactive and creative in shaping a volunteer opportunity. Think about how your unique skills and gifts could help one or more target organizations. Remember that even though you are trying to make a career transition, you are already a professional in your creative field—that is, don't forget that you have something unique to offer! Find a way to "package" your abilities in a way that offers *specific benefits with little risk* to your target organizations.

Jenny, an actress who wanted to break into the field of corporate training, volunteered for her State's Department of Labor to teach a workshop on utilizing acting skills in job interviews. "The subject sounds off-beat at first, but it's actually quite legitimate. It isn't something the Department would have paid for, but it was a natural extension of what they did. It gave me a great hands-on sense of what it would be like to do corporate training, and confirmed my sense that it was a good field for me. Better yet, it was something I was eminently qualified to teach; I was able to present myself to them not as someone needing experience but as someone with experience to share. I was eventually paid a small amount for my work. But much more importantly, I built legitimate, even prestigious credits for my resume. The fact that a large and well-known state agency was willing to use my services added hugely to my credibility and also gave me some references who could speak directly to my presentation skills." After some additional volunteering and some low-paying work, Jenny landed an excellent position at a prestigious consulting firm. She now travels around the world to give sessions on presentation skills to corporate executives.

To give you one more example, Lynn is a writer who wanted to move toward a lifeline career as a freelance business writer and editor. To do so, however, she needed to build a resume that had something other than literary publications on it. She offered to write brochures without charge for ten neighborhood businesses, which she chose carefully for their relatively small size, different fields, and prestigious reputations. Four took her up on her offer. She then volunteered to edit the newsletter of a local conservation foundation for free. "After I'd worked successfully on the first issue, thereby proving to the organization that I had real value to them, I asked for a credit line as editor. After only six months, thanks to my various volunteer jobs, I had four reputable writing clients and an editorial byline, all in different fields. That experience made it much easier to get good business-writing jobs. I also had a really invaluable sense of both the potential and the pitfalls of freelance business writing! I'd learned what kinds of problems arose and gotten a much better sense of what I'd need to charge."

The questions below will help you ensure that the volunteer work you choose will truly help you build a new lifeline career. Note that these questions are equally valuable to ask before you choose an internship.

- **What are my principal duties?** Make sure that you are not just performing clerical tasks such as filing, answering phones, or making copies. These jobs may be perfectly appropriate for an intern or volunteer to do, but they will not serve your particular agenda, which is to find out about what a particular field is like and build your skills in the process.

- **What is my work schedule?** It's important to make sure that you are not being taken advantage of just because you are working for free or for very little! An internship or volunteer situation associated with a school or training program—either of which may carry course credit—might involve as much as two days a week. In other situations, it is completely appropriate that your time commitment be less.

- **What skills and/or knowledge base will I develop through this work?** When you ask your supervisor this question, you may identify new skill areas you had not even thought about. In addition, you'll make sure that your time will be spent in a manner which will genuinely support your new lifeline career.

- **Will I be working for more than one supervisor?** Reporting to more than one person is often harder, but you will probably learn more than you would from a single individual.

- **Will I be interacting with other workers, managers, customers, or clients?** Here again, the more interaction, the more you will learn.

- **Will I receive an evaluation at the end of my duties?** Verbal or written feedback is an important part of professional growth. It will help you gain confidence in a new field and/or target area in which you need work.

- **Might this situation be part of the organization's recruiting process?** This is an indirect way of asking, "If I do a good job, is there a possibility that you will hire me?" It's wiser not to ask for a job directly, as your main goal is to gain experience and knowledge and to build a resume.

Internships

Internships allow you to work at a job related to your field of study or career goal. In exchange for the intern's work, professionals provide on-the-job training on requisite skills or offer mentoring support. Sometimes the work is relatively low-level; for example, interns can end up entering names in a promotional database, stuffing envelopes, and so on. In other cases, for example in social work, your internship duties may be very similar to those you'd fulfill in your eventual lifeline job. The intensity and challenge of the work involved in an internship depends on the particular organization offering it. These variations make it especially important to ask the questions above before choosing an internship.

Internships are usually offered—and may even be required—by specialized schools, such as those that offer master's and certificate programs in fields such as journalism, social work, clinical psychology, and arts management. Internships may or may not offer credit but are well worth your time either way. As with volunteer work, it's possible to create your own internship if you are not enrolled in a program or if the internships offered as part of your training don't fully meet your needs.

In the process of researching potential lifeline careers, for example, artist and actor Jeff was given the name of a small but growing graphic arts firm by a friend. He offered to help the two owners in return for the work experience their firm could offer. Because the firm was still in a start-up mode—that is, overworked and understaffed—they jumped at Jeff's offer. Jeff raves about the knowledge he gained about various computer graphics programs, as well as about the understanding he got about the realities of working under tight deadlines. "That's something I could never have learned in school," he says. His bosses are now helping him develop a portfolio and are willing to help him with job leads and references when his portfolio is complete. They have also agreed to pay him at that time. "I think more experiences like this are out there than most creative people realize, especially in an economy where smaller firms can't afford to commit to a lot of full-time staff," Jeff concludes. "I've found that professionals are surprisingly willing to help someone like me who is making a career transition. All you need to get their assistance is a solid plan for how you can help them in return."

Shadowing Programs

Shadowing programs allow you to spend some period of time—typically a day or two—with a professional in your field of interest. Like internships, they are typically associated with formal school or certificate programs or with professional organizations. Here again, though, you can create your own opportunities if necessary.

"After considerable research," a theater director named LeAnne says, "I felt very drawn to a lifeline job in public relations. I always liked the sales and promotional elements of the theater, and I felt that PR would be the perfect use for my flair. But I also felt hampered by my inability to get any actual experience, and I didn't want to invest a year or more in an entry-level position until I had some kind of hands-on confirmation that I'd actually like the field. I wasn't taking a program or courses that could offer internships, and PR firms don't use volunteers.

"Finally, I decided on a pretty bold move. I rewrote my resume to reflect my most relevant experiences and skills and then researched the industry to find out the names and firms of the top five local PR 'stars.' Then I sent a letter to each of the five company presidents. I told them honestly that I was making a career transition and needed help, but I didn't undersell myself as a total novice, either. I included a strong resume and asked only that they let me 'shadow' them for a day. Three of the five contacted me after the letter—a much better response than I'd hoped for, actually. Two were polite refusals, but one took me up on my offer. I had a great and very informative day, and my 'boss' was so impressed with me that she called me a couple of months later with an assistant-level job offer. Even if she hadn't," LeAnne concluded, "the insight I gained into the nuts and bolts of PR would have been invaluable."

Education and Training

Education and training are an increasingly important part of the world of work today, given cultural and technological changes that can transform entire industries, not to mention mere jobs, almost overnight. Training is mandatory for fields that have licensing or other standardized requirements—for example, fitness training, teaching, and many health-care careers. But proper training has several other advantages, too:

- Education and training help you evaluate a potential new career even before you begin to practice it and give you the tools and knowledge you need to succeed once you begin.

- Training programs allow you to meet peers interested in the same lifeline career you are, helping you create a new support network.

- Certificates or degrees from training programs "beef up" your resume with relevant credentials and are of especial value when your work experience or credentials in your new chosen career is light.

- Training programs can open to the door to internship or other early work opportunities in your new career.

- The educational process in a given field helps you begin to build invaluable links with mentors, contacts, and referral sources in that field.

For these reasons, you should explore training programs even if your chosen lifeline career does not have mandatory education requirements.

"Yes, but I'm trying to find a career to make money, not to spend it on training," you might be saying. Training may seem unnecessary, too. You probably know several people with great educations who are in the same financial or creative bind as you are. As Fats Domino once said, "A lot of fellows nowadays have a B.A., M.D., or Ph.D. Unfortunately, they don't have a J.O.B."

Happily, an entirely new—and practical—educational system is emerging in response to changing workforce conditions. Adult education centers throughout the country now offer a wide range of short-term, work-related, nondegree courses at reasonable prices. Even traditional universities are expanding their offerings to include weekend seminars or "online" classes that can be taken from home. Whatever their format or sponsor, these programs share a practical approach and a focus on the current needs of the job market. These new training formats make it much easier and less expensive for you to get quality education about your new lifeline career.

Programs of this type currently available include the following (some, such as the real-estate program, are licensing courses):

- Entrepreneurship/Small Business Management
- Real Estate
- Public Relations
- Foreign Language Interpretation/Translation
- Fundraising/Nonprofit Management
- Book Publishing
- Technical Writing/Editing
- Alcohol/Drug Abuse Counseling
- Microsoft Certified Teacher Training
- Conference/Event Management
- Art and Antique Appraisal
- Multimedia Technologies

Some such programs offer some form of financial aid; in any case, tuition is often lower than for traditional degree programs. A number of organizations also offer scholarships and/or career counseling to eligible constituents nationwide. A partial listing of such organizations, plus books that list other financial assistance, including that of an emergency nature, are given in the Resources section at the back of this book.

Personal Contacts and Networking

Publications and programs are not the ultimate informational resource; *peo-*

ple are. Your relationships with others—both in and out of your prospective new field—are a powerful but as yet probably untapped source for help in:

- Researching new fields of interest
- Generating the desired new job or clients
- Building and growing your new career
- Ensuring that your new career continues to meet your needs

More than any other method of job research or search, building and using a network of friends and professional contacts will help you meet your unique goals. Networking is invaluable for those aiming toward employment and self-employment alike. As Paul McCartney said, "I get by with a little help from my friends!" When you use employment agencies or want ads, your starting point is what the *employer* wants and how you can fit into those needs. When you use your network, your starting point is what *you* need to know and what *you* want.

I once broached the power of the personal and professional network to Dan, a struggling actor who was just beginning a search for a new lifeline career. In response, he gave me a look that mingled confusion, amusement, and dismay. "A network?" he asked ruefully. "Basically, at the moment, my network consists of about twenty starving artists just like me, the family that's just about given up on me, the waiter at my neighborhood diner, and my dog."

You may be feeling the same. Like Dan, however, you'll be surprised by the breadth and power of your network. To make full use of this unique resource, you must simply learn to *mine the hidden potential of the contacts you already know* and to *expand your circle of contacts continually.*

In their book *Career Renewal,* a job-transition guide for scientists, Stephen Rosen and Celia Paul break down a good network into three different types of contacts. Understanding these three distinct groups is a helpful way to begin using and building a network.

- "A", or primary, contacts consist of your current friends, family, peers, service providers, neighbors, and colleagues.

- "B", or bridge, contacts, often reached through A contacts, are generally experts in their fields who can offer you useful information. They do not have the authority or need to hire you on either a staff or freelance basis, but they can offer helpful advice and industry knowledge. Often, they are an excellent source of other industry experts, including those who might hire you or retain your services at some point.

- "C", or hiring, contacts are individuals in an organization with hiring authority, are part of the hiring decision-making chain, or are potential clients.

Subsequently, I'll describe each group in more detail and review how best to use all three types of contacts. Notice from the start, however, that there is a distinct difference between the A and B groups, which are essentially information-gathering resources, and the C group. The approach you use with A and B contacts, who do not have the direct authority to hire you, is very different from the approach you must use with C contacts, who are potential employers. With individuals in the A and B groups, you can be quite open and honest about your need for information. With C contacts, every encounter is in essence a job interview, and at all times you must be conscious of the impression you make.

A Contacts: Your First Line of Inquiry

These are the people who are already in your life. Normally, their value in terms of professional networking is their ability to introduce you to those who are expert or experienced in your potential lifeline career. Sometimes, though probably less often, your A contacts may also be B contacts, who have direct information about your potential lifeline career, or even C contacts, who possess hiring capacity. (When categories overlap this way, treat the contact as though he or she belongs to the more important of the categories.)

Since these relationships already exist, A contacts are not hard to use. In the words of Iris Murdoch, "There is no substitute for the comfort of the utterly taken-for-granted relationship." A contacts are typically very open to sharing information about fields you may be pursuing or referrals to additional people who may be of help to you. You need only be careful with them when they overlap into the C group.

Typically, my clients have never thought about their existing network of relationships this way. To help them get started, I encourage them to make a complete written listing of their existing contacts. I urge you to do the same. Include space not just for listing your A contacts but also room to note if they can give you relevant career information themselves or introduce you to someone who is closer to your goal. Aim to make your listing as comprehensive as you possibly can. To do so, include both local and nonlocal A contacts and people from all of the following groups:

- Relatives
- Friends

- Your Christmas card list
- Classmates, former or present
- Teachers, professors, and mentors, former or present
- Fellow artists and creative people
- Neighbors
- Fellow members of professional organizations
- Fellow members of churches, support groups, or clubs
- Local merchants
- Service providers (bankers, travel agents, accountants, lawyers, even hair-dressers or barbers!)
- Health-care practitioners (dentists, physicians)
- Fellow members of volunteer organizations
- Fellow members of political groups or organizations
- Local information sources such as librarians or newspaper reporters
- Advertising and promotional officials you may have worked with
- Employees, including personnel directors and managers, at past and present employers or companies
- Any career counselors you have worked with
- Previous or current clients of your freelance services
- Previous or current purchasers/users of your art form (i.e., those who have directed your plays, bought your artworks, etc.)
- Parents of friends or of your children's friends; friends of your parents
- E-mail correspondents

Even if you are the "classic" artist who lives a somewhat isolated life, you may be astonished at how long your list is and how much potential information it represents. Ben, a poet, is a case in point. "My goal for a more stable, non-artistic career is to be a private writing tutor for children who need extra composition help in elementary grades, junior high, and high school. I started compiling my A contacts pretty reluctantly, figuring that they would all be totally irrelevant to that career. Once I started looking at the people I knew from the networking viewpoint, though, I was dumb-struck by how many possible sources of help my life already contained."

He continues, "A total of sixteen people were parents of children or close friends of people with children; they all agreed to help spread the word of my services. My dentist has a son who became my first client. Most importantly, a neighbor is a teacher at a large local school. She first introduced me to a fellow English teacher, who was helpful in alerting me to the kind of writing problems her students struggle with. This teacher in turn introduced me to the principal, who let me use the faculty mail-box system to distribute my brochure, alerting teachers to my availability. Without doing anything more than talking with people I already knew, I totally jump-started my new business." Ben's experience shows how effortlessly A contacts can lead to or even become B or even C contacts.

"Assessing myself and the world of work led me to serious consideration of a lifeline career in alternative medicine, preferably in acupuncture. I researched the field and even tentatively chose a training program, but I didn't have any hands-on sense of what the daily life of an acupuncture physician would be like," said Michaela, a painter by training. "When I was asked to list my A contacts, though, I suddenly remembered that a cousin of mine swore by her acupuncturist, who lived only about thirty miles away. I asked my cousin to introduce me, then took the acupuncturist out for lunch. He was delighted to help me and gave me a huge amount of insight into acupuncture and the whole world of alternative medicine. Our meeting left me feeling inspired, reassured, and much more confident about proceeding with my training."

As the experience of both Ben and Michaela demonstrates, you don't want to make your search for further contacts too narrow at this point. You will have plenty of time to hone in more specifically when you get to B and C contacts.

Michaela's A contacts, for example, might not have yielded an acupuncture physician immediately, but they might have allowed her to meet a yoga teacher who could have given her good insight into her community's openness to holistic treatments or a health store proprietor whose alternative medicine support group would eventually be a good source of clients. Ben's A list might not have introduced him to a school principal, but it might have offered the chance to speak with an accountant who could advise on small-business structuring or a newspaper reporter willing to write a feature on a published poet now helping the community's children. At this stage, be open to whatever help is available.

For A contacts, use a basic pitch that alerts them to the kind of help you need. Ben's pitch might have gone as follows:

> "You may know that I'm forming a new business to act as a writing tutor for children in grades six through twelve. The more information I can get at this preliminary stage, the more effectively I can do this work. Do you know any tutors or English teachers in the area? What about parents of children in that age range? Are you aware of anyone else who might be helpful in this regard? That's great. Would you be willing to let me use your name when I contact them?"

Michaela's A contact talk, in contrast, might have sounded like this:

> "Did [relative, friend, etc.] tell you that I'm planning on entering the Southern School for Acupuncture in the fall? Until then, I'm interested in talking to as many people as I can about holistic and alternative medicine services in this

area. Do you know of anyone who practices here or anyone who goes to see an alternative practitioner like an acupuncturist, homeopath, or massage therapist? Do you know anyone else who might be able to help me?"

B Contacts: Your Source for Detailed Information

B contacts are the bridges that will take you into the world of job offers or business clients. As I've already suggested, they can give you specific and relevant information that can help you assess aspects of your new career including its work style, prospects, training requirements, and more. Because they are already working in or around your new chosen lifeline career, they are a wonderful source of hands-on insight. They can often give you hints, tips, and shortcuts that are virtually priceless— things you might have taken years to learn on your own. They are not, however, in a position to offer you an actual job (at least, not at this time).

Therefore, B contacts, like the previous group, can usually be treated with relative informality. Still, you will have fairly detailed questions for a B contact, and that individual could eventually be in a position to assist you further in your new career. Obviously, you are not helping yourself if B contacts remember you as pushy, disorganized, or in any other negative manner.

Glenda, the writer who publishes literary works under her own name but also makes a lifeline income writing mystery novels under a pseudonym, sees the issue from both sides. "Having started with only the most precarious artistic existence myself and having been helped a great deal by the advice of more experienced authors, I'm very open to helping other writers build a more stable writing career," she says. "I often speak to writer's groups for free, for example, and equally often talk with acquaintances who'd like to get some advice.

"Usually, the folks I meet this way are a pleasure, but not always. I recently agreed to talk with a friend of a friend, a young guy who wants to write a suspense novel. He insisted on meeting in the morning, which is my writing time—I only gave in out of respect for our mutual friend and, quite frankly, a desire to get him off my back. He asked quite probing and uncomfortable questions about my book advances, put down the traditional mystery field—which I happen to write in—as 'moronic,' and ended by dumping a four hundred plus-page novel draft on my desk so that I could give him comments! When I explained very politely that I just wasn't able to offer that kind of detailed help for free, he was quite rude. The sad thing for people like him is that writers, like any other profession, are a relatively close-knit community. Once you've burnt your bridges, it's hard to repair them. One of these days, this man's application will end up in front of one of the many admissions and awards panels I sit on. I would never go out of my way to hurt him, but I won't be able to recommend him, either. He just didn't have a clue."

As this story demonstrates, your goal is to establish as reciprocal and respectful a relationship as possible, even if your current ability to help your B contact in return is nil. To do so, you must structure your dealings within the B group with some care. Some specific guidelines are given below. Many of these "rules" sound obvious, but they're so important they are worth stating anyway.

- **Make an appointment in advance,** at the contact's convenience. If you have not met the contact previously, mention the name of the person who suggested you call or, better yet, ask that person to make the initial contact so that your name will be familiar when you call.

- **Do not press too hard** if you don't get an immediate callback; allow one to two weeks to go by before following up.

- **Do not assume the contact automatically has a free hour to talk to you during the working day;** follow his or her lead about what time period (workday, after work, weekends) would be the most comfortable meeting time.

- **With important B contacts, consider offering to take them for coffee, a post-work drink, or a modest lunch.** Even if they don't take you up on your offer, it creates a more reciprocal atmosphere, reassuring them that you respect the value of their expertise and do not take their time for granted. The relatively small expense involved pays for itself, since you'll capture their time and attention more fully than you ever could by meeting in their busy office in the midst of a demanding day.

- **If you must reschedule the appointment, be sure to give ample warning.**

- **Be careful about asking for further assistance** once your meeting or conversation is through. Although it can sometimes be appropriate for you to ask them to review your resume, introduce you to a specific third party, or sponsor you for a professional organization, it is safer to follow their lead. If they want to give you further help, they will offer it or make clear that they are open to future interactions.

- **Although your questions can be detailed, they shouldn't be intrusive or insensitive.** It's fine to ask if a B contact knows what typical starting fees or salaries are in your area; it's inappropriate to ask what he or she is currently making. Remember, in this regard, that depending on their position, some B contacts may perceive you as future competition. Don't appear to be asking for sensitive information. Though you may make it clear that you will be looking for work, you should not ask the contact for a job, client referrals, or other business. Doing so is simply too pressuring.

- **A follow-up thank-you note is an excellent idea.** It helps your B contacts remember you as an admirable future colleague who is grateful for their assistance and willing to be of help to them some day.

When you meet with your B contact, make sure you are prepared with questions that are appropriate to your need and their expertise. If you are not detailed enough in your questioning, your meeting will not be of maximum value to you. You can be quite forthright and open in your questions. Some inquiries you might make are:

About work experience:
- How long have you worked in this field?
- How did you decide to enter this field?
- What experience prepared you for the job? What training?
- How has your career progressed?
- How does this job fit into your overall career plan?
- How would you describe a typical day?
- What gives you the most satisfaction in your job? What is the most frustrating part?
- Would you have done anything differently if you were beginning this career today?

About the field:
- What kind of training and preparation is necessary to enter this

field? What kinds of experience would be helpful for a person to have before entering this career?

- What personal qualities do you think successful people in this field share?

- How is the job market currently? Are there any positive or negative trends that I should be aware of?

- How do you see the opportunities for professional growth?

- What do you see as the advantages of this field? The disadvantages?

- How can I become most competitive if I enter this field?

- What are typical entry-level jobs? Do you have a sense of what I could expect in terms of an entry-level salary?

- What kinds of organizations hire people in this field?

- What kinds of hours do people work? Are they standard, or can they be flexible?

- If you could choose one thing, what do you think is the single most important thing I should know before entering the field?

- Do you know of anyone else who may be helpful to me as I explore this career further?

Notice that last line. No matter how you adapt the rest of the list to your career goals, needs, and the type of contact you're talking to, you should always make that your last question.

C Contacts: Your Job Offer or Client Resources

C contacts are the individuals in an organization who either have the authority to make you an actual job offer, are close to those in decision-making roles, or could be either clients or spheres of influence. They are the VIPs of your network!

As you begin to meet and talk with C contacts, your focus shifts. It is no longer on gathering information, but on presenting yourself as someone who has something to offer in your new field. For this reason, you must be much more prepared when you meet or speak with a C individual than with any other kind of contact in your network. If you are given the name of a C contact before you're ready to present yourself knowledgeably, hold off on the call until you are confident about your skills and career goal.

Obviously, all C contacts must be treated in a highly professional manner. Follow the basic guidelines for networking etiquette given in the section on B contacts. You might also want to look ahead to chapter 9's interview guidelines before meeting with C contacts, as each encounter you have with them is in some sense an interview.

In addition, when you meet a C contact, you need to be able to produce a strong resume targeted specifically at your new lifeline field and speak briefly and confidently about your goals, abilities, and experience as they relate to that field. (I call this presentation a "personal commercial.") All of the research you have done so far—about your own needs and skills, as well as about potential new careers—has given you the foundation you need to develop these two essential tools for selling your skills. Chapter 8 will help you create both a great resume and a great personal commercial, so let's move right on!

In Summary

As you research a potential new career, be sure to ask the following questions. You'll note that most can be answered through the Occupational Outlook Handbook at the Department of Labor (*http://stats.bls.gov/ocohome.htm*), and in the other resources described in this chapter.

1. What kinds of skills does this job require? How do those skills fit in with those I have identified in my reassessment? (See chapter 3.)

2. Will I need further training to work in this area? If so, will I need courses, a certificate or licensure program, or a degree program?

3. If training is required, what are the names of two or three schools where I can get it?

4. What is the cost of the completed training? Can I afford the cost and the time involved? If not, are there ways to get scholarships or financial aid, or is it possible to accelerate the program?

5. Are internship opportunities available so that I can "check out" the work before I commit to it fully? If not, can I create my own opportunity?

6. How much money can I expect to earn when I start out? How much will I earn with more experience?

7. Is this field typically pursued on a freelance/self-employed basis or as an employee? Or, is either format possible?

8. What is the typical work environment like, including people, workplace, pace, and hours? How does this fit with my needs and preferences?

9. Based on all of the above, how might this work positively or negatively impact my creative endeavors?

10. What are several books or magazines I could read to learn more about the field?

11. Who do I know who can give me information about this area?

12. Where can I write for more information? What are the professional organizations affiliated with this field or career?

Chapter Seven

Popular Lifeline Careers for Creative People

If you want to succeed, you should strike out on new paths rather than travel the old paths of accepted success.

—John D. Rockefeller, Jr.

Famous poets William Carlos Williams and Wallace Stevens were a doctor and an insurance executive, respectively; well-known fiction writers Scott Turow and John Mortimer are lawyers. At the other end of the spectrum, actor Harrison Ford was a carpenter before he found fame and fortune! One might think that Ford, now an acting superstar, would be embarrassed by his former lifeline career, but the opposite is the case. In fact, he speaks gratefully about the inner security that came from having a solid non-arts career. "I found a certain value in being a person who'd come for auditions not as an out-of-work actor but as a person who had come from someplace and was going back to someplace with something to do," the actor has been quoted as saying.

In other words, as long as it is *outside* of the unstable, unpredictable field of the creative (as opposed to applied) arts, virtually any field can provide potential for a good lifeline career. Yet there is also a group of fields that are very commonly chosen by creative people as lifeline careers. On the surface, these careers—Web designer, social worker, paralegal—look vastly different. What they share, however, is *a balance between attractive rewards and substantial flexibility.* In other words, they are positions that not only will compensate you at least reasonably well and give you emotional and intellectual satisfaction but also will leave you enough time and energy to pursue your creative dreams. For this reason alone, they're all worth a look if you don't already have a lifeline career clearly in mind.

Though many of these careers require at least some formal training or retraining, you'll often find that the ones that appeal to you will allow you either to use your existing skills or transfer skills from your existing creative field. Teaching and corporate training, for example, make use of presentation skills that performing artists already have in abundance; editing and journalism jobs require the same language skills that creative writers use every day.

As you scan these listings, be aware that:

1. **Each field I describe is capable of almost infinite adjustment to a particular individual's special interests and skills.** You can be a yoga teacher who teaches only children and pregnant women; you can be a corporate trainer who takes her special seminars on stress management to businesses all over the country; you can be a nurse who specializes in geriatric or hospice care. Yes, it takes time and experience to build up such a specialty, but after you've paid your dues, only your own creativity limits the directions in which you can take a lifeline career. For that reason, don't look at the listings that follow as being generic, ordinary, or dull. Brainstorm about which ones might not only offer you a stable living but also ultimately match up with your most unique talents, values, and interests.

2. **Many, though not all, of the following careers can be pursued either as an independent businessperson or as an employee.** If either independent or employee status is the overwhelming norm, I've indicated as much in my description. However, in many cases you can make that decision yourself. For more guidance on that choice, see chapter 4, "Employment Versus Self-Employment: Which is For You?"

3. **Though a number of the careers listed below require no degree, certification, or licensing, it's advisable to obtain formal training if at all possible.** It's understandable that the absence of degree, certification, or licensing requirements may make a particular lifeline career especially attractive to you, because it reduces both the cost and the downtime involved in making a career transition. However, I'm a strong proponent of training programs even when they are not

strictly required. Often, the investment of money and time you make at the start turns out to be hugely helpful later on.

A certificate or degree is an instant credibility builder, which, as I note elsewhere, is especially valuable before you have been able to build a strong client base, resume, or portfolio in your new career.

Moreover, even a brief training program can give you invaluable insights into your new field—information and pointers that might have taken years to gather on your own; a ready-made cadre of peers; contact with experts in the field; and internship, volunteer or job shadowing opportunities that would be much harder to create outside of a formal program.

4. **Though these fields are *commonly* chosen as lifeline careers by creative people, there are many others that might be right for *you*.** My clients have gone on to successful lifeline careers in a wide variety of fields that space limitations prevent me from including here. Some possibilities were omitted because they are not widely available throughout the country, others because they do not generally afford a sufficiently stable income, and still others because the skills they require are too unusual to make them of general interest. However, if a potential career that is not listed here appeals to you, by all means explore it using the research questions and strategies described in chapter 6, "Discovering a New Career"; you might also refer to the additional entrepreneurial careers listed briefly in chapter 4.

Career #1:
Arts or Cultural Administrator/Manager

What You Do: Arts administrators may be involved in many if not most aspects of the operation of cultural or arts organizations. Work is available in the areas of audience or membership development (marketing), grant writing or development (fundraising), programming, finance/accounting, technology/information systems, and general administration. These administrators or managers may be employed by theaters, museums, libraries, archives, historical societies, arts-in-education agencies, or foundations. Alternatively, arts managers may serve such organizations on a freelance or contract basis. Fundraising, grant writing, and special events planning, in fact, are typically done on a part-time or project basis rather than through employment arrangements; in smaller organizations, bookkeeping and technological support may be outsourced to freelancers as well.

Pros and Cons: Arts administration careers let the creative person remain in the congenial and personally rewarding world of the arts. These jobs often offer flexible arrangements or schedules, as arts organizations are by their nature more sympathetic than most other employers to the needs of an artist. Since their budgets tend to be tight, they may also be more interested than other employers in flexible arrangements, to possibly compensate for lower salary. However, arts administration jobs are prevalent mostly in medium-sized to larger cities and often pay less than their counterparts in the for-profit sector.

What You Need: Though some colleges have certificate or even degree programs in arts or nonprofit management, such formal training is not necessary if you can document relevant experience. Many creative people gain such experience through volunteer work and/or internships. In fact, because arts organizations depend heavily on volunteer and intern support, such programs are already in place at many such institutions. (See chapter 6 for more information on these issues).

Special Note: The same administrative/managerial functions listed here can also be done within the broader nonprofit world—which includes philanthropic organizations, "cause-related" or social services agencies, foundations, and public hospitals—or for organizations in the academic sphere, which includes private schools, colleges, and universities. The information above is generally accurate for those venues as well as for organizations in the arts.

Career #2: Arts-in-Education Teacher

What You Do: Arts-in-education encompasses three basic components: teaching children and teenagers traditional subjects in a way that utilizes your artistic background (i.e., teaching spatial relations through dance, foreign cultures through music), performing for children and teenagers who have little other exposure to live performance, and training teachers to plan and execute lessons using artistic viewpoints and techniques.

Pros and Cons: Creative people involved in arts-in-education are able to make a real contribution to society using their artistic gifts. Government funding for these programs has increased greatly in urban, suburban, and rural areas alike in recent years, making this a growing career. On the downside, it is still a relatively narrow field, so networking and personal contacts are crucial; especially in smaller school districts or with private schools, you may need to approach the parents' association and/or the after-school program directly with a proposal on a specific topic or use of your talents.

What You Need: No formal training, degree, or certification is required; you must simply love youngsters and the learning process. Arts-in-education programs generally offer training to their new teaching artists, although information on training is also available from several organizations.

Career #3: Business and Technical Writer

What You Do: Business and technical writers work on projects with practical applications or purposes rather than for purely creative meaning. Such projects may include business, medical, legal, or scientific books; instruction manuals; annual reports; newsletters; training materials; marketing packages; and corporate procedures or policy statements; catalogs. Technical writers work for corporations, government agencies, and service businesses on either a project basis or on staff. Most technical writers are self-employed and may serve a number of client businesses on contract.

Pros and Cons: Business and technical writing offers dramatic and creative writers the chance to use their language skills while making a steady income. The demand for good business writers is currently strong, thanks to a thriving economy and the explosive growth of the Internet, which has added a whole new medium for which text must be created. Compensation is attractive. Be aware, however, that technical writing is quite different from creative genres in that it demands excellent attention to detail, the ability to work within strict legal or technical restrictions, the capacity to grasp complex concepts quickly and fully, and the willingness to work within a business environment.

What You Need: No formal training is required, though courses in business or technical writing are offered by many technical colleges and adult education programs and can help you get started in the field.

Career #4: Caterer

What You Do: Caterers provide food (and sometimes serving pieces, linens, and staff as well) for events and parties given by individuals and/or businesses. Their role includes menu development, food preparation, food transport, warming and serving of food, and food disposal/cleanup. Catered events may be as small as a boardroom luncheon or as large as a 500-seat charity ball. Caterers are typically independent contractors or companies that price their services by menu item or by event.

Pros and Cons: Though catering is hard work, it also offers a great deal of creative scope, attractive compensation, and attractive flexibility for the creative person; some caterers work only weekend events, for example, while others work only in the "high season" in their location.

What You Need: Culinary training is helpful in establishing credibility. In practical terms, caterers need a sizeable personal or professional kitchen where food can be prepared and stored before its transportation to the event site.

Career #5: Chef

What You Do: The most skilled of all kitchen workers, chefs plan meals, develop menus, and prepare meals that are pleasing to the eye as well as the taste buds, using one or a mixture of cuisines. Junior chefs may help prepare ingredients; senior chefs may help direct kitchen staff. The terms "cook" and "chef" are often used interchangeably, though the title of chef implies greater skill and, often, greater control over menus and presentation. Chefs are employed by restaurants, institutions, caterers, or, in rarer cases, affluent individuals or families.

Pros and Cons: With ingredients and recipes from all over the world now a part of American dining, visual appeal a growing part of food preparation, and even informal foods more innovative than ever before, the job of chef has become an increasingly creative and visible role. Successful chefs are also well compensated, though beginning salaries can be low. On the downside, work as a chef demands substantial training and almost always involves evening and/or weekend work, possibly conflicting with the scheduling needs of performing or other artists.

What You Need: While chefs often learn cooking under the tutelage of an experienced mentor, professional training is an increasingly important part of a chef's success. There are culinary institutes all over the country; accreditation by the American Culinary Federation indicates that a school meets recognized standards and provides formal recognition of skills for the prospective chef.

Career #6: Computer Specialist

What You Do: The computer field is the fastest growing vocational area at the turn of the millennium. Jobs in this field are highly diversified and will only get more numerous and varied as time goes on. Please note that the computer field is changing extremely quickly; the information here is meant to get you started on your research but should be double-checked against current standards, norms, costs, and fees in your area. As of this writing, the most popular computer related fields include the following:

- **Computer Graphics Designer.** See Career #13, "Graphic Designer."

- **Web Site Designer/Developer.** Web site developers plan and create a site's structure, from its design to its interactive links and options. Though it requires a good visual sense, the increasing interactivity and complexity of Web sites has placed a growing emphasis on the technical side of this field; a site designer must now have extremely strong fundamental computer skills and knowledge of programming languages such as HTML, XHTML, Java, GUI, AWT/Swing, and/or JDBC.

- **Computer Network Engineer.** Computer Network Engineering, or CNE, comprises the installation, creation, management, and troubleshooting of linked or related computers in a business setting. A knowledge of DNS servers, operating-system specifics, networking principles, and other highly technical information is required. Demand in this field is extremely high; employment is generally generated through consulting firms.

- **Microcomputer Specialist.** Jobs in microcomputer technology involve the installation, maintenance, security, and support of personal computer hardware, software, and telecommunications. Work can be done as a small business owner (i.e., installing and repairing computers), as a tester/evaluator, or as a help desk administrator for an organization.

- **Computer Programmer.** A computer programmer translates a business's needs into customized computer record-keeping, data generation and storage, and other functions. Knowledge of Cobol, C Programming, C++, Visual Basic, SQL, Lotus Notes Application Development, and/or Oracle is required.

- **Computer Trainer, Teacher, or Tutor.** Computer skills are becoming such an integral part of many jobs—not to mention such a fundamental part of life in general!—that the demand for qualified instructors is very high. You can teach computer skills at schools or colleges; work as a private tutor with individuals (either children or adults) or businesses; and/or train groups of company staff or executives on new programs or skills.

Pros and Cons: Individuals with specialized computer knowledge are likely to be in very high demand in the foreseeable future, and experts in the field can command exceptionally good compensation for their work. Scheduling is often quite flexible as well. Many computer jobs have become increasingly competitive, however; as the technology that supports them has changed and developed, these same jobs have come to require greater technical sophistication than ever before. If you choose a lifeline career in the computer field, therefore, be prepared to invest in excellent training and then make sure you get ongoing updates to keep your skills and knowledge current.

What You Need: No specific degrees or licenses are required for computer-related work, but, as noted above, it is difficult if not impossible to get work without both a high degree of skill and considerable knowledge of current hardware and software packages. Training on computer use and software is available at colleges, business schools, and adult education programs; the cost varies depending on the institution and the complexity of the course.

Career #7: Corporate Trainer

What You Do: Corporate trainers develop and conduct training programs for business, service, or government organizations. They typically meet with company managers to create appropriate course outlines and materials, then make a presentation to one or more groups of employees. Typical topics can include employee orientation; sales, computer, or other job-related training; health and safety; leadership; presentation skills; and time management. Topics intended to improve employees' overall well-being, such as stress management and goal setting, have become more common as well.

Pros and Cons: The corporate training field is glamorous and well compensated. However, it is also highly competitive, and staff jobs can be hard to secure, primarily because most organizations do not consider training to be part of their mission and therefore do not have large training staffs.

What You Need: Most performing artists could easily teach presentation and related topics to corporate employees, and the field of corporate training as yet has no standardized licensing or education requirement. Typically, however, it is difficult to make a transition into this field unless you can not only prove you have excellent presentation skills but also show a history of presentations made. The best way to do this is to start by volunteering for nonprofit programs and then network with corporate training professionals.

Career #8: Decorative Painter/Muralist

What You Do: Decorative painters contribute interior decoration schemes. They may create special paint effects (sponging, stippling, ragging, etc.); imitate stonework, brickwork, stucco, marble, or other materials; paint *trompe l'oeil* flora or fauna; or even create complete scenes on walls or ceilings. Most decorative painters work on a freelance or independent contractor basis.

Pros and Cons: Decorative painting allows visual artists to use their artistic talents in a potentially lucrative lifeline career. Unique and elaborate works such as those such as those provided by decorative painters have become highly popular for upscale homes and corporate settings, creating a steady flow of work; moreover, because such work is by nature part of a luxury package, budgets can be large. Experienced decorative painters with excellent skills and good portfolios of past work are well compensated.

What You Need: No license is required, merely experience in one or more techniques.

Career #9: Editor (Film/Video)

What You Do: Film and video editors cut and splice moving images to create a clear, effective whole.

Pros and Cons: The editing process is an essential part of film, documentary, commercial and/or videotape production, meaning that skilled editors—especially those up to date in the latest computer-based Avid technology—are in steady demand. Pay is attractive. Thus, mastering Avid technology is actually a better way for an aspiring film producer to gain financial and professional security (and, possibly, useful contracts) than producing a small independent film. It is also relatively easy to break into this field, either by producing your own "reel" as a way of building experience or by arranging a formal or informal internship with a small production company.

What You Need: Training in Avid technology and equipment is available in schools specializing in the visual arts, film schools and programs, and media departments of colleges. Your own Avid equipment is a definite plus if you want to be a freelance film or video editor.

Career #10: Editor (Text)

What You Do: Editing always involves either acquiring or improving written material but beyond that includes a wide variety of roles in a wide variety of settings. Common editing positions, some of which can overlap, include:

- **Copy editor.** Copy editors "clean up" grammar, spelling, spacing, phrasing, and punctuation on a given piece of writing and bring it into consistency with a given company's or publication's "house style." They also prepare a piece for publication by inserting any marks or directives the typesetter or formatter will need. Newspapers, magazines, reference series, publishing houses, and virtually any and all other organizations that turn out texts regularly will have at least one in-house or freelance copy editor. Demand for good copy editors is steady.

- **Technical or business editor.** A technical editor may handle copyediting, style editing, or both, but works on material that is specialized rather than general in nature. Technical editing overlaps with the field of business and technical writing; for more information, see Career #3, "Business/Technical Writer." Experienced technical editors can work in-house or freelance.

- **Acquisitions editor.** When most people think of an editor, it's actually an acquisitions editor they're picturing. An acquisitions editor searches for, screens, and buys materials for a publication or publishing house. Acquisitions-editor positions appeal to many creative writers because they permit a total immersion in the world of books. However, the field is increasingly competitive, workdays tend to be extremely long, and pay is typically low. If this field remains of interest to you, be prepared to break into it as a lowly editorial assistant (i.e., office drone!), the traditional point of entry.

- **Managing editor.** The managing editor of a press or publication actually does more management than editing. Depending on the size of the publication, he or she may manage editorial budgets, set submission deadlines and schedules, oversee the hiring of writers and copy editors, work with the advertising and subscription departments, and become involved in any or all of the business aspects of the publication. Managing editors typically have prior text-editing experience and business experience.

Pros and Cons: Editing is one of the most appealing lifeline careers for creative and dramatic writers because it allows them to use and hone their language skills, yet does not compete with their own writing. Also appealing is the fact that editorial projects can be structured in a wide variety of arrangements, including flexible freelance ones.

What You Need: No formal training is required, though the certificate programs in publishing and/or classes in technical editing now offered by some colleges can be helpful ways of breaking into the field. Before being hired, copy editors are tested in their knowledge and usage of standard copy-editing marks, which can be learned through books or many adult education or vocational programs. Other types of editors are hired based on relevant background and experience rather than tested knowledge.

Career #11:
ESL (English as a Second Language) Teacher

What You Do: ESL teachers help foreign students, business people, immigrants, and others gain a working grasp of English. They may work as tutors to individuals or teach in group settings. ESL teaching is in demand in all metropolitan cities worldwide and in most medium to large American towns with immigrant populations. ESL teachers may work for private language institutes, church programs, business and secretarial schools, adult education programs, tutorial services, corporations, colleges, and public schools.

Pros and Cons: The variety of settings in which ESL is taught and the variety of places in which such teaching is needed give it a flexibility that is highly appealing to many creative individuals. Many performers, for example, teach English in Asian, European, or American cities while they are on tour; others stop teaching when they are needed for a production, knowing that the demand is high enough that they will be able to find work at the same or another organization when the show closes. Compensation is attractive, given the flexibility of the job and the limited training needed.

What You Need: You do *not* need to be fluent in another language to teach ESL; since the purpose is for the student to learn English, that is the only language spoken in the classroom. You should, however, enjoy languages and be facile in the language arts. ESL training requirements vary, and thus training can be quite informal. Most colleges, for example, do not even require a certificate, though public school systems require a bachelor's degree and a teaching license for ESL teaching (like all other subjects). Some ESL teachers enter the field simply by observing some ESL classes, brushing up on their grammar, and going to work; others enroll in ESL teacher certificate classes, which are offered by many college adult education programs.

Career #12: Fitness Trainer

What You Do: Fitness trainers work with clients individually or in groups to teach exercise modalities including weight training, aerobics, Pilates, and spinning, and to engage clients in a regular, committed exercise routine. They may become involved in some nutritional consultation as well. Most trainers begin by working for a spa, gym, or health club; once they have built up a strong and loyal clientele, they often branch into private practice, traveling to clients' homes and developing individual regimens for them.

Pros and Cons: Fitness training is a highly flexible career that many dancers, performers, or athletic individuals enjoy. In today's busy but health-and-appearance-conscious society, fitness training is no longer a trend, but a way of life. Health clubs, gyms, and individuals therefore have a strong and growing need for fitness trainers.

What You Need: Most health clubs and gyms require national certification; certificate programs are offered by many adult education schools.

Career #13: Graphic Designer

What You Do: Graphic designers create design for printed matter ranging from simple invitations, stationery and flyers to far more complex items including brochures, newsletters, reports, advertisements, corporate logo and signage packages, and books. Graphic designers can work for large companies or organizations, advertising or publishing firms, graphic design firms, and other companies. Many designers act as freelancers or independent contractors. Temp work is even possible, though it often requires a long-term commitment (i.e., a month or more of full-time work), as it is done on a project basis.

Pros and Cons: With the incredible—and incredibly sophisticated—abundance of computer-related design technology available today, graphic design has become an extraordinarily creative field. It is also typically flexible in terms of schedule. Experienced designers are well compensated.

What You Need: Virtually all graphic design today requires strong computer skills and knowledge of software programs such as Basic Macintosh, Adobe Illustrator, Adobe Photoshop, and/or Quark Xpress. Knowledge of graphic design principles and production issues is also a necessity, as are strong visual skills.

Career #14: Journalist

What You Do: While most of us think of high-profile investigative reporters like Woodward and Bernstein when we think of journalists, the field encompasses everything from such media "stars" to the freelancers who provide radio, magazine, television, and newspaper coverage in small, local markets. Newspapers tend to employ the reporters who produce the main body of their news, though local news and some features may be produced by independent writers. Magazines, on the other hand, are mostly written by freelancers.

Pros and Cons: Journalism is a challenging and varied field that allows creative people to make use of their innate curiosity as well as their verbal and/or presentation skills. Compensation varies widely depending on location, working arrangement, and other factors.

What You Need: A degree is not required, though it can be helpful in learning the trade and establishing credibility. Journalism programs are offered by many colleges and universities and classes in magazine writing, reporting, etc., are available in some adult education programs.

Career #15: Massage Therapist

What You Do: Massage therapists stimulate blood circulation, relax muscles, and remediate various physical problems by kneading, rubbing, and otherwise manipulating the body. Special techniques such as the use of essential oils may be added. Massage therapists typically start out working at gyms, spas, sports-medicine centers, or chiropractic centers; once they have built a strong client base, some then branch out into a wholly or partially private practice, working out of their own home or office or visiting clients' homes.

Pros and Cons: The work schedule is extremely flexible—especially once a private practice is opened—and the pay is good. Many creative people enjoy the tangible, hands-on nature of the work, and dancers and performers in particular have a built-in affinity for tired or straining bodies! Finally, the demand for qualified massage therapists is growing; once used primarily by dancers, athletes, or patients with health conditions, massage has recently become much more widely accepted by the general public as a means of stress reduction and life enhancement. One of the relatively few downsides to a career in massage therapy, surprisingly, is physical debility. The strong and constant pressure a therapist exerts can be tiring and in some cases may cause problems, including carpal tunnel syndrome.

What You Need: Formal training is a requirement, as is state licensure. Education can be costly, but government scholarships are available at certified institutions.

Career #16: Office Administrator/Manager

What You Do: Office administrators or managers may handle a variety of tasks depending on the size and nature of the business involved. They may be responsible for such concerns as office finances, including payroll, budgeting, and petty cash; mailings; purchasing; hiring or management of temporary or clerical staff; record keeping, including word processing and/or spreadsheet file creation and management; meeting and event scheduling; and other administrative functions. Jobs are typically full time, although some small and nonprofit organizations may use part-time or even freelance administrators. Although the huge majority of office administrators work on-site, creative people should be aware of the new career of "virtual" assistant. Virtual assistants are freelancers who assist clients (whom they have usually never met) with office tasks, bookkeeping, record keeping, etc., online.

Pros and Cons: While office administration is not the most glamorous of careers, it is one that can be pursued in virtually any location and/or type of organization. In smaller businesses, flexible schedules can often be arranged. Office administration involves a more rewarding variety of tasks than many other office jobs (such as word processing) that are traditional fallbacks for creative people but that are typically too repetitious and unchallenging to provide a fulfilling lifeline career. Though it is too new to be fully evaluated as a potential lifeline career, virtual assistantship may offer creative people good potential in the future, since it permits maximum flexibility of location and time. This administrative field permits you to do light clerical work at home, where you may choose your hours and pace.

What You Need: All types of office work, from word processing to management, now demand computer skills. Microsoft Word is the most frequently used word-processing program, while Excel is popular for charts and spreadsheets. Office administrators also need to be well organized and detail oriented.

Career #17: Paralegal

What You Do: Paralegals, also called legal assistants, work under the direct supervision of lawyers on the background and preparatory work involved in the legal process. Duties can be general or specialized depending on the firm, but may include such tasks as preparing cases for trial, investigating case facts, researching legal precedents and issues, organizing and analyzing information, and/or drafting documents. Paralegal work is generally performed on an employee basis, though some paralegals act as freelance legal assistants and contract their services out to attorneys or corporate legal departments. Paralegal work is available primarily in large private law firms but can also be obtained at some corporations, banks, brokerage houses, insurance companies, real-estate companies, and federal, state, and municipal agencies.

Pros and Cons: Paralegal skills and training afford creative people steady work at attractive rates of pay. It can also be flexible in its time commitments, as full-time, part-time, and evening schedules are available at many large private firms.

What You Need: Many continuing or adult education programs offer a short-term program leading to paralegal certification. Alternatively, some organizations train their own employees (usually, either legal secretaries or college graduates) as paralegals. Beyond training, you'll need strong written and oral communication skills, good research and investigative abilities, and the capacity to understand complex legal language. You may also need to develop a familiarity with common legal software packages and online resources, as computer work is increasingly part of a growing number of paralegal jobs.

Career #18: Photographer

What You Do: Professional photographers take and sometimes print photographs of individuals and groups; parties, such as weddings; newsworthy events; objects, from houses to automobiles to food, that will be pictured in advertisements; and many other subjects. Compared to artistic photographers, who are primarily concerned with the aesthetic or social impact of an image, professional photographers tend to focus on clarity and meeting a client's particular needs. Some photographers specialize in a particular area, such as headshots or portraits, while others (especially those in smaller communities) cover many subjects. Professional photographers may run freelance businesses of their own, work for photo studios, or be employed by newspapers, magazines, ad agencies, large businesses, or other organizations.

Pros and Cons: Except when the photographer is employed by a company, magazine, or newspaper, professional photography can be a somewhat uncertain field. Successful freelance pros typically market themselves aggressively; obtain steady work from newspapers, advertising agencies, or other organizations; and/or develop unique "niches" that distinguish them from competitors. Nevertheless, it is a flexible career, an opportunity to work outside a traditional office or business environment, and a field which may allow a visual artist to build a lifeline career while using highly creative skills. Compensation rates are difficult to estimate, since employment arrangements and types of jobs vary so widely.

What You Need: No formal training is required; talent, a portfolio, and the requisite camera equipment and skills are all you need.

Career #19: Real-Estate Salesperson

What You Do: Real-estate agents help buyers, sellers, and/or renters of homes complete transactions that are often the most important financial events of the clients' lives. Real-estate agents are generally independent sales workers who provide their services to licensed brokers on a contract basis. They receive a commission rather than a salary for their work.

Pros and Cons: Some creative people like the fact that much of the work is conducted outside the office; can be done night or day, workday or weekend; and can be lucrative. At the same time, agents must be available at the times clients need them, and hours can be long before a good base is built and word of mouth provides a sufficient clientele. The real-estate business is also highly competitive; it's not for shrinking violets!

What You Need: Real-estate agents must pass a licensing test in their state; business schools and adult education programs offer a relatively inexpensive course that prepares you for the exam. Beyond licensing requirements, real-estate agents must maintain a thorough knowledge of the housing market in their community, the neighborhoods that will best serve particular clients' needs, and trends in the housing industry generally. They must also be familiar with local zoning ordinances, tax laws, and financing sources.

Career #20: Sign-Language Interpreter

What You Do: A sign-language interpreter translates spoken material into sign language for hearing-challenged individuals and translates sign language into verbal or written material for hearing individuals. Sign-language interpreters work at hospitals, schools, courts, social-service agencies, cultural organizations, conferences, businesses, and theater and television companies.

Pros and Cons: Sign-language interpretation is a rewarding (yet not overly draining) career that is in growing demand due to legislation that mandates equal access to educational and other opportunities for disabled or handicapped individuals and due to the consequent broader participation of such individuals in the country's business and cultural life. Though it requires training and application to master, it yields attractive payment. Finally, the wide variety of situations in which sign-language interpretation is needed may allow a creative person some flexibility of schedule.

What You Need: Training in sign-language interpretation is available at schools specializing in sign language and in some colleges and community colleges. Once you are "conversational"—that is, have reached a minimum standard of signing competence—most programs can link you to work experience through internships, volunteer opportunities, or job listings. After you've had some work experience and fully mastered basic signing, you may wish to enter a certification program, the curriculum of which will involve classes on interpretation theory, deaf culture, signing skills enhancement, and ethics/decision making for interpreters. Certification maximizes your professional credibility and qualifies you for the highest paying interpretation jobs.

Career #21: Social Worker

What You Do: Social workers render assistance to individuals, families, and groups with problems, including physical and mental illness, poverty, family maladjustment, inadequate housing, and addictions. Part- and full-time jobs are available in settings such as hospitals, clinics, social-services agencies, government agencies, and the public school system. Social workers can also conduct private practices working as therapists with individuals and families.

Pros and Cons: Social work appeals strongly to the sensitive, compassionate, and altruistic side of many creative people; their ability to imagine and empathize with the plight of people in various difficulties often makes them excellent at this job. Remuneration is good for social workers in private practice. On the downside, for some creative people ongoing interaction with individuals in painful or problematic situations—particularly for social workers also dealing with the bureaucracy of government or social-services agencies—can be draining.

What You Need: A Master's in Social Work (MSW) degree is generally required for school, health, and mental-health settings, although a Bachelor's in Social Work (BSW) may satisfy hiring requirements for agencies in smaller communities. MSW training typically requires two or more years to complete both coursework and fieldwork requirements and can be costly; be sure to check with the financial-aid offices of any schools you consider to learn about potential grants, scholarships, and other sources of funding.

Career #22:
Speech or Language Pathologist/Audiologist

What You Do: These careers both serve individuals (children and adults) with hearing loss, brain injury, learning disabilities, conditions such as cerebral palsy, mental retardation, physical disabilities, or emotional problems, and are thus closely related. Speech/language pathologists identify and treat speech and language disorders, whereas audiologists determine the nature and extent of hearing impairments and implement corrective measures and plans. Full- and part-time employment is available in hospitals, health care facilities, nursing homes, and the school system. Many creative people establish private practices once they become experienced and well connected in the field.

Pros and Cons: Speech-language pathologists and audiologists work with a wide range of challenging problems and populations, ranging from young children to seniors, and the demand for this profession continues to grow. Patience, compassion, and good listening skills are necessary in assisting clients, whose progress can be slow. The repetitive nature of clinical treatment techniques and the emphasis on diagnostic testing and measurement may not appeal to those artistic types who value change and variety.

What You Need: To become a speech or language pathologist or audiologist, you must have a Master's degree from a school accredited by the American Speech-Language-Hearing Association (ASHA). The training program is rigorous and contains a substantial amount of medical content.

Career #23: Teacher

What You Do: Teachers work on a long-term or temporary (i.e., substitute) basis in schools ranging from preschools and kindergartens to colleges. Teaching positions commonly sought by creative people include elementary, junior high or high school teacher, substitute teacher, university teacher, and teacher in nonschool settings. If you prefer to teach on a purely private basis, see the information on Career #24, "Tutor."

Pros and Cons: With the exception of permanent or tenured university positions, overall pay rates for teachers are not especially high compared to other jobs. On the other hand, demand for teachers from preschool through grade 12 is strong, especially in specialized fields such as special education, early childhood education, and special needs. Teaching is attractive to creative people who enjoy helping others, using their communications skills, and working with children; many creative individuals find that it offers a congenial atmosphere and also welcome the time flexibility of vacations and summers off.

What You Need: Private schools require no degree or license for their teachers, though in practice it may be difficult to get a teaching job at a good private school without at least a bachelor's degree. Teaching in the public school system requires a college degree and, after a specified period of time, a master's degree, as well as licensure through your local board of education. College-level teachers must typically have at least a master's degree (a Ph.D. is virtually essential to get a permanent university position).

Career #24: Tutor

What You Do: The general title "tutor" covers a multitude of jobs. Tutors always work privately with students in either their own or the students' homes; what they tutor, however, can range from SAT or GRE preparation to computer skills, reading, math, ESL, music, and many other subjects. Tutors in today's market are often highly specialized. For example, there is a demand for tutors who can prepare small children for the ERB exams required for private school entrance or who can work with students suffering from dyslexia, ADD, and other disorders. Some tutors create even more unusual niches based on their own unique experience. Tutors are virtually always independent contractors. Many successful tutors, however, have informal relationships with schools who know of their expertise in a given area and are willing to make students and/or their parents aware of them. Such relationships help take the self-marketing burden off the tutor and stabilize income by assuring a steadier stream of potential students.

Pros and Cons: The growing competitiveness of top college and private school programs, coupled with a growing ability on the part of medical and educational specialists to diagnose learning problems and disabilities, is increasing the actual and perceived need for good tutors and therefore creating steady demand. Tutoring is a highly flexible job, with hours that you can set based on your own needs. It permits the building of one-on-one relationships with students in a nonbureaucratic setting, which helps make it appealing to many creative individuals. Experienced tutors with specialized fields of expertise can be quite highly compensated.

What You Need: Tutoring has no specific education or licensing requirements. In practice, however, most specialized tutors, such as those who work with ADD or learning-disabled children, are or have been special-education teachers in either public or private schools or have obtained other relevant training.

Section III:

Building a Better Balance through Lifeline Employment

Chapter Eight

Your Personal Selling Tools: The Personal Commercial and the Resume

The difference between the almost right word and the right word is really a large matter—'tis the difference between the lightning bug and the lightning.

—Mark Twain

I have nothing to declare except my genius.

—Oscar Wilde

To paraphrase a popular advertisement, you've come a long way! You're now committed to a specific type of career transition and equipped with a clear goal, a file full of research, and a network of professional contacts. You're on the way to getting the training and on-the-job experience you need, even if you haven't completed it yet. You are ready to begin presenting yourself to potential employers in your new marketplace.

Later chapters will deal with the mechanics of searching out specific job possibilities. Before you can job hunt effectively, however, you'll need the right tools to market your unique capabilities. There are two such tools you simply can't do without.

- **Selling Tool #1: Your Personal "Commercial."** This is a brief, to-the-point *verbal* distillation of your abilities, experience, and new job goals. I refer to it as a commercial for reasons we'll review shortly.

- **Selling Tool #2: Your Power Resume.** This is the concise but detailed *written* document that highlights the same information as your commercial, but supports it in more depth.

Your Personal Commercial

A performing artist once told me a story that highlights the importance of having a strong personal commercial. Bethany is a dancer who wanted to supplement her performing income with a teaching career. Specifically, her goal was to teach adults of all skill and fitness levels how to use movement to enhance their flexibility and overall health. At a benefit cocktail party for a small ballet company she had danced for, she met the dean of a local college that offered a broad continuing education curriculum. "I summoned my courage and mentioned that I was hoping to move into the field of teaching," Bethany says. "She said they were always open to new courses, and immediately asked me what I could offer."

"What a great opportunity—and what a waste! Here, right out of the blue, was a potential employer. But I was utterly at a loss," Bethany admits. "I had a great resume sitting on my desk at home, and I think I have a clear picture of who I am, what I want to do, and how I can help others. But for the life of me, I just couldn't express all of these thoughts. I ended up sounding like an over-eager novice rather than a professional who had something to offer. Eventually I was able to set up an interview at the college, which I handled much more gracefully and effectively. But it was really luck that I got a second chance. That incident taught me how important it is to be prepared to 'pitch' my skills and goals at any moment."

Bethany's all-too-common experience is a classic example of why the first tool of your job search is what I call a "personal commercial"—a succinct, powerful statement of the skills and services you offer to others. Like Bethany, you will sometimes meet up with potentially valuable B or even C contacts unexpectedly, in venues where handing over a resume is impossible or inappropriate. Like Bethany, you will sometimes need to state your goals and skills verbally. Like Bethany, you may have only a moment or two to summarize yourself well.

Enter the personal commercial.

What It Is—And What It Can Do For You

I use the term "personal commercial" because like an actual product commercial, your verbal self-presentation is an *informative, powerful, memorable, highly focused marketing tool that is prepared in advance, of very short duration, and designed to encourage further exploration.* Let's review those characteristics in detail.

- **Informative.** Your personal commercial must tells the recipient about the skills or experience you have that can benefit them.

- **Powerful.** Bethany didn't actually say anything dreadful in the encounter she described, but she did not present herself powerfully. The confidence, conciseness, and polish that would have signaled to the dean that she was a highly capable professional were missing. Your personal commercial should not only say the *right things*—i.e., be informative—but say them in the *right manner*—i.e., convey your strength and professionalism through speech, tone, gesture, and organization.

- **Highly focused.** Obviously, you have a lot to offer! You cannot possibly showcase all of your goals, skills, and background in a sentence or two. Instead, you must select only a few essential elements, ruthlessly weeding out any characteristics, talents, or experiences that are not *essential* to the kind of job you are looking for.

- **Prepared in advance.** When you're actually "on the spot," it is simply too difficult to think in a focused way about large themes such as your goals and your abilities. When you have a brief summary already in your mind, as I will show you how to do, encounters like the ones Bethany had become far easier. All you need to do then is make the slight adjustments that adapt your presentation to the situation you're in and the person you're speaking to.

- **Brief.** Companies like Ford, Microsoft, or General Foods do not have hours of airtime to extol the virtues of their products to consumers, and neither do you! They—and you—usually have a minute or less to catch someone's attention. Even in the formal setting of a job interview, your prospective employer does not want to listen for twenty minutes as you answer the questions "Tell me about yourself" or "What do you think you can bring to our organization?" Nothing loses interest faster that than overly detailed, rambling replies. Your resume can give more detailed backup for the claims you make verbally. The verbal claims themselves must be crisp and concise.

- **Encouraging further exploration.** The makers of a television ad do not expect you to go out and commit $50,000 for a luxury car just on the basis of their sixty-second spot. All they want to do is pique your interest enough to get you to explore their product further. Similarly, your personal commercial is not intended to get you a job. It is only designed to get someone interested enough to explore a relationship with you further.

Once you have developed your personal commercial, you'll find that it's useful in a wide variety of situations—both when you are job hunting and later, when you're building your new career. You'll be able to use your personal commercial

- When you meet potential employers or contacts in a social setting;

- When you are asked "Tell me about yourself" in a job interview;

- When you send a cover letter along with your resume in response to an ad;

- When you make "cold calls" to potential employers;

- When you are asked to introduce yourself at professional, social, or organizational gatherings; and

- When you need to describe your job to people in your own and other organizations.

In these and many other situations, the personal commercial has tremendous power, not only because it focuses the content of what you say but also because it allows you to present yourself with poise and confidence. One of my clients, a musical-comedy performer, created a commercial that summarized his business and acting credentials. When he met an executive socially, his commercial allowed him to begin a business dialogue that led to a job offer. Ultimately, he got a lucrative second career working in marketing for a Fortune 500 company.

Similarly, a former model and make-up expert highlighted her talent and enthusiasm for the cosmetics industry in a personal commercial she delivered by phone to a New York entrepreneur. She gained not only an interview but a part-time job at the executive's upscale pharmacy as well.

How To Write Your Personal Commercial

So what exactly is in a personal commercial? Basically, it is a two- or three-line presentation which incorporates your job title (or the job you are seeking); a cluster, or general grouping, of your skills (for example, marketing); one or two specific skills directly related to that cluster (for example, direct-mail promotion); optionally, one major accomplishment you want to emphasize, again related to your general cluster of abilities; and finally, also optionally, a line or statement that mentions your goal or desired outcome and serves as an invitation or closer, depending on how you're using your commercial.

Though the personal commercial always follows this basic format, it will look different for each person. A recent graduate from a degree or training program might emphasize educational background, for example, while a more seasoned professional will prioritize career accomplishments or a strong client base. It doesn't matter what the precise content is, as long as it powerfully communicates your abilities and experience and is appropriately targeted toward your particular lifeline career goals.

To begin writing your own commercial, use the following format. Later, you can change the order or phrasing slightly, to suit the content you've developed.

"My name is _____. I am an experienced _____ with skills in _____, _____, and _____. Currently, I'm _____; one of my recent accomplishments is _____.

Obviously, the second line, referring to "experienced" in terms of your career, will be a bit tricky if you are looking for your first lifeline career job. To handle gaps and omissions in your experience or employment while creating a powerful commercial, use the following strategies.

1. Stress civic involvement or even leisure activities that demonstrate skills and experience related to your objective.

2. Include related skills and experience acquired in the past, even many years ago. (This does not typically work well in a resume, but can serve you in a verbal statement.)

3. Speak about current education or training, if relevant.

4. Mention your active role in professional organizations (if necessary, become active for just this purpose!)

5. Mention the relevant skills and experience gained as a volunteer or intern, stressing the skills used rather than the work format. See chapter 6 for information on volunteering and interning.

6. If possible, have a friend who owns a business vouch for you as having experience and/or give you a job.

Sample Personal Commercials

To give you an even stronger sense of what your own commercial might look like, let's look at some examples. Here is my own current personal commercial:

> "Let me introduce myself. My name is Ronda Ormont. I am an experienced career development specialist with expertise in all aspects of vocational counseling, including knowledge of the business world, resume writing, and interviewing techniques. I have a doctorate in psychology, conduct job-search programs, and write articles for professional publications."

In contrast, this was the commercial Bethany developed:

> "My name is Bethany Jergenson. I'm an experienced dancer with strong skills in tap, ballet, and modern dance and a bachelor's degree in physical education. For the past fifteen years, I've danced for many troupes and companies, including the Seattle and San Francisco Ballets. I'm now making a transition into teaching people of all ages how to increase their well-being through movement. My first course was offered at the Fitness Connection sports center this fall and got a very positive response. I'm exploring further teaching opportunities for next year."

Where my commercial demonstrates a typical format for a longtime professional, Bethany's example illustrates how someone who is just beginning a lifeline career can still present herself powerfully. She cites credentials (her dance credits, her degree) that establish her credibility as someone with experience and expertise. She succinctly captures her new goal and offers an actual teaching credit—she does not need to mention at this point that she is a volunteer teacher at the sports center. She makes clear that she is looking for new teaching jobs, but the verb she chooses—"exploring"—sounds strong, not needy. Overall, you can see how Bethany's commercial positions her clearly and powerfully, with an emphasis on the experience and abilities she brings to her new career choice.

Here are several other examples of commercials for creative artists looking for new lifeline careers. You'll see that they represent several different levels of experience and achievement as well as different types of job goals. You may also notice that while in two cases the speaker identifies his or her creative field, in the other two artistic interests or experience are not mentioned at all. The deciding factor, of course, is relevance to the *new* career area.

> Since the day I graduated from college five years ago, I've worked in the Broadway company of Les Miserables, understudying the lead role. I am currently

studying arts administration at New York University as I begin a career transition to management of arts-related organizations. I serve as a union representative of Actors' Equity, which has given me experience and sparked interest in my field.

I have a wide variety of experience in teaching young children and am state certified as a substitute teacher. I live in this neighborhood and am very interested in working at your school.

I am an experienced office worker with skills in scheduling appointments, greeting clients, and handling heavy phone work. I am knowledgeable in Microsoft Word and am interested in temporary assignments.

I'm a trained artist and am very familiar with computer software, including Photoshop, Illustrator, Quark, and Pagemaker. I am currently seeking freelance work in computer graphics and desktop publishing.

In contrast, here are several commercials for longtime professionals seeking a new and more flexible job. As you can see, it is easier for them to present their credentials compellingly, although the issue of their transition to a lifeline career must be handled carefully.

I worked as a vice president in the Information Technology department of ABC corporation for almost twenty years. I've now opened my own firm, which provides computer consulting to small businesses. I plan, set up, and troubleshoot networks and train workers in their use.

I write brochures, reports, and other marketing materials for businesses. My specialty is coordinated marketing packages. In my work, I build on the ten years I had as the marketing materials director for a Wall Street firm.

I'm an interior designer, and I do one-weekend home makeovers that transform your living area, even on a tight budget. I can also realign your home decor according to the principles of Feng Shui. After a career as the head stylist for the XYZ home furnishings store, I enjoy working with people to make their homes more attractive and harmonious.

Now that you've created a personal commercial, it's time to move on to your second selling tool: a power business resume.

Your Power Business Resume

Just like your personal commercial, your resume is a selling tool that helps you introduce your capabilities, experience, and goals to contacts and potential employers. It simply extends the information in your commercial into a more detailed—but still tightly focused, powerful, and succinct— written document.

What Your Resume Can Do—And What It Can't

Perhaps the single-most important point to realize about a resume is that it is *not* meant to be a comprehensive summary of every professional accomplishment since your first lemonade stand. Instead, it is a highly selective document, just as consciously crafted as any advertisement and just as specifically slanted toward a certain audience. It cannot be emphasized enough that employers are short on time. They have little incentive to wade through long or complicated data to find out how you could help them—especially if one or more of the other resumes on their desk is succinct and to the point. The only people who have time to browse in a leisurely way through resumes are Human Resources departments, and they rarely if ever have final hiring authority over nonclerical or temporary jobs.

Nor is the resume meant to stand alone as a job-search tool. Mailing out scores of resumes in response to job advertisements or personal contacts, for example, virtually never works, even when the resume is very powerful. Your resume will not get you a job until it is put into the right hands and appropriately supported by your other selling tools, such as your personal commercial and your ability to complete a strong interview.

By itself, a resume is simply meant to *impress people enough that they wish to continue to pursue a working relationship with you.* In other words, it is a way to *enhance your relationship* with people who can lead you to or give you the job that you want, not to *create a relationship* by itself. It is a step along the road, a means to an end, a tool that allows you to create more in-depth awareness of your potential.

Writing The Power Resume

As I'll discuss in detail below, there are two basic types of resumes: the *chronological* resume, which lists your relevant employment in reverse order, with your current position first; and the *functional resume,* which organizes pertinent information by the kinds of functions you have performed rather than the actual job titles you have held. The focus of the chronological resume is work history; the focus of a functional resume is skill areas. The chronological resume is the most common and the most generally preferred, but either can be used successfully. You might try both or shift from one to the other over time. Since resumes must be updated and revised frequently, which type you choose to use is not a long-term decision.

Before we begin to discuss formats, you need to familiarize yourself with the characteristics and rules that apply to any strong resume, whatever organizational principle it uses.

You'll notice that the issues I'm about to name are related to resume content, not appearance. Naturally, you'll want to highlight your professionalism by using classic (preferably white or off-white) paper of good quality and a clear and simple font. But the key to a successful resume is substance, not form.

With that in mind, note that a strong resume has five basic characteristics:

- It has *a specific interest or appeal* to the individual (i.e., employer) reading it.

- It is organized and written so that it is *easy to read.* The resume and cover letter will typically be read in approximately *thirty seconds.* To capture an employer's interest in that time, it *must* be well organized, well edited, and formatted with boldface headings and other tools that direct attention to key areas.

- It speaks in *powerful, active* terms.

- It presents your background succinctly. Because of the thirty-second reading average mentioned above, one page is ideal. Additional details can always be discussed during an interview.

- It is *impeccably neat and error-free.* Not just the content but the form of your resume communicate your value to a potential employer. It goes without saying that if your resume is sloppy or scattered with typos, potential employers are justified in thinking that your work for their organization will be careless, too.

Resume Rules

Whether you are using a chronological or a functional resume format, you can achieve those five strong-resume qualities by following these rules:

Resume Rule #1: Remember That This Is YOUR Resume

You are the person who must be satisfied and comfortable with the resume you create. *You* are the person who will be expected to support your resume's claims during interviews. You can use standardized formats, and you should get others involved in giving you feedback, but ultimately it is your personal approval that is necessary, no one else's. Don't let anyone—friend, relative, counselor, or potential employer—talk you into a resume that makes you uncomfortable.

Resume Rule #2: Focus Your Entire Resume around Your New Career Goal(s)

There is no such thing as a good "general resume." Whether they look like it or not, all powerful resumes are slanted very specifically toward a particular professional objective.

To create this kind of resume requires consolidation. Career counselors use this word to describe the fine-tuning or refocusing process in which you review your past work experience in the light of future career goals and moves. Even for those who are not actively seeking new jobs, consolidation occurs at important junctures throughout a career. An executive of a major corporation is consolidating when she begins to move out of everyday management tasks into high-level strategic planning. You are consolidating as you move from an existence of sporadic or low-paid "day jobs" into a new and more stable lifeline career.

Classical musician Beverly, for example, was unhappy with her career as a legal word processor. After several meetings with me, she realized that she liked most of her job duties, as well as the good money she earned through word processing. What she *didn't* like was the world of law and lawyers! "I began to realize that working in a more creative environment would be much more satisfying to me," she says. "I decided to target major advertising agencies and see if I could get a similar position in one of them. I constructed a new resume that downplayed the legal element in my work history and focused only on my strong word-processing abilities. I eventually landed a good job for a big ad agency. The funny thing is that I'm actually doing much the same work as I did before, but it's infinitely more satisfying now that I'm doing it in this high-energy creative context."

Stage and screen actor Peter, in contrast, wanted to change the actual nature of his work. He came to see me feeling frustrated by the hectic and scattered schedule of his professional life. "I had been doing adjunct teaching in the theater department of a local university, supplemented by temp clerical work when money was tight—which was most of the time," he says. "The instability of moving from temp site to temp site was exhausting, and the work itself wasn't rewarding. Through the course of my career counseling I realized not only that I really wanted to teach but also that I would need to downplay my office skills—both in my actual life and on my resume—in order to make that transition. I rewrote my resume to emphasize only the theater and teaching credentials that would get me a full-time teaching job within my area's private school system. It took time, and at first it made me nervous to shoot for this more ambitious goal. But I eventually got a full-time teaching position. These days, I don't use my office skills at all, except to prepare handouts for my acting classes!"

As the experiences of both Peter and Beverly suggest, the refocusing involved in consolidation must be reflected accurately on your resume. In fact, resume writing always involves elements of consolidation, since a strong resume must slant one's job history toward new objectives and/or the new job being sought. Undesirable or irrelevant aspects of your experience can and should be downplayed or restated in light of the kind of work you are seeking *now*.

Resume Rule #3: Omit the Irrelevant

This one is the natural corollary to Rule #2, but it's so important that it's worth stating as a separate guideline. As I said above, a resume is not meant to be comprehensive. It is a single encyclopedia entry, not the whole twenty-four-volume set!

By asking you to omit irrelevant information, I am not telling you to lie, nor am I saying that you can never share the information you leave out of the resume. What I'm suggesting, instead, is that you focus on information that is helpful and appropriate for someone to know now, in a specific professional context.

Writer Jeremy demonstrates why this is important. "I used to include all of my published writing—including my poems and so on—in all of my resumes. I felt that these publications gave me more credibility, since my experience in my new field of technical writing was still spotty. But including my literary career on my business resume clearly worked against me," he notes. "When people saw those credentials before meeting me, they made all sorts of assumptions: that I was a snob who would look down on business people, that I wasn't committed to my business writing career—you name it. I could have countered these assumptions, but I often didn't even get the chance, since my resume didn't get me into the interview stage."

"I finally decided to create different resumes for these different aspects of my work," he adds. "I felt a bit odd, at first, about omitting from one resume information about the artwork that is so important to my life. It felt as though I was hiding something. Gradually, though, I realized that wasn't true. I don't keep my life as a creative writer a secret. I often mention my publications later on in the process, once I have established a comfortable relationship with a potential or actual client. By that point, they already trust my professionalism, my commitment, and my business writing capability. The fact that I have a whole different creative life no longer distracts or worries them. They have a context. It's appropriate for them to know extra facts about me, just as I have learned new things about them."

You should therefore *start* the resume-writing process by compiling a full and accurate record of your work history. Capture the experiences of each job as powerfully as you can. Repeat the following format for each employer in order to record the essential information:

Resume Worksheet: Work History

Employer: _____

Dates of Employment: _____

Major Duties and Responsibilities: _____

_____

_____

Major Accomplishments: _____

_____

_____

Once this series of brief summaries is complete, however, you must then *end* the resume creation process by omitting from the final resume those elements that do not relate to your current work goals.

Sometimes this feels hard to do. You may be proud of job accomplishments that don't relate to your new goal, or you may fear that leaving out irrelevant items will make your resume seem too scanty. But to create a good resume, you'll need to move both pride and anxiety out of your way. Hiring executives are not looking for a "good all-around person" or a "Renaissance (wo)man." They are looking for a professional with solid potential, demonstrated by relevant recent experience, in a particular job. It is their needs, not your worries, that count.

For further proof of that statement, read the resume on the following pages. Mary Mistake has many talents and much potential. She might well have the capacity to build a lifeline career as a Spanish teacher, a copy editor, a word processor, or even a fundraiser or publicist. *Yet her resume does not sell her as a focused, expert professional in any of these fields.* Instead, it allows each of her talents to cancel the others out. It makes no linkages between apparently disparate jobs. Employers in *all* of her possible fields will perceive her as a dilettante, someone unable to commit to any one career. They may question why, with higher-level skills such as teaching and fundraising credentials, she ended up doing something as menial as word processing. Do *not* use Mary's resume as a model!

Resume Rule #4: Consider Having More Than One Resume

If your new lifeline career could take several different forms, you may need more than one resume to reflect its different aspects. The extra work involved in creating several different documents will more than pay for itself by helping you land the kinds of jobs you want.

Martha, a screenwriter working as a teacher and private writing tutor while hoping for her first big sale, has three different resumes: one for teaching, one for private coaching and tutoring, and one, emphasizing her own creative work, that she uses only in film-related situations. These resumes overlap, but are far from identical. The tutoring resume, for example, describes her past full-time teaching positions in far less detail than the teaching resume, while the teaching resume groups a number of important tutoring relationships into a single general category. Each resume mentions selected aspects of her experience that are related to film—her teaching resume, for example, mentions a course taught in film history for the summer session at a major university, while her tutoring resume cites several experiences coaching adults working on screenplays—but neither discusses either her film training or her screenwriting skills specifically. "By splitting the two aspects of my lifeline career into two resumes, I keep each document powerful, focused, and short—one page," Martha asserts. "I would never go back to a single resume again."

You may wish to use two or even three resumes if the *users* of your lifeline services are different, as Martha's are (schools for her teaching, private individuals for her tutoring); if the actual *services* you provide vary (for example, you are a painter who does both mural work and decorative/faux painting as a lifeline career); or if you are simultaneously looking for more than one type of lifeline job (for example, you would like to get a job as a Web site designer but are also open to a job in traditional graphic design).

Resume Rule #5: Use "Power" Language

The most crucial words in your resume are the verbs. They must be powerful *and* specific. You are looking for language that emphasizes, both directly and subliminally, the *actions* you took, the *influence* you had, the *results* you achieved, and the *changes* you accomplished. Your resume should have as little vague, general, or static wording as possible. Verbs in the description of your current job should be in present tense; those in descriptions of former jobs, in past tense.

A detailed listing of power words follows. To prove why you need them, let's look at two examples of resume entries—one that doesn't use power language and one that does. The writer of this first resume excerpt is currently doing part-time work for a local preschool. She is looking for a full-time management or administrative role in an elementary-school setting.

> **1994 - Present: Program Coordinator.** On a part-time basis, handle all aspects of community-based preschool arts program from grant writing to budgeting. Also do application review, session scheduling, guest coordination. Fill in for absent teachers. Applications grew 17% in five years.

You'll immediately notice that "do" and "handle" are not especially compelling terms and that the improvements made are not specifically credited to the coordinator herself. The description is also rather vague. In contrast, read how the same material has been "powered up" below (crucial power words are in italics).

> **1994 - Present: Program Coordinator.** As coordinator of a prestigious community-based preschool arts program, *direct all aspects* of administration from grant writing to budget management. *Review* and *evaluate* student applications, *orient* teachers and parents, *promote* the program through advertising in local media, *identify* and *contract* with guest artists and educators to *broaden* program offerings, *research* and *coordinate* the transition to a new and more efficient computer system, and *am designing* a special outreach program to low-income families. As a *result* of this work, *increased* application volume by 17% and grant funding 23% during my tenure, while also *reducing* program expenditures and *diversifying* the student body.

This entry is specific, compelling, and dynamic. It demonstrates that the coordinator plays an active shaping role in the program's operations and attests to the resume writer's energy and ability to generate results and make changes. It is chock-full of action verbs that are used specifically and with quantified results wherever possible. It also follows the other Resume Rules. For example, it does not comment on the part-time nature of the work, as that information is irrelevant at the resume stage. It cites a wide range of skills within the field, from technological knowledge (the reference

Power Words For Resume Writing

Accomplished	Edited	Modified
Achieved	Educated	Monitored
Activated	Eliminated	Motivated
Administered	Enforced	Negotiated
Advised	Established	Originated
Analyzed	Estimated	Organized
Approved	Evaluated	Performed
Assessed	Expanded	Persuaded
Assisted	Explained	Planned
Attained	Facilitated	Prepared
Audited	Focused	Presented
Balanced	Formed	Produced
Bought	Formulated	Promoted
Calculated	Founded	Proposed
Chaired	Framed	Publicized
Changed	Generated	Published
Clarified	Handled	Recorded
Compiled	Headed	Recommended
Completed	Helped	Recruited
Composed	Identified	Reorganized
Conceived	Implemented	Reported
Concluded	Improved	Researched
Conducted	Increased	Resolved
Controlled	Influenced	Restored
Converted	Informed	Revitalized
Coordinated	Initiated	Revised
Corrected	Inspired	Simplified
Counseled	Interpreted	Solved
Created	Instructed	Sold
Decreased	Interviewed	Strengthened
Defined	Introduced	Succeeded
Demonstrated	Invented	Supervised
Designed	Investigated	Supported
Determined	Launched	Taught
Developed	Led	Trained
Directed	Maintained	Translated
Documented	Marketed	Tripled
Doubled	Managed	Widened
Drafted	Mastered	Won
Earned	Maximized	Wrote

to computer transition) to people skills (the reference to teacher and parent orientation). It proves that the writer is sensitive to *both* social issues (through the mention of outreach and diversification) and realities like money issues (through the mention of cost reductions and grant increases). It does not distract from its powerful focus by including irrelevant information such as substitute-teaching responsibility.

Resume Rule #6: Count Volunteer Work Experience as Genuine Work Experience

If you have performed the kind of career-related volunteer work discussed in chapter 6, you can and should list those positions along with ordinary, paid jobs. The same goes for freelance or temp jobs. It is not the arrangement under which you were hired that matters in the context of a resume—it is the actual work that you did. Volunteer or intern experiences do not have to be cited in your resume as unpaid work.

Resume Rule #7: Head the Resume with a Strong Summary

The summary is a key element in both chronological and functional resumes. A concise, powerful summary statement allows potential employers to grasp your key qualifications immediately, just by scanning the page. It tells them quickly how the diverse experiences on the resume come together and lets them begin to assess your fit within their organization very rapidly.

You'll sometimes see resumes that begin with a statement of objectives rather than this type of skill/experience summary. I prefer the summary because it is less limiting (i.e., does not tie you to a particular job), more powerful, and more helpful to potential interviewers who want to know what you can do for *them* rather than what you wish to do for yourself!

The summary at the top of your resume will be similar to your personal commercial in virtually every respect. The only difference is that it is generally a bit briefer, as the more detailed information in the body of the resume will supplement and support its statements. The basic summary format is as follows:

"Expertise in all aspects of _____, with skills in _____, _____, and _____. A recent major accomplishment is _____ (OR) I am currently employed by [generic description of firm or field]."

You can adjust this form a bit if necessary, but basically it's just that simple.

Here are some examples of strong summary statements. As you can see, they all answer the question, *"What related skills and experience do you bring to the job and field you now seek?"* Even though each of the summary statements reflects very different skills and goals, you can see that they all respond to that query with a concise, highly focused format and powerful language. Any glamorous or prestigious experience is highlighted, as are special accomplishments.

- Knowledge of all aspects of office work including reception, record keeping, and word processing.

- Experienced in all aspects of teaching English as a Second Language, including grammar, accent reduction, and conversational techniques from beginner through advanced levels.

- Expertise in all aspects of special-events planning, including weddings, parties, corporate outings and meetings.

- Expertise in fundraising, grant writing, public relations, and special-events planning. Currently, I work for a large nonprofit organization.

- Excellent office manager with skills in Microsoft Word, Excel, and Powerpoint. I am currently employed by a large Wall Street brokerage firm.

- Expertise in all aspects of arts management, including theater administration, special-events production, fundraising, and audience development.

The Chronological Resume

As I noted above, the chronological resume is ordered by the specific jobs you have held over time, listing your most current work first and moving in reverse order through your career. Your current position is considered the most important, so it will include the most detailed description and take up the most space on the page. Chronological resumes work best when that position is impressive, when your work history demonstrates advancement in a single or several closely related fields, or when your employers were well known or prestigious. Where those qualities are not the case, a functional resume (see below) may serve you better.

Employers typically prefer the chronological format, since it makes it easy for them to read and document "hard facts" such as your actual employers, your job titles, the length of time you held each position, and so on. For this reason, there are distinct advantages to choosing a chronological resume. Yet as you shift to a new lifeline career, creating a chronological resume can be tricky. You probably haven't yet accumulated substantial employment in your new field. Much if not most of your work background appears unrelated to your new objective.

Happily, there are methods you can use to select and refocus elements of your past experience in order to present yourself as a strong, viable candidate—even using a chronological format. Mary Mistake, for example, could have used these techniques to produce three very useful resumes in teaching, office administration, and fundraising. For evidence, see the sample resumes that follow. *All* of these resumes were created by individuals with spotty or highly disparate work experience! They simply made use of the following basic techniques to *fill in experience gaps* and *communicate a stable career direction.*

Guidelines for Masking Flaws and Gaps in a Chronological Resume

1. **Don't overcompensate.** You only need a few items that connect to your new job objective for the resume to be sufficient. It's better to use a few recent citations than a long history that includes a lot of gaps. (In the sample resumes that I provide, you'll see that most feature one or two recent jobs.) If there is a substantial gap in the sequence of employment you do choose to include, you can explain that you took time off on a one-time basis for travel or family matters. It is best to give such reasons rather than artistic ones at this stage, to avoid giving the impression that you are unable to commit to a job for the long term.

2. **Don't be afraid of short employment gaps.** It is better to have a short gap than to include work that is hugely different from or contradictory to your goal.

3. **Look for links.** Even apparently disparate jobs and fields may share common themes. The shared elements may have seemed like minor aspects of the job at the time, but that doesn't matter. As an example, see the sample office resumes on pages 172 and 174. The employers listed there are very different, but the experiences are linked through their shared emphasis on elements of administration. Even Mary Mistake's very scattered resume has common themes; for example, she could have highlighted the common theme of written/verbal communication (evident in her experiences copy-

editing, reviewing, and teaching a language) or a flair for office work (her knowledge and use of software on many different jobs). Reviewed carefully enough, your own resume should reveal similar connections.

4. **If you haven't done so already, find the kind of volunteer opportunities discussed in chapter 6.** Then, as recommended above, list them just as though they are paid employment. As I've said before, volunteer situations are often the best and fastest way to build your resume with focused work experience.

5. **Cite relevant education and memberships.** Listing continuing-education courses you have taken in your new field, or unions, clubs, and other professional organizations you have joined (again, in your new field), help demonstrate involvement in and commitment to that field. This information is placed at the bottom of a chronological resume.

6. **Try to arrange to get relevant work or a relevant job title through a friend, relative, or contact owning a business.** Such personal contacts are often glad to help out in this way. Even when you are volunteering, you can often arrange to have a distinct job title that will help you gain paid employment.

7. **Include only goal-related functions for each place of employment you list.** Omit functions of any job or position that don't relate to your new objective. Through this technique, you can use the elements of a single job as the springboard to many different careers. For example, let's say you worked as the department administrator for a college's graduate theater department, but are looking for a new and stronger lifeline career.

   - If your goal is to move into *teaching*, you would omit purely clerical or administrative elements of the job but include interactions with students, liaison roles with faculty, and curriculum-management functions. You would cite only special projects or accomplishments that relate to the teaching role. For example, you might mention that you were responsible for coordinating meetings of the faculty curriculum committee— this role gave you an overview of the course development process—but you would not mention that you shaved 10 percent off the department's budget, since that achievement has no direct bearing on your teaching skills or experience.

- If your goal is to get a *better administrative job in a different field or environment*, you would omit counseling and liaison functions and elements specific to theater and emphasize nuts-and-bolts office-management tasks such as budgeting, working with accounts payable, staff hiring, or supervision. Those functions are universal for all administrative positions. You would cite special accomplishments specifically related to administration: your ability to streamline the budget, improve office efficiency, redesign the record-keeping system, etc.

- If your goal is to move into *a higher-level management role in a local or regional theater*, you would omit clerical functions and interactions with students while including management-level tasks such as staff hiring and supervision, marketing and promotion, or budget accountability. You would cite accomplishments such as increasing ticket sales for the student play series by 15 percent or attracting grant funding for a special college theater program.

You'll notice that *none of these descriptions* involves falsehood. All of them accurately describe the job you held; they just do not describe the *entire* job you held.

8. **Group freelance or temp assignments together.** Rafael is a painter who has worked at decorative faux painting as a lifeline career for years, taking on projects only when he needed the money. Now he'd like to commit more strongly to that career, developing a broader client base and gaining more important jobs. On his resume, rather than list each assignment as a separate job, he could use a more general heading such as "June 1993 to Present: Decorative Painter" to create the impression of greater continuity and focus. The description under that heading could read something like this: "Created faux marble and wood effects and interior murals for clients including architects, interior designers, and private individuals. Projects included faux paneling for the library of the Royal Elm Design Showhouse, 1992; extensive interior murals for the Cooper Square Cafe, 1995; and decorative paint finishes for all interiors in a private townhouse in Manhattan, 1997." This entry does not hide the fact that these projects were spread out across many years and many different employers. But by grouping them together, it creates an impression of professional commitment and focus.

The Functional Resume

As I have mentioned, the functional resume emphasizes your major skills rather than your work history. Creative people tend to use functional resumes when they have utilized their skills in a wide variety of industries. Raul, for example, had worked in restaurants, as a retail sales person, and as a telemarketer. "When I listed my employment chronologically, it looked totally random. I knew that few employers would see value there. Then I realized that the theme in all of my jobs was customer relations. Using that as the heading in my functional resume made my experience appear linked for the first time." A functional resume might also work for you if your employers have not been prestigious or well known, as it lists but does not truly highlight the names of employers.

In a functional resume, you first give the same summary statement that would be used in a chronological resume—the summary that, as I noted before, answers the question *"What related skills and experience do you bring to the job and field you now seek?"*

You then identify two or three skill clusters that relate to and support the summary. Commonly used categories build on the same basic list of transferable skills you used in the reassessment from chapter 3. In summary, the skill groups most commonly used in a functional resume include:

- **Communication Skills**
  Editing
  Writing
  Fundraising
  Proposal or Grant Writing

- **Human Services Skills**
  Advising
  Coaching
  Teaching
  Customer Relations
  Public Relations
  Mediation

- **Information Management Skills**
  Budgeting
  Auditing
  Computer Skills

- **Managerial Skills**
  Administration
  Supervision
  Coordination
  Organization
  Problem Solving

- **Manual/Physical Skills**
  Assembly
  Repair
  Construction
  Working knowledge of instruments

- **Analytic Skills**
  Research
  Interpretation
  Evaluation
  Compilation

- **Design/Planning Skills**
  Conception/Development
  Initiation of Plans
  Drafting

Look for headings that link together the basic skills you have or the functions you have performed. Career counselor Susan Julia describes this section of the resume, which is usually entitled "Relevant Experience," as answering the question *"How did you demonstrate these skills on the job?"* Your employment history is briefly listed at the bottom of the page, answering the final question, *"Where were your skills demonstrated?"*

Because the functional resume downplays actual work experience, some employers are wary of this style. Remember that just as in a chronological resume, you must prove that you have direct, current work experience in the relevant field.

Examples of strong functional resumes are given at the end of the chapter. These resumes effectively highlight their subjects' strengths in a forceful, easy-to-read manner.

A Final Word: Job Applications

Once you have a strong personal commercial and resume in hand, your personal selling tools are taken care of. However, you may still need to negotiate one more hurdle as you market yourself: the job application.

Job applications are used by the human resources departments of most mid- to large-sized organizations, as well as by employment agencies. Guidelines for completing them successfully are similar to the rules for creating a strong resume, and indeed, the application and the resume should contain the same basic information, since the two will typically be used and filed together.

Many candidates mistakenly see the job application as trivial. Though the application per se will not "sell" you, most employers see applications as a firsthand indication of your work habits. Sloppiness, carelessness, and inability to follow directions precisely may count against you. Don't let the application end your candidacy for trivial reasons! You can avoid this by following these three rules:

1. **Be neat.** You will typically be filling out the form by hand. You may want to purchase an erasable pen or write a draft on a separate sheet before handing in the application. Neatness does count, because all

aspects of your self-presentation will factor into a potential employer's impression of you.

2. **Follow directions.** Read the questions carefully before answering. Make sure you understand the directions—such as whether to list work history in chronological or reverse chronological order—thoroughly.

3. **Offer positive information.** Questions regarding "salary history" or "reasons for leaving last job" can be tricky and, if not answered correctly, may present the individual with an unconventional working history in a bad light. Here are some strong answers to typical application sections. Note that while you should not lie on a job application, it is better to leave a question or section blank than to present a potentially damaging answer.

- **Salary History.** Leave this blank if your salary was under market value or you cited volunteer work. While many potential employers may check former employment as listed on your application, most will not check your salary at a former position; if they do so, former employers will typically not answer questions regarding your salary.

- **Reasons For Leaving Job.** Answer with a positive phrase. "Career advancement" and "Desire to learn new skills" are both good reasons to cite. Negative reasons that indicate dissatisfaction with your job are not helpful.

- **Pay Desired.** Never offer a specific rate of pay. Doing so can hurt you whether you cite an amount under that they are willing to offer (because you will be offered the amount you list, not the going rate) *or* an amount that is higher (because they may discard you as a candidate). Leave the negotiations on salary until you have received an offer. Answer this question with "Open" or "Negotiable."

- **Position Desired.** Cite broad skills categories rather than narrow job titles so that you don't limit your opportunities. Refer to the summary statement of your resume for guidance.

- **Gaps in Employment.** As with your resume, you can account for periods in which you cannot list employment by citing that you were "self-employed," "raising a family," "taking time off to travel," or "attending school." If the gaps occurred some years ago, simply skip the ancient history and focus on more recent jobs.

Resume 1: Weak Resume

MARY MISTAKE
123 45th Road,
Beverly Hills, CA 90210

Work Experience

1986-Present   Freelance word processor: Wordperfect, Lotus, Excel, Power-point, Pagemaker, Msword, DOS, Quicken, Soft Solutions, Dbase III+

1986-Present   Adminstrator, The Beverly Language Institute
Coordinated office services of Language Foundation including publicity and fundraising; parttime Spanish teacher at the Insitute

1978-Present   Professional Actress—film, commercials, theatre, voiceovers, television

1992-1993   Spanish Teacher, The Colverdale School
Taught Spanish to middle school children, grades 7, 8 & 9

1991-1992   Columnist/Film Reviews, The Beverly Hills Gazette

1990-1991   Producer, Beverly Hills Rep

1984-1990   Part-time Legal Word Processor, Stuart, Simon & Co.

1978-1982   Copy editor, Time Warner Books

Related Skills

Speak, write & read Spanish
Word process 115 wpm
Narrator, Publisher, Fundraiser, Writer, Producer, Publicist, Teacher

Education

B.F.A., UCLA 1977
Spanish—Escuela del San Martin, Mexico City, Mexico
Numerous acting course—New York and Los Angeles

Professional Affiliations

Actors Equity Association
Screen Actors' Guild
Association for Professional Fundraisers

Resume 2: Sample Arts Administrator Resume

PROFILE

Expertise in arts administration and management including staff supervision, planning, scheduling, budgeting, projected management, fundraising grantswritting, and creating publications

PROFESSIONAL EXPERIENCE

Marketing Consultant   ***New York Times* Credit Union**
Direct all aspects of marketing to the organization's 7,500 members.
- Write, design, edit, and oversee publcation of annual report, newsletters, brochures, posters, and other promotional materials using Word, MacWrite, Illustrator, and PageMaker.
- Plan and budget annual marketing strategy using Excel and Lotus 1, 2, 3.
- Implementing Web page.
- Plan and lead monthly staff training in member service.   **1995-present**

Grantswriter   **Freelance**
Clients including New Perspectives Theatre Company, The Work Shop, Gerber's Playshop.
- Proposals and pitch letters, brochures and flyers.
- Samples on request.   **1988-present**

Administrator   **Young Audiences**
Managed office communications and operations for the national office of the arts-in-education network.
- Designed and managed databases using FileMaker
- Created financial and statistical spreadsheets with Excel.   **1994-1996**

Producer   **Amiable Productions**
Financed, produced and promoted Off-Broadway shows, showcases, readings, and scene nights.

RELATED EXPERIENCE

As a stage director and Production Stage Manager for 15 years, I have worked with Ensemble Studio Theatre, LaMama ETC, Bruno Walter Auditorium, Playwrights Horizons, Wilma Theater, Riverside Shakespeare, The Writers Theatre, Chicago's Body Politic, Akademi der Kunste-Berlin, and the Munich Int'l Theatre Festival

EDUCATION

NYU, Certificate in Fundraising Management
Commercial Theatre Institute, Certificate
Hope College, BA cum laude

Resume 3: Sample Office Resume #1

PROFILE
- Experienced writer with expertise in Office Administration
- Word Processor, Editor, Researcher, Translator
- Excellent interpersonal and organizational skills
- Independent self-starter who thrives on teamwork yet works well alone

EXPERIENCE

HARVEST Information and Technical Center, NYC   **1997-Present**
Editor/Computer Assistant
　　Create all written materials: letters, resumes, flyers, business cards, and obituaries. Redraft written documents: business plans, proposals, brochures, and newsletters. Organize and maintain mailing lists for clients. Heavy customer contact, especially troubleshooting: assisting patrons with word-processing programs, Excel & Internet research. Main Spanish translator for all incoming jobs. Photocopy Assistant (B&W/Digital Color).

ACTORS' WORK PROGRAM, NYC   **1995-1997**
Administrative Assistant
　　Prepared written correspondence including memos, letters, and flyers. Scheduled meetings and maintained appointment calendar for Program Director and Counseling Staff. Also, filing, reception, photocopying, and heavy phone interaction.

NUAGE ANGECY (NY CONNECT), NYC   **1994-1995**
Case Manager
　　Counselor/Advocate for new teen mothers. Evaluated client needs and referred them to appropriate Social Programs (i.e., Educational/Parenting Skills). Led conflict resolution sessions between parents and teens. Tracked and followed-up client progress. Performed administrative duties: wrote progress reports, correspondence. Maintained case files.

RELATED EXPERIENCE
　　An award winning freelance writer, I have written numerous screenplays, plays, young adult novels, and children's books. In 1987 I helped establish Danit B. Film Corp., an independent film and video production company where I was part of a creative team that produced media products, e.g., industrials, promotional and music videos, Public Service Announcements, and commercials. Bilingual in Spanish: I have translated scripts in addition to other materials.
- Writers' Guild of America, East
- Geri Ashur Award/New York Foundation of the Arts for *Best Intentions* (Columbia Pictures)

EDUCATION:　　City College of New York & University of Seville, Spain BA
　　　　　　　　English/Creative Writing Minor; Spanish/French
SKILLS:　　　　Windows98, MSOffice 2000, Excel, PowerPoint, 50 wpm,
　　　　　　　　IBM Proficient, Mac aptitude

Resume 4: Sample Teaching Resume

Expertise in all aspects of teaching English as a second language, including pronunciation, grammar, and conversation, by utilizing various methods including the Rassias method. Setting up curriculum for groups of various backgrounds. My students emerge ready to enter the real world secure in the knowledge that they have a firm grasp of the language.

TEACHING EXPERIENCE:

1993-present   **43RD STREET KID'S PRESCHOOL**
         New York, New York

- **Develop and teach ESL course to families new to the country.**

- **Organize and create all materials and assignments.**

1995-1996   **THE TUTORING SCHOOL**
         New York, New York

- **Instructed students of High School level in grammar and vocabulary in both Spanish and English.**

- **Prepared student to enter into proper grade level.**

RELATED EXPERIENCE

43rd Street Kids Preschool: Music teacher and summer camp supervisor for children ages 3-10.
Private voice teacher.
Office manager for doctor's office.

EDUCATION

University of Hartford, Bachelor of Music
Rassias Method workshop, Baruch College

Resume 5: Sample Office Resume #2

NEIL SILVER
345 Main Street
Denver, CO
456-678-9876

HIGHLIGHTS OF QUALIFICATIONS

- Expertise in MS Word office software
- Superior communication and interpersonal skills
- Organized, accurate, and detail-oriented administrative assistant
- High ability to function under stress and meet deadlines
- Experience in corporate and legal settings
- Dependable, energetic team player
- Demonstrated skill in interfacing with senior management

RELEVANT EXPERIENCE

Administrative/office
- Expertise with heavy workload of word processing assignments, including correspondence, mailings, and data entry
- Maintained extremely large legal files and appointment schedule
- Researched and compiled corporate sales data
- Managed secretarial staff of four as well as temporary workers

Public Relations
- Coordinated annual fundraiser, including telephone and written solicitation
- Established solid, ongoing relationships with suppliers
- Consulted and planned large private parties for executives
- Served as Secretary for statewide charitable organization

EMPLOYMENT HISTORY

1997-Present	Administrative Assistant	Alexander Law Offices, Denver, CO
1995-1997	Personal Assistant	Charity Party Planners, Denver, CO
1994-1995	Production Assistant	CDE Productions, Denver, CO
1993-1994	Word Processor	Joseph & Sons Law, Denver, CO
1988-1993	File Manager	Joseph & Sons Law, Denver, CO

EDUCATION

1987 BFA Colorado State College

Resume 6: Sample Food Management Resume

ALICE BAKER
123 San Diego Street
San Jose, CA
415-123-4567

SUMMARY OF QUALIFICATIONS

Expertise in all aspects of restaurant management, including superior customer service, knowledge of food and wine, and problem-solving ability

RELEVANT SKILLS AND EXPERIENCE

Customer Relations
- Developed effective approach for training staff in advising customers on food and wine selections
- Created and implemented an extremely efficient reservation system
- Increased business by consistently excellent treatment of customers and repeat customers
- Fostered positive word-of-mouth reputation through excellent communication skills

Management
- Demonstrated excellence in staffing, scheduling, and budgetary issues
- Excellent problem solver regarding both staff and customers
- Trained assistant manager and wait staff in restaurant policy and procedures
- Earned position as role model regarding honesty, fairness, cooperation, and attendance

EMPLOYMENT HISTORY

1997-Present	Manager	Texas Mexas Restaurant, San Diego, CA
1994-1997	Assistant Manager	Jewel Restaurant, San Francisco, CA
1992-1994	Assistant Manager	Kathy's Place, San Francisco, CA
1990-1992	Waiter	The Kingdom Diner, San Francisco, CA
1989-1990	Sales staff	The Gap, San Francisco, CA

EDUCATION

B.A. 1988 San Francisco State College, Theatre Arts

Resume 7: Sample Functional Resume

Anita Noble
215 Highlands Road
Seattle, WA 91345
814-678-2189

Summary of Qualifications

Record of excellence in the field of teaching dramatic arts, including scene study, speech, and theater history. Directed musical and dramatic works on the high school and college level. Professional acting credits include Broadway as well as an Obie Award nomination.

Teaching

- Taught wide variety of classes, including speech, scene study, theater history, and monologue preparation
- Created theater games and exercises for dramatic arts majors and nonmajors

Directing

- Selected musical and dramatic works for production
- Supervised casting and performance aspects of two major productions per school year.

Marketing and Promotion

- Conceived advertising design for school and local papers, wrote press releases
- Developed audience-outreach programs and supervised ticket sales

Employment

Instructor, The College of Seattle, 1998-Present
Actress/Promotions Director, Seattle Theater Workshop, 1990-Present

Education

University of California at San Diego, 1988
University of Washington, BFA, 1986

Chapter Nine

The Official and Hidden Job Markets: How To Get the Job You Want

Though this be madness, yet there is method in it.
—Shakespeare

Talent is cheaper than table salt. What separates the talented from the successful one is a lot of hard work.
—Stephen King

Now that you have a strong personal commercial and a power resume, where do you actually begin your search for a job?

If you're like most people, the places that spring to mind immediately will be classified advertisements and employment agencies. These two resources together reflect what people in the career-counseling industry refer to as the "official" or published job market—jobs declared to the general public and to which anyone with the required qualifications may apply.

Both of these sources can, and do, work effectively for some people. Later, I'll share some tips on how to make them work as well as possible for you if you choose to use them as an option.

But if you are like most creative people, neither classified ads nor employment agencies will be the most effective means of getting the job you want. Here's why:

- **Since they are distributed to a huge readership, newspaper job ads create fierce competition.** Scores, sometimes hundreds of individuals may apply to a single ad. As Dawn (the playwright we met earlier, who wanted to work in Web site design) discovered, the competition that a creative artist faces when job hunting through ads can be extremely stiff.

   "I applied for a number of Web design jobs through the want ads and never got a single response," she comments. "As it happened, I met an executive from one of the companies at a party a few months later. She told me that her company usually got upwards of a hundred applications from each Web design job posting—and that almost all of the applicants had years of experience in computer and graphic design. Compared to these folks, I was a beginner. I felt very discouraged."

- **Employment agencies tend to feel more comfortable with "standard" employment candidates.** They are paid to streamline an organization's hiring process, to screen out unlikely candidates, and to fill work slots while wasting as little of the organization's time as possible. They work with the odds, not against them. Thus, they are rarely if ever willing to take risks or send along an unusual or nontraditional candidate.

   "Five years ago, I had a job-hunting experience I'll never forget," says Jimmy, a musician and composer. "I had worked in marketing for years, but then went back to graduate school to pursue my first love, musical composition. When I finished the coursework for my graduate degree, I needed to find a job that would give me some kind of stable income while I completed the thesis required for my degree and built my career as a composer.

   "I decided that rather than return to marketing—which is too high pressured and demanding to give me time for my music—I would aim for a lifeline career in office work. I took the time to get excellent training in common computer software packages and wrote a powerful resume. Then I visited six employment agencies . . . none of which would even put me on their books, despite the fact that every one of them had suitable jobs for me! This experience taught me that employment agencies had an entirely different perspective than I did. I saw myself as a bargain: a responsible worker with both office and higher-level skills who was willing to work for a relatively low salary. The agencies saw me as a risk: someone who looked overqualified, who would get bored with office work quickly and who might backfire on them if sent for an interview. I finally realized I was going to have to go outside traditional channels to find the job I wanted."

- **Finally, and perhaps most significantly, the vast majority of jobs listed through *both* ads and employment agencies are traditional positions that require full-time work on a standard schedule.** As an artist looking for a lifeline career, these jobs rarely provide the flexibility you need to pursue your creative dream. This is particularly true if you are in the performing arts, as auditions and interviews are usually scheduled during the working day. By the time they are posted, these jobs have usually been rigorously defined; they force you to fit into their demands, rather than allowing you to shape the job to your needs.

    For all of these reasons, you will almost certainly need to turn to the "hidden" or unpublished job market to get the kind of position you want. Almost all of the artists whose stories are given in this book found positions through the hidden market. Most career-guidance professionals—myself included—estimate that over 80 percent of *all* jobs are filled through hidden rather than official sources. In addition, of course, most freelance jobs are filled through these unofficial channels as well. Together, the positions that comprise the hidden job market represent the unseen bulk of a huge iceberg, compared to the tip of the iceberg that is visible through the published market.

The hidden job market consists of all positions that are created and filled without going through published channels. Hidden jobs are created when organizations

- **Offer positions arising through company plans, retirement, promotions, or reorganizations—that have not been officially published but are searched through word of mouth.**

- **Prefer to reduce salary and benefit costs, as well as advertising or employment agency expenditures, by creating consulting or freelance arrangements rather than permanent full-time positions.**

- **Find that their special or unconventional needs are best met by searching outside of published channels.** "I would never bother to advertise any of our jobs in a newspaper, much less use an agency," says Robert, the director of a prestigious nonprofit arts organization. "I don't have the time or the staff to sift through hundreds of resumes from people who, while qualified in terms of actual skills, won't fit into our organization's culture. We're looking for a particular kind of person—someone who has the skills for the job but also someone with a deep commitment to the arts. I find those people by putting the word out within the arts and education community—by letting my colleagues in the field know we're looking, by posting flyers at arts programs in the city, asking staff to alert their contacts, and using my network of contacts. It's a much more effective way for us to search."

- **Fill positions as a result of their decision-makers with hiring authority (or with links to those who hire) who meet individuals with relevant or attractive skills and goals.** These decision-makers have the power to create or adapt jobs to make a match between what a candidate can contribute and what the organization needs. Robert's viewpoint, discussed above, again underscores the importance of this kind of link. "Whether or not we have a job open at the time, I'm always alert when I meet people with interesting skills and qualifications. I keep their names and numbers on file, and I encourage them to keep in touch with us. Often, that's the kind of contact I turn to when new needs arise in our organization. On one occasion, I even created a job for someone I met. She was a graduate of a film-production program, but she had strong writing, business, and grant writing skills. Talking to her made me aware of how those kinds of skills could benefit us—and because she was looking for stable work, there was a natural fit. I went back to the office the next day and juggled the budget to squeeze out a part-time position. It's not a hugely lucrative job. But the steady salary benefits her, and her skills are a great advantage to us."

As these examples illustrate, the hidden job market is much more likely than the official channels to provide the kinds of interesting, flexible jobs you want than official channels. Even better, the things that act to your detriment in the official job market—your unorthodox career path or your need for flexible work—can actually become advantageous in the hidden job market.

Though you might not realize it, you have already begun tapping into the market of unpublished jobs. This market is accessed primarily through your contacts—the same A, B, and C contacts you began to identify and use in chapter 5. Continuing to use this network is the first of eight steps to getting the job you want.

Eight Steps to Getting the Job You Want
Step 1: Expand and Work Your Contacts

Continue to expand and work your B and especially C contacts in every way you can. Doing this effectively requires an active, consistent, steady approach. You'll need to follow up on referrals or introductions promptly, invest the time and effort to schedule appointments, write thank-you notes, and so on. Don't let this process get pushed aside by other distractions or deadlines. If necessary, make an appointment with yourself at a specific time each week and use those hours only for your networking activities. Or, consider joining a professional organization or a special-interest group related to your field if you haven't already done so. Such clubs and associations may be formally organized (like Kiwanis, the Rotary Club, Toastmasters, and the Chamber of Commerce) or not. The Independent Computer Consultants of New York, for example, is an informal but useful group. Either way, the regular meetings will "force" you to network!

As you network, explore creative ways to broaden your contacts. Flora, for example, is an actress who has a lifeline career as a real-estate broker. In her recurring role as a lawyer in the television drama *Law and Order*, she always makes time to hand out her real-estate business cards to cast and crew members on the set. "You never know when someone might want a new apartment," she says. As Flora proves, there are many ways to broaden your contacts.

Resist the temptation to give up once you've exhausted your first round of contacts—those contacts that come easily from your original A list. Dig deeper, go broader. Keep asking these contacts if they know of anyone else who might be helpful to you, and never forget that your goal is to link with C contacts who have the authority to hire you. Even after you move to step 2, continue to work whatever contacts you can.

As you continue to network, review chapter 5 for guidelines on how to deal with these contacts. Make sure that everyone knows you are looking for a lifeline job and that you are, by now, well trained and versed in your new field. If people ask you how your job search is going, be confident and upbeat rather than defensive. "Thanks for asking. I'm still exploring to find the right position, but I'm excited about the information and contacts I've gained," is a good and appropriate answer.

Above all, be aware that this process takes time. Identifying and meeting contacts is a bit like planting seeds; it can take a long time for new growth to germinate, and some seeds never grow. Networking rarely generates great jobs overnight. But if you are persistent, it almost always yields excellent results in time. The experiences of both Dawn and Jimmy, whom you met earlier, are evidence of that.

After her futile search through the want ads, you may recall that Dawn met an executive from one of the companies she'd applied to at a social gathering. "This woman was a real power in the organization," she says. "Though the news she delivered (about how stiff the competition was) felt discouraging at first, I maintained a positive attitude. I used my personal commercial to introduce her to my abilities. Without putting any pressure on her to find or offer me a job, I asked her if she'd be willing to share some advice about how someone like me could break into the field. She was very helpful, and, when we met briefly later that week, gave me very sound guidance. Four months later, it was her introduction that helped get me a job at another company."

After his failed attempts to get hired through an agency, Jimmy knew he needed to redirect his job search according to his goals and talents, not the needs of employment agencies. After some thought, he decided that New York's large network of smaller film, music, art and entertainment-related organizations would be a good focus for his search. Such employers, he reasoned correctly, would not feel put off by his unorthodox background and would be more likely to be receptive to a flexible working arrangement.

"I went back to my graduate school and started asking people in the music and film divisions where they did their sound recordings, bought their instruments and equipment, edited their films, and so on. In less than two weeks I had a list of over thirty businesses that provided some kind of technical or business support in arts-related fields. I contacted these companies by letter, then followed up by phone. Less than three weeks later, I was offered the position of administrator by a stock-photography organization that provides photographs for use by advertising agencies, publishers, and artists. I now handle their billing and correspondence and share reception and photo-filing duties. They're happy to let me begin work at 10:30 rather than 9:00, so I have the early mornings free for work on my music. Plus, I really like working in an environment that supports the arts."

Step 2: Supplement Your Existing Network through Research

To supplement your existing network, begin researching agencies, organizations, institutions, or companies where you might like to work—even if you do not know anyone there and even if no appropriate job is currently available. You should aim to develop a list of twenty-five to fifty or more such target employers, whom you'll then contact using the steps that follow. The purpose of this process is to lay the groundwork for potential positions that may arise or be created in the future.

Begin by asking yourself, "What are the categories of organizations for which I would like to work?" Sometimes, only one category of organization will apply. If your lifeline career is, say, personal training, the answer (at least until you can build up a private practice) will obviously be fitness clubs, spas, and gyms. On the other hand, if your lifeline job is office work, computer graphics, or proofreading—if it involves a skill that could be used in a wide variety of environments—you will need to narrow down possible employers. In such cases, you should consider both practicality (which category of organizations is most likely to *need* the skill you can provide) and personal preference (what type of environment—artistic, business, nonprofit, technological) you would most *enjoy* working in.

Once you have identified one or more categories, you can use your contact network to help you identify the names of specific organizations within that group. Your local yellow pages can also be helpful in compiling your list; your library will have yellow pages for surrounding towns and possibly nearby cities as well. Libraries will also have company directories, organized by various types of trades, in their business reference section. Finally, you can use the Internet, searching by keyword, locality, profession name, and so on.

Step 3: Get the Names of Relevant Decision-Makers

Having the full name and correct title of the right contact person for each organization on your list is crucial. Don't waste your time contacting the personnel or human resources director, as your response will most likely be a "No positions are currently available" form letter. Similarly, don't send letters addressed to vague or generic titles such as "To Whom it May Concern" or "Dear Vice President of Marketing." The person you are looking for will be a chairperson, chief executive officer, director (in a smaller organization), or the vice president or manager in charge of a department (i.e., marketing, finance, public relations, accounting, sales) within a large company. Again, make absolutely certain that your information about who holds this position is current and that you have the proper title and spelling of the name.

The best way to get this information is through your existing contacts. This gives you the advantage of being able to provide a reference in your letter; executives are far more receptive to letters that mention a contact than they are to those that come in "cold." If you have no such referral, you can check the organization's Web site or call the organization and inquire. Staffers working at the switchboard or reception generally respond positively to requests for name, spelling, title, and address if you politely explain that you "wish to correspond with" or "have a letter that needs to be sent to" an executive. Don't give too much information, and be persistent but impeccably polite to anyone you speak with. This sounds obvious, I know, but it's nonetheless crucial. The secretaries, assistants, or receptionists you speak to may well interact with others in the organization. If you become frustrated or treat them with less-than-perfect respect, word may get around.

Make sure you have a considerable list of organizations targeted. Never count on just one; if your first contact with a company or institution yields a "watchdog" type who won't help you, simply move on to the next company. As you gather information, keep a record on each organization. Otherwise, you'll find your many "irons in the fire" will begin to blur over time. Your record might look like the following:

Target Organization Information Checklist

Organizational name:_____

Organizational format (i.e., nonprofit, government agency, corporation): _____

Organizational address: _____

Contact name and title: _____

Contact address, if different from main headquarters: _____

Referral contact, if any: _____

Other contact/organizational information (news you've gleaned from the paper, etc.): _____

Date of letter (attach copy for your file): _____

Results/response: _____

Date of follow-up call: _____

Results/response: _____

Step 4: Write to Your Contacts

Write and send a strong and concise letter to each contact. Several sample "broadcast" letters follow. Use your personal commercial and/or the summary statement from your resume as a basis for the information about your background and abilities. Mention a referring or other linking contact if possible. Always address the contact specifically, by name and title and with the complete company address. Include your resume with the letter, but always and without exception, keep the letter itself to one page. You'll notice that all of the sample letters I provide would fit onto a single page without my annotations.

The sample letters below show you how the basic broadcast form is adapted to three very different situations. Some features appear in all three; others vary by letter. By reviewing these life situations in conjunction with the letters themselves, you can begin to see how different challenges and issues you face might be handled.

- Suzy Garofalo, a dancer, has chosen massage therapy as her lifeline career. She is now writing to spas, gyms, and health clubs for positions, as this is how massage therapists generally begin a practice. These jobs are usually part time, with flexible hours depending on how many appointments are booked. Because such jobs require a relatively minimal commitment on the part of the employer, Suzy's letter need not be quite as detailed as the others, nor does she have as much significant experience to show as either Amy or Daniel. However, it's interesting to note that Suzy could strengthen her candidacy for top facilities by using her dance connections to arrange for massage work at one or more local dance or theater companies. Being able to say in her letter that she is the "massage therapist for the Cedar Rapids Ballet" would be a real plus.

- Daniel Jefferson, a full-time psychology-textbook editor for many years, now wants to work on a freelance basis in order to make time to write a screenplay. He has already secured some projects from his current boss, who in this downsized environment is actually delighted to have Daniel's expertise without having to pay him for vacations, sick days, or benefits! Wisely, though, Daniel doesn't want to rely on any single client relationship. He's therefore broadcasting his editorial services to other textbook publishers as well as to magazines that have self-help or psychology features.

- Amy Longfield is an actress. She genuinely likes administrative work and now wants to focus on steady, higher-level administration as a lifeline career. She has targeted advertising as her preferred field, as she likes the color, drama, and intensity advertising companies tend to have. Amy's work record is in fact quite spotty, with lots of temp work. However, she has worked hard to use training and volunteering to bolster her skills; hence, she is able to write a strong and quite detailed letter. Her letter copes gracefully with the fact that she has no referring contact to "introduce" her to this executive.

- Painter Tawana Sundell had an unsatisfying career working as an office manager for almost ten years. She has now decided to make her living doing project work in computer graphics instead, as that will allow her more flexibility to paint and provide an outlet for her creative and visual talents. Like Amy, she has carefully trained herself in the necessary computer programs and skills. However, her letter has the additional challenge of dealing with her ten years in an unrelated field. It is directed to the owner of a small but successful graphics design company because she has decided that one-man shops and other small businesses will be the most open to affordable freelance help.

Suzanne Garofalo
3 Everycity Lane
Everycity, NY 10500

October 3, 2000

[insert full contact name, title, facility name, and address]

Dear Mark Manager:

Your longstanding client Mr. Sam Slim has spoken highly of your facility and recommended that I write to you. [**Suzy uses her contacts to open her letter. Had she no personal connection to this gym, she would simply omit that sentence and begin with what follows.**] I am interested in a position as a staff massage therapist and am available for weekend and evening appointments.

I am a licensed Swedish massage therapist. [**A license is required for this work, so Suzy has waited until she got it to begin her broadcast letters. She does not need to specify here that she received it less than a year ago.**] In addition to my private practice, I have worked with the touring cast of *Chorus Line* and the Cedar Rapids Ballet Company. [**Suzy does not mention that she was not paid for this work, nor that she was a *member* of both companies. Also, because this single paragraph summarizes her work experience, she does not enclose a resume. She will, however, bring it with her to the interview.**]

I look forward to meeting with you personally to discuss how my experience and credentials might help meet the needs of your clients. [**Suzy chooses not to mention that she plans to call Mark Manager one week from the date of the letter, but she will in fact do so.**]

Sincerely,

Suzanne Garofalo

Daniel Jefferson
3995 Main Street
Emeryville, FL 33333

January 15, 2000

[insert contact name, title, business name, and address]

Dear Mr. Managing Editor:

I am writing at the suggestion of Lou Blank, who recommended that I contact you. I am currently making the transition from a position as a full-time book editor into freelance editing. I am interested in discussing potential future openings for such work at your publishing company.

I have enclosed my resume for your review. As you'll see, my background includes:

- Six years experience at University Texts, primarily editing psychology titles such as *Psychology and Your Life* and *Current Psychology.*

- Expertise in editing shorter journal and magazine articles for a variety of prestigious publications. [**The managing editor is probably only interested in book-length work, but Dan includes this point because it underscores his versatility in his field and because the managing editor might at some point refer him to journals or magazines.**]

- A Master's Degree from Harvard University. [**Dan's degree is actually in English Education. He specifies this on his resume but need not say it here.**]

I would welcome the opportunity to meet with you personally to discuss how my editing capabilities might be of use to your organization. I will call you next week to arrange a date at your earliest convenience. [**Unlike some of the other letter writers, Dan does specify when he will call. That's fine, as long as he does it!**]

Sincerely,

Amy Longfield
30 Anytown Drive
Anytown, MA 06395

July 2, 1999

[insert contact name, title, business name, and address]

Dear Ms. Account Executive:

I am currently exploring part-time administrative work in advertising and would be very interested in discussing possible future openings at your organization. [**Amy does not have a personal contact to refer her. Instead, she simply opens by reassuring the executive that she understands that there may be no openings at this time.**] I have been impressed with Anytown Advertising's fine and imaginative work for the Anytown Arts Museum account and congratulate you personally on your award as our Kiwanis Club's Woman of the Year. [**Specific references show that Amy has done her homework on the executive and company.**]

I have enclosed my resume for your review. Items that might be of particular interest to you include:

- I have five years of experience in office and administrative work and have worked in both smaller firms and larger organizations. [**Amy does not need to mention here that the first few years were temp work; that is clear from her resume, as is the fact that a number of her temp assignments were long-term.**]

- I am knowledgeable in Excel, Microsoft Word, and Word Perfect, as well as in basic office-administration skills. [**Because Amy's goal is administrative work, her first two "highlight" items are related to that specific skill.**]

- Since 1983, I have been the audience development director for the Anytown Players, which has recently expanded its playing season thanks to growing audience support. This experience gives me a hands-on understanding of advertising and promotion. [**Having established credibility as an administrator, Amy now shows that she has knowledgeable about advertising, not mentioning the volunteer nature of this work.**]

- My training includes coursework in computers, the Internet, marketing, advertising, and sales promotion. [**Again, Amy shows knowledge about the company's field, as well as demonstrating ambition and the desire to improve and learn.**]

I would be most grateful if we could meet briefly to discuss my credentials and your company's needs in further detail. I will call you shortly to set up such a meeting. In the meantime, many thanks for your consideration.

Very truly yours,

tawanda sundell
111 Elm Street • Treetown, CA • 94000

June 3, 2000

[insert contact name, title, business name, and address]

Dear Fred Founder:

Frannie Polk of the Computer Graphics Guild suggested that I write to you. [**Tawanda uses local networking well to make such contacts.**] I am currently looking for free-lance computer-graphics work with high-quality firms such as Vivid Graphics. Vivid's work on the packaging and Web site design for Pets Products especially impressed me and, you may be pleased to know, has been complimented several times at Graphics Guild meetings for its innovation. [**Like Amy, Tawanda has done her homework and can mention specific company references. In addition, this helps her underscore the fact that she is knowledgeable about and interested in the field.**]

I am fully familiar with the latest versions of Adobe Illustrator, Photoshop, Quark, and other software programs. I have been a visual artist and printmaker for many years and have exhibited at several galleries, including the Great Gallery in Manhattan. [**This mention of Tawanda's creative pursuit is appropriate only because it is so closely allied to her new lifeline career. However, note that the reference is brief. By mentioning it, Tawanda also distracts attention from the fact that she is not explaining what she has done for a living!**]

I'd like the chance to show you my portfolio, which includes a variety of materials, including newsletters, brochures, posters, Web sites, and packaging designs. [**These samples are work Tawanda did for free for friends and arts organizations while taking classes in computer graphics. She need not mention this now, during her interview, or in her resume.**]

I'll call you in the near future to set up a personal meeting. In the meantime, many thanks for your consideration.

Very truly yours,

As these letters demonstrate, in the course of your background research, you may discover particular facts about an organization, its goals, and its achievements. Added to your letter appropriately, references to this information tell your readers that you have done your homework and are not merely including them in a random mass mailing. If you add such material, your tone should be positive but not effusive, and your reference to the item brief. Lines such as "On each visit to your spa, I have been impressed by your up-to-date class offerings, excellently maintained facility, and wide variety of exercise equipment" or "Congratulations on your recent Rotary Club award for community service" are appropriate and help to distinguish you from other potential applicants. You may also wish to mention some relevant information about your referring contact, if applicable. Here again, the reference should be brief.

You may recall Peter, the actor whose consolidation efforts were described in the preceding chapter. Once he had refocused his goals on full-time teaching, he used local and area yellow pages to create a listing of nearby private schools. To more than a dozen decision-makers at these institutions, he wrote a letter that delineated his teaching credentials and was delighted to be invited to a personal interview shortly thereafter. Other schools recommended that he recontact them before vacation in June. Peter planned to do just that. Though it hadn't yielded a job yet, Peter felt much better about his search than he did a few months before. "Just to be hunting for a job on my own terms and targeting my search on organizations that I like and have chosen gave me a new sense of control. I never expected to land a full-time position instantly, but I felt very optimistic that it would happen within the near future." Peter's experience shows that even letters sent without the help of a referring contact can yield results.

Step 5: Call Your Contacts

Call each recipient two to three days after the letter is likely to have been received and ask for fifteen minutes of his or her time to discuss possible *future* openings. You need to make this call whether or not you choose to *say* you'll make it in your letter. Without such a call, the letter is unlikely to yield results, since only the most highly motivated recipient will take the time to call and schedule an appointment with you in the midst of his or her busy day.

When you call, acknowledge that you are aware that there are no positions currently available but that you'd like to "connect your face with the documents you sent." This takes the pressure off the executive and increases the chance that he or she will be willing to give you some time.

Approximately 30 percent of the people you have called will typically invite you for a personal meeting or interview. Whether or not a job offer results from any of them, you have built another potentially useful connection in your new lifeline career. You should consider yourself successful even when organizations do not agree to a meeting, since your concise, professional letter and follow-up call have differentiated yourself from other individuals. Be aware, too, that failing to get an immediate response does not mean your interest has fallen on deaf ears. Managers today tend to be pressured and overworked. Some will simply file your resume until an actual job opens up, potentially contacting you weeks or months after your letter was sent.

When you make your follow-up call, you will typically speak first with a receptionist, assistant, support staffer, or secretary who is responsible for protecting the executive you're calling from unwanted or unnecessary calls. It's important to understand that the "watchdog" role is part of the person's job, so handle the call, as I mentioned earlier, with grace and politeness. The impression you make on this individual, particularly if it's negative, will often be transmitted to the person in charge.

When you identify yourself at the beginning of the call, say that you are calling "with respect to the documents" or "with respect to the personal information" you sent. Commenting that you are calling about your resume or a job will only elicit a response like "There are no positions currently available"—information that doesn't help you, as you are trying to lay the groundwork for *future* job possibilities. It may also be useful to call slightly before 9 a.m. or after 5 p.m., when executives may answer their own phones. (However, calling *too* early or late may be considered intrusive.)

Step 6: Meeting with Contacts

Handle any meetings that result from this process as professionally as if they were interviews. Even though a job may not be available immediately, the meetings actually really are interviews. Detailed guidance on interviewing effectively is given in chapter 10. While the guidance there about such specifics as negotiating salary may not be appropriate, most of the other rules do apply.

Step 7: Send a Thank-You Note

This gracious gesture is a way of demonstrating your interest, enthusiasm, ability to follow through, and tenacity. A sample thank-you note follows. You'll notice that it is quite brief, but that it mentions a specific point covered in the meeting. Both brevity and specificity are key to a good thank-you letter.

Amy Longfield
30 Anytown Drive
Anytown, MA 06395

August 3, 1999

[insert contact name, title, business name, and address]

Dear Ms. Account Executive

Thank you for giving me the opportunity to meet with you on Monday. **[This note is timely—sent within the week.]** I enjoyed our meeting and especially appreciated the helpful insights you gave me about advertising at the local level. **[Amy paid attention, and she shows it here by citing one brief reference.]**

As I said during our meeting, I continue to be very interested in a position at Anytown Advertising, and I was pleased to hear that positions do open up from time to time. I hope that you will keep me in mind if any such jobs arise. Please do not hesitate to call me if you have any questions or if there is any other information I can provide. **[Though Amy chooses not to say that she will contact Ellen Executive periodically, she does intend to do so.]**

Thank you again for your time, and best wishes for a pleasant and productive late summer.

Very truly yours,

Amy Longfield

Step 8: Keep in Touch

Stay in contact with your targeted firms—especially those with whom you've met personally—at regular intervals as long as you're still searching for a job.

Your follow-up letter can use the same basic format as your first, adding simply that you are still interested in speaking with the executive there. Try to highlight some new experience or training you've received and include another resume.

The timing of this follow-up letter is something of a judgment call. I often suggest that clients send them after either January 1 or Labor Day, which are major seasonal shifts in the business year and times when work often speeds up or refocuses after the summer or holiday season. Referring to the New Year or hoping the executive and company had a pleasant and productive summer fit your letter naturally into this flow.

My clients sometimes fear that sending this type of follow-up mailing will seem pushy. Sometimes they'll even tell me that an executive or manager suggested they check in again in a few months, and they didn't do so! (Don't make this mistake yourself. Always follow up if invited.) In fact, as long as your letter is nonpressuring, organizational decision-makers will very rarely see appropriate persistence as anything but professional. The key, of course, is the word "appropriate." Needless to say, letters sent too frequently, criticisms of the fact that the organization did not contact or hire you last time, or impoliteness to the staffers who answer your calls, will not be perceived as appropriate.

"None of us want to admit it, but the truth is that in this environment of corporate downsizing, most of us are crisis managers, at least in part," admits one vice president of a large business. "We tend to have lots of urgent projects under way at any given moment. The people who want to catch our attention need to be willing to give us a reminder now and again."

Sarah, a short-story writer whose lifeline career is university administration, agrees. "My department was trying to get approval to hire a part-time assistant. Around the same time, we got a letter from a writer who wanted to talk about future job possibilities. I found his credentials impressive and appropriate to our needs. But I didn't respond, partly because I didn't know anything definite and partly because I was so overwhelmed with more urgent responsibilities—that was the reason I needed an assistant in the first place.

"Three months later, I received a very polite second letter from that same writer, stating that he was still interested in speaking with our department. When he called to follow up, I was able to tell him that I expected to get approval for a new position shortly. I ended up hiring him a week later! It's worked out great. But to be honest, I'm not sure I would have searched him out when the job came through if he hadn't written and called again. As busy as I was, I might have been tempted to take someone else who was closer to the forefront of my mind."

If You Also Search through the Official Market . . .

Although it is not wise to search *exclusively* through the official job market for the position you want, it may make sense to do *part* of your looking through traditional channels as a supplement to the outreach and networking activities described above. If you choose to do so, there are books that cover this subject specifically, several of which are listed in the Resources section. In the meantime, here are a few key techniques for making this part of your search as effective and efficient as possible:

- **Remember that it's a numbers game.** Anyone reading this book almost certainly has a nonlinear career path and needs a nontraditional working arrangement. For both these reasons, as explained earlier, the odds are against you when you apply for jobs through the official markets. Therefore, you must be consistent and disciplined if you are going to use resources such as ads or agencies. Check the paper every day; apply promptly to all ads that are appropriate to both your needs and your skills.

- **Don't waste time mass-mailing resumes.** "But you said that it was a numbers game," you may be thinking. "Doesn't it make sense to send as many resumes as I can?" Paradoxical as it may seem, the answer to that understandable question is an emphatic *no.*

    Used by itself, through mailings that may or may not get it further than an organization's Human Resources office, your resume is simply not effective. As I said in the previous chapter, it is primarily of value as a tool that enhances your relationship with contacts developed through networking channels, rather than a tool that builds relationships on its own. In my long experience, I've found that the only real benefit of high-volume resume mailings is usually to make the sender feel productive. That's a small gain for a rather costly process. Based on current prices for postage, good-quality resume paper and envelopes, and copying or laser printing, each resume-and-cover-letter packet you mail could cost $1.25 to produce and mail—and that's not counting the value of your time!

- **Don't neglect published but less accessible sources of jobs.** To give just one example, many schools—at elementary, high school, and college levels—are required to publicly post all administrative or officer-level openings for a given period, often a week or two. These jobs are not always widely advertised; instead, descriptions may simply be posted on a bulletin board near the institution's Human Resources, Employment, or Career Development offices.

"I got a job as an admissions officer at a college by taking the subway up to check the school's postings each week," says Beth, an aspiring film director. "Many of the postings were filled with internal candidates, so it's not as though the competition wasn't stiff. Still, I did find that it was easier to get callbacks and interviews through this source than through want ads in the paper. I also love working in the university environment—it's full of young people with a passion for the arts, and it reminds me of my own undergraduate degree in film ten years ago. For both reasons, it's much less isolating than working in an office. I'd encourage any artist looking for a stable job to give college or university postings a try."

- **For cover letters, use the same letter format already given in this chapter.** Simply match the list of your qualifications to the job that is listed.

Beyond Networking

If diligently pursued, this ongoing process of company contacts—supplemented by any results from your personal networking—should generate a series of meetings with potential or future C contacts. Over time, one or more of these meetings should transition into discussions about a specific job. The final step to getting the job you want, then, will be learning to interview effectively, the subject of the following chapter.

Chapter Ten

A Guide to Successful Interviewing

To know oneself, one should assert oneself.
—Albert Camus

I celebrate myself and sing myself.
—Walt Whitman

That's it, baby, when you got it, flaunt it.
— Mel Brooks

You must stir it and stamp it
And blow your own trumpet
Or trust me, you haven't a chance.

—W. S. Gilbert

Just as a theatrical opening night is the culmination of a long behind-the-scenes process of study and preparation, the job interview is the culmination of the entire self- and market-assessment process described in the chapters you've just read. This single meeting can not only make or break your chance to work for an organization but also help define the role you'll play and the salary you'll be offered.

The guidelines below are designed to help you prepare for, handle, and follow up after interviews effectively. Some of these guidelines reflect basic common sense; others are procedural pointers that I've gleaned from many years of working with clients during the interviewing process. Together, they will enable you to feel comfortable in an interview setting, avoid common interview "traps," and present yourself as strongly and positively as possible.

The Five Fundamental Interview Realities

The five basic facts below distill the fundamental realities common to any interview situation. Virtually all of the smaller interview "mistakes" job seekers make arise from lack of understanding of one or more of these basic realities. Simply by keeping them firmly in mind, you will give yourself a tremendous advantage over many of your competitors.

Reality #1: The interview is *not* reality. It's an unnatural situation, and many of its "rules" can't be extrapolated from everyday social norms. Like a fencing match or a Japanese tea ceremony, it is full of protocol that will only become familiar to you over time. Much of the behavior I'm about to suggest requires you to go against the grain of what feels natural. As you'll see, the goal is the paradoxical one of trying to "be yourself"—that is, trying to communicate the strength of your own particular personality, being extremely positive, and highlighting appropriate skills—and yet still conforming to the established, artificial rules of the interview format.

Reality #2: It's not really an interview, it's a sales call. Many job seekers envision an interview as a mere meeting. That's an unproductively static, neutral perspective. In fact, the interview is a dynamic situation that should be regarded as a sales call—with the product, of course, being you. The point of a sales call is to close a sale, and the point of an interview is *to get a job offer*—not to network (though it can happen), not merely to meet your potential employer, but to get an actual, firm offer. Once you are officially offered a position, you can evaluate how well the job will work for you, turn it down, use it as leverage to get a better offer from another organization, or negotiate whatever changes are necessary to make the job better suit your needs. But for now, simply aim for that offer.

Reality #3: Success isn't in the product (you!); it's in the match. It takes more than a good product to make a sale. It takes a strong match between the product's benefits and the buyer's needs. The importance of directly relating your *particular* skills and experience to the needs of the *particular* position and organization for which you're applying simply can't be overemphasized. Just knowing, say, that you'd be "good in advertising" because you're creative and good with people isn't enough. You must be able to demonstrate that your skills and experience match up with the *specific* jobs of copywriter, copy editor, account executive, art director, and so on—jobs which may call for radically different and perhaps even opposite qualities.

Reality #4: When candidates are equally qualified—as is often the case—who gets hired will often come down to who shows the most interest. In other words, the candidate who is hired has researched the job and company most thoroughly beforehand; has asked the best questions at the interview; has demonstrated the most positive, professional energy; and has followed through with a thank-you note and call. For that reason, you want to make sure that you are *always* the person who shows the most interest.

Jenny, the actress and corporate trainer we met earlier, shared this scenario: "At the end of an interview I was given the card of the CEO of the consulting firm. I'm sure that 95 percent of the other candidates didn't, but a day later, I called him. I told him how impressed I was with the organization and how suitable I felt I was for the job. I would not have made the call if I hadn't gotten his card, but I would have contacted everyone else I met. I think that I got the position partly because I was willing to take the initiative and demonstrate how strong my interest was."

Reality #5: No matter how hard you prepare for an interview, there are factors you simply cannot control. You can't control your personal chemistry (or the lack thereof) with the interviewer. You can't control your competition. You can't control the fact that the interviewer may be having a terrible day or that funding for the position might be cut. The only thing you *can* control is *how effectively you interview in any given situation* and, just as important, *whether you keep yourself in a position where you have the potential for numerous other interviews at numerous other organizations.* Preparation and the guidelines below will enable you to enter each interview at your personal best and remain in as much control as possible. Enter every interview aiming to get a job offer, as I said before; but remember that no single job represents the "be all and end all" of your future.

An Action Plan for Great Interviewing
Research the Organization

Look for facts about the organization's history, philosophy, products or services, and mission. To get this information, you can request company materials in advance—most organizations have a plethora of printed matter, including annual reports, brochures, newsletters, product guides, and so on. Information about larger organizations is available in libraries. You can also visit the organization's Web site.

In addition, try to get as much specific information as possible about the position itself. Your main source will be the interviewer, but your referring contact, other company staff, and even secretaries may be able to help. (Use the latter carefully, however. Interviewers will be annoyed if they feel you are "pumping" their secretaries for information behind their backs, and the perspective a clerical staffer has on your potential position may or may not be accurate.)

Such research will obviously involve a lot of work if you've set up many interviews. However, it's well worth the extra time it takes. It will make you feel more confident as you interview, allow you to respond appropriately to interview questions, and help you to ask relevant, informed questions yourself.

Peter, the actor whom we met earlier in this book, wrote me the following letter about the research he conducted before interviewing at a private school. "First, I got information about the school—scads of it—from its Web site," he noted. "I then walked into the theater department where I now teach one course and asked if anyone knew anything about the school. A faculty member had a daughter who had just graduated! I called her and we had a great talk. Feeling quite confident at this point, since I had so much information, I also called the person with whom I was interviewing to see if he had some sample lesson plans before the official date of our interview. He said he didn't have any, but he must have been interested, because he called me back the next day—just to talk! He gave me more information over the phone than I could have gotten from any lesson plan. Needless to say, I aced the interview. There were still a lot of people to see, but the department was really keen on me."

Bone Up . . . On Your Own Background

You know what you've done—or do you? Can you succinctly discuss the relevant duties and accomplishments for each and every job you've cited in your resume, and explain with equal brevity how they relate to the position at hand? If not, visualize a typical day at every job you list on your resume. Include in your visualization your interactions with the colleagues, suppliers, supervisors and clients; your personal workflow and style; the types of skills you used (analytical, creative, interpersonal); and the impact of deadlines or goals, if any. Return to the job summaries you completed at the start of your resume-creation process for help; take brief notes as you go. This concrete re-visioning of each job will help you tie your experience and talents to the position for which you are interviewing.

Prepare and Organize Your Materials Carefully

You should bring several copies of your resume even if you have sent it to your interviewer beforehand—never simply assume they'll have it handy. Also bring a reference list that you've printed out on a separate piece of paper. It should have two or three names of people you have called before including them on your list. They can be colleagues, supervisors at a volunteer or intern job, teachers, or friends who know your work; none has to be your boss or supervisor. Ideally, you will have a good enough relationship with the individuals you choose to guide them about what the position entails and which of your qualities might be highlighted.

If appropriate, you may also need to bring a small quantity of any other materials that testify to your relevant skills. For example, an artist interviewing for a job in Web site design might well bring printouts from her own personal Web site or the one she's designed for a friend, while a writer applying for a journalistic job might bring some related writing samples or testimonials.

The key words here are *small quantity* and *relevant*. Keep this portfolio as compact as possible, with just a few very carefully chosen items that highlight key skills and accomplishments. Interviewers dislike being inundated with materials; you can always show more samples later if asked. Also, consistent with Interview Reality #3, make sure that the material you bring speaks *directly* to the position for which you are being interviewed. Naturally, you're proud of your creative endeavors, and you should be. Nevertheless, someone interviewing you for a word-processing position does not care about your interpretation of Caliban in a summer stock production of *The Tempest*. An interviewer may decide you're not truly interested in the job at hand if you focus too much attention on unrelated skills.

Consider the Issue of Salary or Compensation

Before you enter the interview room, you must be prepared with a sense of what the job should pay, your ideal salary, and the lowest salary you can afford to accept. It's especially important to have an understanding of normal pay scales in the type of job you are interviewing for, because many interviewers will query you about what you want rather than name a specific amount. If the salary you name is too low, you are penalizing yourself; if it is too high, it may remove you from the running.

In some interview situations, it is easy to know what salary is appropriate; a specific salary was posted with the job, for example, or the pay scale for the position is fairly standard. In other circumstances, it can be difficult to ascertain the appropriate salary. You can often get an idea of the pay range by reviewing classified ads, consulting relevant guidebooks on your new lifeline field, and/or speaking with your B contacts. If that doesn't work, you may wish to consult a career counselor, who will typically have a good sense of salary ranges.

To ascertain your ideal salary, adjust the average pay for the job to your experience and skill level. Then, determine a lowest-possible salary as well. This preparation will set a floor on any negotiation and will ensure that you don't take a job that is not realistically able to meet your personal needs. Needless to say, both your ideal and your "lowball" salary figure should be within the normal range of compensation for the position, given your particular experience.

At The Interview
Dress Conservatively

This guideline sounds obvious, but it's often ignored by creative people . . . usually to their detriment!

In an ideal world, how you looked and dressed would have nothing to do with whether or not you were hired. In the real world, interviewers make both conscious *and unconscious* judgments about you based on appearance, and some of the judgments may be quite valid. If you are unwilling or unable to adapt your dress to the culture of the organization you're interviewing with, isn't it fair for an interviewer to assume that you won't be willing to adjust your working style, either?

Please note that dressing conservatively does not necessarily mean dressing with great formality. Today's workplace is somewhat more relaxed in terms of dress than it was ten years ago, which makes the issue of interview clothing just a bit more tricky. It's also true that corporate cultures vary. The dress code at IBM differs from that at a software company in Silicon Valley, where the CEO may well be a twentysomething former hacker who thinks "formal" means putting on a clean tee shirt. The faculty of a private boarding school may wear silk dresses and suits, while teachers at a community college may wear khakis or even jeans.

Here is another way your preliminary research can really pay off. What are people wearing in the photos in the company's brochure or annual report? Is the text of the Web site full of words like "tradition," "history," or "stability," suggesting a more conservative corporate profile, or does the company seem to pride itself on its innovation and pizzazz? What about the industry itself? Banking and finance are notoriously conservative in dress as well as politics. Advertising, fashion, and entertainment, on the other hand, are industries noted for their flair and individuality. A navy blue suit, starched white shirt, and regimental striped tie will look right at home in a brokerage firm, but may raise some eyebrows at a fashion design house . . . unless, of course, the position you're interviewing for is in Accounts Payable.

Never forget, however, that no matter how wild or casual the organization, *dress standards for an interview are always significantly more formal than those for an ordinary workday.* "My company is totally comfortable with me wearing quite casual clothing on the job," says Ben, a sculptor who is working on his first gallery show while doing color consulting work at an architectural firm. "Still, I would never interview in anything less formal than a good sport coat and tie, and I typically wear a suit. I just wouldn't take the risk of appearing disorganized, disrespectful, or discourteous by dressing down."

When it comes to appearance, then, caution is the key. No one has ever been rejected because they *didn't* have an eyebrow piercing! Here are more tips:

- Skip the jewelry—particularly the trendy items like thumb (not to mention nose) rings.

- Keep tattoos hidden if you can.

- Wear only the lightest, most subtle cologne or after shave, or skip the fragrances altogether.

- Keep your hair simple and neat. Do what you can to tame your usual hairstyle if it is on the cutting edge. Men and women with long hair should choose a pulled-back style rather than a wild and flowing one.

- Avoid both an overly casual look (sandals, baggy shirts or trousers) and an overly dressed-up one (stiletto heels, big jewelry, bright makeup).

- Leave clothing items designed to broadcast your personality your funny tie, your astrological earrings, your organizational stickpin—at home.

- Finally, if the interview clothing you've chosen is new or rarely worn, "road test" it a bit before the actual interview date by wearing it out of the house. "I bought a beautiful and conservative linen jacket specifically to interview in, only to find out that it wrinkled horribly when I wore it in the heat," says Layla, a dancer and teacher. "I looked like a rumpled paper bag by the time I got off the subway, and I felt untidy and unprofessional during that entire interview. I now check out all of my potential interview clothes in advance whenever I'm meeting with new schools that might have teaching positions. Only the most comfortable shoes, sturdiest and most run-resistant pantyhose, and wrinkle-proof clothes make the cut!"

Arrive (Slightly) Early

You don't want to appear harried or breathless, and you certainly don't want a traffic jam or subway stoppage to make you late. Ten or at most fifteen minutes early is ideal.

Do a quick check of your appearance in the restroom if necessary. Then, use your waiting time to get a "feel" for the organization. You might be surprised at how much you can learn about its pace, its dress code, and other elements of its corporate culture merely by observing the office life that goes on while you're in the reception area. You may also have the opportunity to read company materials such as brochures, annual reports, and newsletters while you wait.

Act Positive

Again, this point sounds obvious, but you'd be surprised at how often it's ignored. Being positive about yourself means presenting your qualifications in a thorough, straightforward manner. Don't be afraid to substantiate your skills with examples from prior jobs, giving appropriate details where you can. Don't hesitate to claim your successes and strengths. Employers expect you to "blow your own horn" to some extent at an interview.

But it's also important to be positive about life in general. This tells the interviewer that you are a resourceful, cheerful person—someone who will be pleasant to work with and who will solve problems when they arise. This is an area in which Interview Reality 1 holds especially true. In everyday business life, a certain amount of griping is perfectly normal—in fact, in many offices it's part of the employee bonding ritual! In an interview, however, negativity is extremely risky.

As proof, consider the experience of a colleague of mine, who once interviewed an actor for a well-paid administrative position. When asked how she was, the candidate complained at length about the difficulties of the subway system and the terrible time she'd had getting there. When asked why she wanted to work full time after a period of freelancing, she spoke about how impossible it was to make a living freelancing these days; when asked why she had left a previous job, she spoke about how companies have no loyalty. All of her points may have been true for her, but the impression she gave was of a complainer who lacked even the most basic coping skills. Needless to say, she didn't get the job—despite a very impressive resume.

Avoid Defensiveness

It's natural to *feel* a bit defensive about gaps in your resume, a lack of relevant experience, or other perceived flaws in your hiring potential. Still, I encourage you to avoid *acting out* that defensiveness in your interview.

Defensive people just aren't very likable. They often come across as whiny, self-absorbed, or insecure. Just as important, your defensiveness may lead you to point out flaws or concerns that weren't even on the interviewer's mind! There you are, earnestly explaining at great length that your lifetime commitment to your work as a ceramic artist won't interfere with your duties on the job . . . while your interviewer, an amateur watercolorist herself, is perfectly comfortable with creative types.

To avoid defensiveness, troubleshoot your resume in advance to pick out potential problem points. Find a way to respond to questions on these issues in a confident, simple, positive, and, above all, brief manner. Memorize it, practice it, and in your interviews stick close to that "party line"—do not invent or extrapolate on the spot. Here are some example questions with possible answers.

Q. I don't see any employment for the end of 1993.
A. I was taking care of some family business. I don't expect that kind of situation to come up again.
A. I was taking classes at the Everytown Design School. They really expanded my skills in the kind of computer-aided design your organization specializes in.
A. After many years of work in the field, I gave myself a one-time 'sabbatical' in order to travel.
A. I felt that I had reached my full potential in my previous position. I had been working on writing a book, and it seemed like a good time to take time to complete my first draft before moving on to my next professional position.
Q. How will we know that your work as a [painter, writer, actor] won't interfere with your responsibilities here?

A. I have always had to balance both a creative commitment and a career. I'm confident that I can continue to do so effectively, and give full effort to my position at XYZ Widgets.

A. My work as a [painter, writer] has always been done in the evenings and on weekends.

A. Although I will continue to work as an actor some evenings, I no longer accept work out of town.

Q. Your experience seems mostly to be clerical, but this position is at a higher level.

A. [**This is the time to use your volunteer or internship experience . . . without acknowledging that it's unpaid (that doesn't matter).**] My role as Director of Fundraising for the Smalltown Theater Guild is an executive position with management-level responsibilities. I'm responsible for identifying, contacting, and making presentations to potential funders; working with the organization's treasurer to allocate funds effectively; and acting as a liaison with the marketing and advertising directors. Corporate and individual sponsorships more than doubled during my tenure there.

Q. Why did you leave XYZ Corporation's employ?

A. Unfortunately, my position was eliminated when the company was taken over, and there was no appropriate position to which I could transfer. Much as I enjoyed my work there, I'm excited about the opportunity to contribute to another organization.

A. There were no further opportunities for growth at XYZ.

For other strong, nondefensive answers to common interview questions, refer to the sample interview later in this chapter.

If you were fired or let go, it's best to claim that you left due to company reorganization that eliminated your position or department or due to an overall firmwide downsizing. If you can't do so, it's best to omit the information from your resume entirely.

If you left a job due to personality conflicts with your boss or department, boredom with the duties, frustration over your salary, or any other negative reason, don't volunteer it. These are perfectly natural reasons to leave a job, but—given that a potential employer knows very little else about you—mentioning them can make you appear easily bored or frustrated, difficult to please, or difficult to get along with.

Listen!

When you are in a performance-oriented situation like an interview, it's natural to focus on what you yourself have said, are saying, and will say later. Yet listening carefully to what the interviewer says is crucial in allowing you to match your skills to the interviewer's concerns. Attentive listening also demonstrates your openness, calm, interest, and respect.

Ask Questions

This is a way both to show that you're knowledgeable about the organization in a natural way and to demonstrate your interest in the organization and the job. Have a short list of questions prepared before the interview, based on the research you've done on the organization. If possible, add a few more specific questions that relate directly to the content of the interview itself. Appropriate questions might include: What are the opportunities for advancement? What is a typical day like? What is the background of the staff in this department? What is the next important project?

Be Pleasant, But Not Over-Friendly

Many of the creative people I've worked with over the years have had trouble with this distinction, but it's nonetheless a difference that is crucial to your success in interview situations. When you are *pleasant,* you're enthusiastic, smiling, and positive. You're tactful and constructive in the way you speak of former employers and colleagues, gracious about any delays or interruptions in the interview, and poised in the face of any surprises (for example, the organization's director "drops in"). Your body language—occasional nods, an expression of alertness and interest, straight posture—indicates strength, confidence, and openness. You come across as warm, but also and even more strongly, as capable. The line between the personal and the professional remains firmly drawn—in fact, you reveal very little of your personal life or beliefs.

When you are inappropriately *friendly,* in contrast, you go a bit too far. Over-friendly behavior might include

- Talking too much about your art, interests, or personal life;
- Asking personal questions about the job itself, querying why it is open, who left, and so on;
- Offering to lend the interviewer a book or other personal belonging;
- Introducing topics of current interest or sharing opinions on current events and trends;

- Referring to something personal—an item of clothing, a trait, a family picture that's on the office credenza—related to your interviewer;
- Sharing a health, professional, or personal problem or a personal achievement not related to work;
- Mentioning that you have seen the interviewer at the movies or grocery store or that you know the interviewer's wife, boyfriend, or dog; and
- Telling overly long, detailed stories about past experiences and future aspirations.

In a social setting, these are natural ways of bonding. In an interview, they send the wrong message. They suggest that you wish to be liked, rather than that you are a professional interested in doing a job effectively. They may open up potentially controversial areas—subjects in which your taste or opinion might differ radically from that of the interviewer. They can quite unnecessarily reveal personal needs and flaws. And they risk presenting you as inefficiently chatty, weak, or insecure.

The experience of Vicki, a writer who has a lifeline career as a news-feature writer, underscores this point. Vicki's first interview when she began looking for full-time work was with a local newspaper.

"They brought me into their newsroom, introduced me to lots of people, and took me to lunch," she says. "The atmosphere was casual and very friendly, with none of the reserve I'd expected in an interview situation . . . in fact, they treated me as though I were 'one of the crew' already. In response, I really let my guard down. Over lunch, I told my interviewer how anxious I was to get full-time work, how much I needed both the money and the experience, and how eager I'd be to take any job he had available, not just the one I'd come to interview for. It was all incredibly pleasant—but when they offered me a job, it was at considerably less than the salary that had originally been quoted in the ad."

In retrospect, Vicki understands that the relaxed "cues" she was given led her to act naively. "I told them way too much. I certainly didn't come across as someone who valued her own skills and was confident that she'd be offered a good job—if anything, my comments suggested that I'd accept anything I was offered. In later interviews with other organizations, I was much more conscious that no matter how friendly an interviewer seemed, they were in a position of power. I worked much harder to stay impersonal and brief, and that approach eventually got me my current job."

As Vicki's experience shows, sometimes it is the interviewer or organization that sets an overly friendly, personal tone. They may be doing this in a mistaken attempt to put you at your ease, or they may be testing you.

Whatever their motives, the rule is the same. They have nothing to lose by being too friendly. You do.

Don't Be Afraid To Say "I Don't Know" or "I Haven't Yet Done That"

Your credibility will suffer if you try to fake it on questions to which you don't know the answer or haven't had the requested experience. People can tell when someone prevaricates. Wild guesses and bluffs, not to mention outright lies, have a nasty way of catching up with you. Steven, a fine artist interviewing for a lifeline job as a draftsman for a construction company, learned this the hard way. "In the course of our conversation, the interviewer asked me if I'd read Tracy Kidder's book on houses. It was clearly just incidental opening chitchat. But I was nervous, so I said that yes, I liked her writing very much. The interviewer looked oddly at me, but didn't say anything. I found out later that Tracy Kidder is a man! I probably failed to get that job offer, thanks to that one idiotic mistake alone . . . all because I wasn't confident enough to say I didn't know."

Instead of bluffing when you truly do not have the necessary information, face the fact that you simply won't be able to answer some questions fully or positively. It may help to remember that you do not have to be perfect to get a job. All candidates bring both strengths and weaknesses to the table. It's also helpful to remember that trying to guess the right answer without all the facts can create problems.

At a very important job interview, jazz-pianist-turned-piano-teacher Phil was asked how he would handle the situation of overly involved stage parents. Instead of trying to second-guess what the interviewers were looking for (something he simply couldn't ascertain from the information he'd been given), he just smiled and said honestly he wasn't sure. Wisely, though, he didn't stop there.

"I restated the problem and agreed that it was an important and difficult one," Phil recalls. "I then explained that I believed that gathering all of the facts was crucial to making effective decisions. I went on to discuss how I would go about getting the information I needed if the situation mentioned arose." By doing so, he proved that he was honest (because he was willing to admit that he didn't know the answer to the question); that he was sensitive to the company's concerns (because he reiterated that the situation would be problematic); that he was a careful and effective decision-maker (because he wouldn't speculate about a response to a situation without having the facts) and that he was resourceful (because he showed how he would actively confront the situation if it occurred). If anything, Phil's "I don't know" response worked in his favor.

Feel Free to Reframe

The fact that a question is asked does not necessarily mean it's the right question for you to answer. Without being adversarial or contradictory, you may sometimes need to reframe or refocus an interviewer's question to present your strengths appropriately. The situation just mentioned is one example. Phil reframed the question he was asked. By focusing on his general information-gathering and problem-solving skills rather than the specific crisis he was actually asked about, he both avoided a potential pitfall and got an opportunity to show off some of his strengths.

As Phil's experience also demonstrates, the key to reframing is a two-step answer. First, you *reaffirm* the fundamental concern voiced as a legitimate or important one. This sets a tone of understanding, deference, and agreement. Then and only then, you shift the focus slightly to highlight the information that is more helpful to your candidacy. For example:

> Q. Why do you feel you can edit our newsletter when you've never worked with a government agency before?
> A. I understand that you would naturally feel concerned that your editor be able to understand your business, its terminology, and so on [**reaffirmation**]. However, as a consulting technical editor, I am always working with clients in new fields—last year alone I edited pieces on commodities trading, fashion, and radio manufacturing. As a result, I am experienced in learning the relevant vocabulary and so on very quickly. In this case, you and your colleagues have the government experience that is necessary for a good newsletter; what I bring to the table are my editing skills and my sensitivity to the vocabulary and concerns of many different industries [**reframing**].

Ascertain Your Status

This is essential *before you leave the interview*. If an offer is not made (which is not unusual), ask when a decision will occur. Who will make it? Is there anything else you can or should do to further your candidacy? Do not hesitate to ask these questions if your interviewer does not volunteer the information.

After The Interview
Take Notes While the Interview is Fresh in Your Mind

Details blur over time, especially when you're going on a number of interviews. Jot down the topics that were discussed, the job information you got, the answers you gave, the date on which a decision should be made, and anything else that might be relevant. Make sure to add the full name and title of anyone who met with you so that you have it on record.

Write a Thank-You Note

The importance of a thank-you letter can't be overestimated. Career counselor Judy Kelso estimates that as few as 20 percent of interviewees extend this basic courtesy. Simply following through with a well-written thank-you letter can set you apart from most of the other candidates.

Peter, whose comments on his job search in the field of private school teaching were related earlier, is a convert to the discipline of writing interview thank-yous. "I wrote a thank-you letter to the department head immediately after my interview," he says. "He had been so helpful and our meeting went so well, I merely reiterated my interest and experience. Even though I felt I already had a good chance at the job, I also made a follow-up call. When he called me back, it was with a job offer."

As Peter's experience suggests, this simple act of courtesy has several potential pay-offs. It keeps you in the interviewer's mind, emphasizes your professionalism and follow-through, allows you to reemphasize relevant skills, lets you rectify omissions in what you said or correct answers that you don't feel you answered ideally, and gives you another chance to reiterate your interest in the job.

Your thank-you letter should be brief but not impersonal. It should demonstrate that you paid attention to what the interviewer said during your meeting by mentioning a topic or two that was covered. If possible, you should also reiterate the way one or more of your particular gifts, skills, or experience areas will help answer the organization's needs or solve particular problems. If you do address a problem answer or issue, make the mention brief and nondefensive.

For example, at an interview for a personal-training position, Deborah was asked how long she was prepared to stay in the job. She gave an appropriate answer; that is, that she was ready to make a long-term commitment. When she reviewed her notes after the interview, however, she recognized that it was a major concern of the manager and realized that she had not addressed it strongly enough. In her note, she reiterated that her interest was in a long-term position and wrote about how her entire employment history confirmed her willingness to stay in a job for a considerable period of time.

As always, type the letter on good-quality stationery (do not hand-write business correspondence) and make absolutely sure that the information on the company and interviewer are correct and correctly spelled. Send it within one or two days of the interview—certainly before the decision-making date, if one exists. See the following page for a sample thank-you letter.

Amy Longfield
30 Anytown Drive
Anytown, MA 06395

September 19, 1999 [**Amy's earlier outreach and networking efforts, in chapter 9, have paid off: She did get an actual job interview with this company!**]

Ms. Account Executive
Anytown Advertising
4500 Anytown Boulevard
Anytown, MA 06394

Dear Ms. Account Executive: [**The executive invited Amy to use her first name at the interview, but in this thank you Amy sticks to the more formal usage.**]
Thank you for giving me the opportunity to interview for the position of your assistant. I am pleased to be considered and very interested in joining your department at Anytown Advertising.

I enjoyed our discussion and was particularly interested in your comments about the problem of keeping your busy office running smoothly while you travel. [**As in her earlier letter to Ellen, Amy shows that she paid attention—in this case, to Ellen's particular employee needs.**] I believe that my combination of excellent office abilities, familiarity with basic advertising concepts and terminology, and strong interpersonal skills would allow me to support you well in that regard, freeing up your time and attention for more pressing matters. [**Having reiterated a need, Amy shows how she can fill it.**]

I appreciate your time, as always, and I look forward to hearing from you on October 1. If there is any further information I can provide to help Anytown Advertising make its decision, please do not hesitate to call me. [**Amy reiterates the decision date and again shows interest and the willingness to go the extra mile.**]

Very truly yours,

Amy Longfield

Call to Reiterate Your Interest Before the Decision Date

Express your enthusiasm again and offer to answer any additional questions the decision-makers have. This call is useful and shouldn't be skipped, even though it (more briefly) repeats the content of your thank-you note.

Remember: the Evaluation Process Goes Both Ways

As I've emphasized before, your main objective during the interview is to get a job offer. Once the organization has decided you're right for them, however, it's time to make a final decision about whether the organization is right for *you*. The interview itself can give you valuable insight in this regard.

Obviously, all employers and all organizations have flaws and limits. I'd never advise you to turn down an otherwise good job just because you didn't like, say, the brusque personality of your interviewer. Yet I do encourage you to pay attention if you feel genuine discomfort or concern. It may be a cue that the employment "marriage" between you and a particular organization simply won't be a good one or that the job doesn't truly suit the values you identified in the self-assessment chapter. You may want to review your values checklist at this point, just to bring the qualities you hold most important to the forefront of your mind again.

Even though no one wants to turn down a job offer unnecessarily, it is better to confront potential problems up front than to discover months down the road that you're painfully uncomfortable in a job. By that time you will have lost significant momentum in your exploration and networking activities. You may also end up with a problematic gap in your resume if you end up having to leave a job.

At this point—before you accept any job offer—your networking, outreach, and job search efforts have given you many different possible avenues for further exploration. As I have said earlier in this chapter, no single job represents the "be all and end all." Consider your answer to an offer from a viewpoint of abundance and strength, not from a standpoint of desperation or scarcity.

The experience of Joelle, whose training was in set design but who was seeking a lifeline career related to interior design, is a case in point. "After a comprehensive job search I was offered a position as the office manager for a small interior-design firm. In many respects, it was just what I was looking for. However, each of the four meetings I had with the company's owner gave me pause. He was obviously a workaholic, and so were the other staff. There always seemed to be a crisis—a deadline for a presentation to a client, a problem with an installation that required late-night work. Frequent mentions were made of the importance of staying late when necessary, pitching in during crises, and so on, while I never once heard anyone state any boundaries or limitations about the hours they would work. I'm certainly not against doing my share, so I just couldn't figure out how to broach the idea that as much as I wanted to be a team player, I also wanted to get out of work more or less on time most nights so that I could continue my work at our regional theater. In the end, I swallowed my doubts and took the job. What a mistake! I ended up having to stay hours late again and again—without overtime, of course. Often, there wasn't even a good reason for it; it was simply the owner's crisis-management technique. It was draining, and of course I had no time at all for the theater. I eventually found a better position, but if I'd listened to my instincts in the first place, I could have saved a lot of time and effort."

Peggy, an artist and teacher, remembers a related experience with more amusement—because she *did* stay focused on her own values. "I was interviewing for a teaching job at a private school. The salary was good and the campus was gorgeous. But the interview was like something out of *The Great Gatsby*, right down to the tea they served in porcelain cups and the incredibly WASP-y students, who all looked like something out of a Ralph Lauren ad. The thought of spending my days in such an uptight, privileged, Stepford-perfect place gave me chills. I didn't let any of that show at the interview; I wanted to get the offer. But ultimately, I turned it down. It took two more months and some jittery nights of worrying, but I found a job teaching at a public magnet school instead. The pay is actually a little lower, and the setting sure isn't as pretty. But I feel at home and happy there, and I just love going to work." Peggy's interview gave her the clues necessary to understand that a potential job did not truly match her values or style.

Fine-Tune an Arrangement That Works for You

If you get an offer and are interested in the job, you may be able to customize it a bit to accommodate your creative needs. However, several variables will affect this issue.

- If you have gotten the interview and offer through broadcast letters, you may have already introduced your desire for part time or flexible work. In that case, it is easy to renew discussion of the issue now. All you will need to work out is the details.

- If you are very comfortable and/or have lots of offers (an ideal and relatively rare situation to be in!) you can mention your preferences as to working schedule at the time you negotiate salary, start date and so on.

- If you really want the job but it is presented fairly rigidly in a conventional full-time manner, you'll probably need to work at the firm for some period to prove your value and dedication before asking for special considerations.

The Anatomy of an Interview

Over time, you'll find that interviews follow a fairly standard pattern. They usually begin with five to ten minutes of informal conversation, then move into a discussion of the job and its relevance to your personal qualifications. The second stage might take twenty minutes or more. After that, the interview draws to a close, either with a job offer or with a time frame for further action.

Below I've provided a "transcript" of one typical interview. In it, Jane Doe, a playwright, interviews with the department chair for a position teaching theater history at a local college. The flow of this interview, as well as the particular questions answered, track those that might be involved in many interview situations.

Review this transcript before you go on any interviews yourself. Your goal is not to memorize these or any other pat answers, but rather to grasp the basic skill of selling yourself in relation to a particular position. Watch the way Jane avoids common interview traps—moments in which she may feel defensive or criticized. Note, too, that she deals effectively with the gaps and flaws in her background, for example the fact that she has not previously taught at the college level. Using her commercial and the guidelines above, she presents herself positively and strongly at all times.

The Interview, Part 1: The Informal Opening

Q. How are you today?

A. Fine, thank you. I've been looking forward to our meeting. *Jane's answer uses a general opening question as a chance to express enthusiasm about the organization and job.*

Q. Did you have any trouble getting here?

A. None at all. There's a bus connection that's quite easy. *This is the correct answer even if it's not true! The interviewer does not need to know that you had difficulties. Be positive!*

Q. I have a long commute by car, but at least I get to catch up on the news on the radio. Did you hear about the latest Senatorial scandal?

A. No, I'm afraid I didn't. I did spend my bus ride reviewing the school's annual report, however. It's very impressive, particularly when it comes to the arts. *Danger! Even if the interviewer is just trying to put you at your ease by speaking of everyday topics, this is shaky ground. You don't want to go into anything controversial—recent crimes or trials, politics, religion, social inequity, animal rights, or anything else.*

Faced with this trap, Jane wisely diverted the interview into neutral ground. In fact, she made an opportunity to show that she had researched the organization well.

The Interview, Part 2: Candidate/Job Matching

Q. We're very proud of our accomplishments. Now, let me tell you a little about the job. As you know, it's an adjunct instructor position that involves teaching two theater-arts courses a semester. With that in mind, why don't you tell me about yourself?

A. As you can see from my resume, I have a strong hands-on background in theater and playwriting, a graduate degree in theater arts and history, and substantial teaching experience, both at the ABC Elementary School and through the Anytown Summer Stock Company. I'm confident that this combination will allow me to be a very effective teacher for your college. *The friendly invitation to "tell me about yourself" can lead to trouble—it's so open ended that it's an encouragement to ramble. Avoid a long, historical "story" about your background. Speak to the point and use your commercial. Jane does this successfully. She does not go back to her childhood, discuss her passion for the theater, or focus on her playwriting. She focuses on what she would be paid to do: teaching!*

Q. You haven't taught at the college level before. What makes you feel qualified to do so?

A. My work with high-school students and graduates at the Anytown Summer Stock program gave me the chance to work with individuals at nearly college age. I enjoyed it greatly, and if you decide to contact my references, I'm confident that the Summer Stock Director will testify to my successful interactions. And, of course, my M.F.A. in Theater qualified me to teach at a college level, as well as providing me with a rich background in all aspects of the theater. I believe that I would be able to make real contributions to your school, its theater department, and its students. *This question is really just a restatement of the question before, but phrased in a more confrontational manner. Here again, stick to your commercial, rephrasing and substantiating it as necessary but avoiding too much elaboration.*

Q. Why are you interested in working for our school in particular?

A. My goal is to work within the field of theater as part of a diverse, effective educational institution. Anonymous U's commitment to the arts is very impressive to me, as I mentioned. I particularly enjoyed reading about your student production series, and I noticed that you had a very varied and thoughtful selection of course offerings. *Jane's* *research pays off here, allowing her to answer this question quite specifically. Having at least one specific element to mention here is tremendously helpful.*

Q. What did you do in the grant-writing position you mention in your resume?
A. I helped a small theater find funding for its programs. During the time I was involved, we raised over $25,000 this way from both corporate and individual sponsors. The experience of working on the financial side of a theater gave me a practical perspective that I believe will be very helpful for the students I teach. *Note that although Jane answers quite specifically, she slants her answer to her potential abilities as a college teacher. She does not want to come across as someone who should be working in an actual theater setting rather than as a teacher of theater history.*

Q. It sounds very enjoyable. Why did you leave?
A. Having completed my degree, I was ready for a full-time commitment.

Q. I learned from John Doe, who recommended you highly, that you are very dedicated to your work as a playwright. Do you think that it would interfere with your teaching?
A. I take my professional responsibilities very seriously and would never let my personal pursuits interfere with them. *Like Jane, you should answer this kind of question briefly and positively. Do not over-defend or overexplain.*

Q. We have very few tenured professorships, while your credentials are very impressive. Would you feel overqualified for this position?
A. No. The job sounds exciting to me, and I look forward to the experience of working within a college setting. *The fact that Jane is asked this question means that she's doing very well. The interviewer's focus has shifted from whether or not she is qualified for the job, to whether she'll get bored and leave once she has it. Note that she cites only one area about which she'd like to learn. Listing too many things she'd like to develop might well make her look inexperienced.*

Q. I am concerned that you might get bored teaching the same two classes repeatedly.
A. I am very excited about working with young people to develop their skills and understanding in the theater. With a new group of students to work with each semester and the chance to refine and strengthen my lesson plans over time, I'm confident that boredom would never be a problem. *Here again, the interviewer is reiterating a previous point more confrontationally. In response, Jane strengthens and restates her earlier answer; she does not try to give a new answer or substantially more information.*

Q. One of the difficulties of college teaching is maintaining discipline with students who are already almost adults. Do you feel you can handle this?

A. I expect to like my students and to enjoy a cordial relationship with them, but I'm very clear that they are students and not friends. At the Anytown School, for example, I worked with students and volunteers of all ages in a comfortable and professional manner. *Jane assures the interviewer of her competence and backs her claim up with an example from her past experience.*

Q. How would you describe your strengths?
A. I consider my strongest points to be my ability to communicate well, my understanding of theater history, my liking for younger people, and of course my passion for the theater in general. *You'll notice that these strengths are directly relevant to the job at hand.*

Q. What about your weaknesses?
A. I am a perfectionist, and sometimes I'm told I'm almost *too* thorough. *Jane states only one weakness and chooses one that is not a major flaw with respect to this job. Another good answer might be, "I like to work relatively independently, without someone looking over my shoulder." If you do choose to mention a "real" flaw, make sure you state how you corrected it; e.g., "I used to miss deadlines from time to time. I took a time-management course, and now I am consistently ahead of schedule."*

Q. Adjunct instructorships are part time. May I ask what else you plan to do?
A. I have another part-time position in the theater field. *This nonspecific response is often the best answer to give. If you decide you'd like to speak about your art, however, make sure you keep it brief and matter-of-fact. "I intend to write. But I am used to balancing my art with my professional life, and my creative commitments will not interfere with this position" would also have been a perfectly acceptable answer, because it is succinct and impersonal. Do not become overly detailed or passionate while speaking of your art. This can detract from the impression of commitment to the lifeline field you're interviewing in, and is really irrelevant to the interviewer's needs and concerns. This guideline is not specific to your creative commitment, by the way. We all have our "outside passions"—our children, our hobbies, our religion, our favorite sports or pastimes—it is just not appropriate to discuss them at an interview.*

Q. Where do you see yourself in five years?
A. My goal is to be a long-term member of a theater department like yours, involved in both teaching and if possible in writing for student and college productions. *It's best to answer with this type of response even if your long-term goals involve a different type of job, a higher level position, or a role in a different organization.*

Q. Is there anything else you'd like to tell me?
A. I am fluent in Spanish and am also knowledgeable with computers. While completing my M.F.A. in theater, I organized an internship program that allowed undergraduate

theater majors to gain work experience in local theater companies. That experience might be useful to your college, as I noticed that the theater department has no internship opportunities. *This is the time to mention a few additional, broader-based skills or talents that have not come up in the interview. (Even if you don't get asked such a question, try to fit the same information in.) As long as you have remained focused on skills and goals relative to the job at hand until this point, mentioning other talents will help make you stand out among the candidates. In another interview, good answers might have been, "I am a fitness trainer as well as professional dancer," "I have an undergraduate minor in psychology and experience in peer counseling," or "I have considerable translating experience." Notice that although these skills may not relate directly to the job at hand, they are still in the professional realm. Jane's answer mentions two unrelated skills, and one further type of experience that makes her an even more attractive candidate for this job.*

Q. Do you have any questions for me?

A. I noticed that the department has no course offerings in Spanish and Latin American theater. As I just mentioned, I'm fluent in Spanish and knowledgeable about the history of plays in that language. If I were to teach at your school, I wonder if the theater department might be open to letting me offer a course on that subject eventually. *This question sounds open-ended, but it really isn't. If you don't have any questions, you may appear uninterested. Try to ask at least two or three questions of your interviewer. They should focus on the work itself, not on issues such as salary, benefits, promotion possibilities, perks, or facilities such as offices. You might ask questions such as, "Why is this job being made available?", "What are the opportunities for advancement?", "What are the backgrounds of the other staff members in the department?", or "What quality do you feel is most important for becoming successful in this firm?"*

Jane's answer is a good one because it once again highlights an exceptional skill, shows that she is highly committed to her field, and demonstrates ambition.

The Interview, Part 3: The Closing

The close of an interview can involve one of several scenarios. The interviewer may need to screen more candidates or meet with colleagues before making a decision; alternatively, he or she may be willing to make an offer, either with or without the possibility of negotiation. The following questions walk you through these three possible scenarios:

Job Offer without Negotiation

Q. We would be pleased to offer you the position. The salary is X. Is that acceptable?

A. Yes. I'm very pleased to have the opportunity to work with you. *In this case, the interviewer is clearly indicating that the salary is not negotiable. Jane is able to say "yes" immediately because she knows both her salary needs and the normal salary ranges for the position beforehand.*

Job Offer with Negotiation

Q. We'd like to offer you the job. What salary are you looking for?

A. I feel that between X and Y would be appropriate for the position we've discussed; toward the higher end of the scale if possible, based on my skills and experience.

Q. Hmm. We were only thinking about offering W.

A. I understand that university budgets are tight. However, I feel that I have significantly more experience guiding young people and in the theater generally than most adjunct instructors. I believe my qualifications would warrant a salary of at least X, with a review and potential raise after I've demonstrated my capabilities. *Jane does not get rattled or intimidated when the interviewer mentions a number that is out of the ballpark and below her minimum salary. She assumes that the interviewer has some room to move, just as she does. Also, again, she has done her research and knows appropriate figures to name. She also knows that she wants this job and will accept a salary that is closer to her low figure than she might have liked. Like Jane, you should always give a range so that there is room to negotiate. Note that the only justification for asking for a salary toward the high end of the range is either skills and/or experience. Simply needing more money is not enough—your personal needs are not the interviewer's concern, and besides, everyone needs more money!*

Q. We would be willing to go to X; we review all new teachers after the first semester.

No Job Offer Yet

Q. We will be screening candidates through Thursday and plan to make a final decision early next week. We'll contact you then.

A. I look forward to it. Please don't hesitate to let me know if you have any other questions or if there is anyone else you'd like me to meet. Thank you very much for your time. *As mentioned above, it is not unusual for a decision to be delayed like this, either because there are more candidates to see or because hiring authority is not in the interviewer's hands alone. It is crucial to respond to this graciously, without showing disappointment or trying to rush the process.*

Final Correspondence

Even when you have gotten a job offer and negotiated its terms successfully, you still need to complete one final post-interview step. Sending a confirmation letter to your new employer serves two functions. First, it starts you off on the right foot, with a continuing image of professionalism. Second, it puts major elements of the job down on paper for future reference. If there is any agreement, at least some of the terms have been stated in black and white. If your new employer sends a confirmation letter, you may choose to skip this step. However, many firms today do not do so. A letter like the one below simply confirms what you have agreed upon in your job offer discussion.

Jane Doe
32 Greene Street
New Brunswick, NJ 00000

June 13, 2001

Dear Dr. Department Chair:

I was so pleased to learn that I have been selected as an adjunct instructor with the Theater Department of Local College. I look forward to a long and productive relationship with the Department and the College's students. I understand that I will be teaching two sections of Theater History 101, with each section meeting three hours per week during the term, and that my salary will be $35.00 per class hour. I further understand that my appointment is contingent upon student enrollment.

I will contact Dr. S. Dullea for my schedule during the week of August 16th as you suggested. Please do not hesitate to let me know if there is anything else I need to do in the meantime.

Again, thank you for your confidence in me. I look forward to seeing you this fall.

Very truly yours,

Jane Doe

Chapter Eleven

Restructuring Your Current Position

Few people do business well who do nothing else.
—Earl of Chesterfield

Don't tell me how hard you work. Tell me how much you get done.
—James Ling

I never knew a man escape failures, in either mind or body, who worked seven days a week.
—Sir Robert Peel

I've assumed for the most part thus far that you will be looking for new work, either salaried or freelance, in order to balance your life more effectively. But what if you already have a job with appealing qualities (money, stability, a good work environment, recognition, or some combination) even though it makes it difficult to pursue your art? Both "starving-artist" and "closet-creative" types may find themselves trapped in this situation:

- Those who have overinvested in their art typically take on a job—teaching, administering an office, doing computer work or graphics—on a temporary and part-time basis in order to make short-term money. Thanks to their exceptional performance, likeability, and willingness to take on more hours, they quickly find themselves working full time or even more. If this is your situation, you may have at first liked the feeling of being needed, becoming part of a working team, and earning extra money. Over time, however, the lack of time to devote to creativity has probably grown more and more frustrating. This chapter will help you refocus on your creative priorities without losing the benefits the job provides.

- Those who have overinvested in career security often have a long-standing professional position but mistakenly perceive their situation in black-and-white terms, believing (mistakenly, as I'll explain) that theirs is an "all or nothing" situation in which they must sever all ties with their current employer in order to make more time for their art. If this is your situation, you may feel that even requesting reduced hours or more flexible arrangements will jeopardize your standing with your firm. This chapter explains which positions and fields are the best candidates for flexible arrangements and how to propose such an arrangement without damaging your security in your firm.

Whatever your circumstances, you may feel so trapped and frustrated by the *status quo* and its incongruence with your artistic needs that you contemplate quitting completely or even changing fields. You may feel at the end of your rope and desperate to get away from a deadening routine at almost any cost. While this kind of drastic measure is warranted in some circumstances, it's important not to overlook the redeeming qualities of your current work as you consider a potential change. Remember, *as a valued employee, you have increased your life options, not decreased them.* You can move to a new job or a new field. You can switch to a freelance version of what you currently do. But you may well *also* be able to use your good standing at work to negotiate a much more flexible arrangement which will better respond to your creative needs while leaving you with many of the same advantages you have worked hard to secure.

It's also helpful to remember that in today's downsizing environment, arranging reduced hours is often perceived as a benefit by *employers,* not just employees. A number of clients have told me that despite their trepidation, their boss was delighted to retain their core services for a reduced cost. Approach your restructuring as a potentially win/win package.

Flexible and part-time arrangements are almost infinitely variable depending on your needs and the nature of your job and business. Options may include:

- Working from home one or more days a week to save commuting time or to be more available for auditions

- Transitioning to a part-time schedule (fewer hours per day or fewer days per week) by giving up specified roles, tasks, or clients

- Working the same amount of hours as before but beginning and ending your work day earlier or later than normal

- "Saving up" lunch hours, ordinary holidays, or vacation time to free up time later (i.e., one afternoon a week, one month each summer)

- Working on selected special projects whose hourly demands may vary, involving full-time work some weeks but little or no responsibility at other times

- Job sharing with another employee

- Continuing to work for your current employer, but on a consulting basis that gives you more flexible and fewer hours, rather than as an employee

The strategies in this chapter focus primarily on restructuring your job to a part-time arrangement, as that is the option most commonly used by creative people. Many of the same guidelines and issues also apply to job-sharing, though that is a much less frequently used alternative. Naturally, if you feel your needs could be served well enough merely by shifting your working hours without reducing them or working at home, your proposal to your employer might be somewhat less formal than the one I recommend. As a general rule, the greater the change from your existing job structure, the more comprehensive your proposal must be.

Are You and Your Position Candidates for Renegotiation?

Attractive as renegotiating your current job may seem, not all positions or personalities are right for this kind of transition. If you and your job are appropriate candidates for a renegotiated part-time or flexible position, most or all of the following criteria will apply.

- **You have a solid base as a valued employee with a sufficiently long history of responsibility and strong performance.** This is the platform you will require in order to "dive" into a new and more flexible arrangement. Your employer needs to feel that you have put the best interests of the organization first and that you will be trustworthy and reliable in any new arrangement you make. Without that level of trust and without a reasonable length of history with your company, your proposal is unlikely to succeed.

If you are just beginning to think about cutting back and feel that you have six months to spare before you make any definitive changes, you are in the perfect position to build this kind of foundation quite consciously. Make yourself as indispensable as possible. Focus on becoming the most valuable resource you can, not just to your boss but to colleagues and subordinates. Develop a history of helping out and making accommodations for them so that they, in turn, will help gladly with your new job structure. Remain involved in your career and field by staying active in professional organizations, attending conferences, and so on. Finally, find out who the decision-makers are in regard to any change in your position. Your boss will certainly be an important part of the picture, but he or she may not have sole or final authority. What is the role of those higher in the management chain and of the Human Resources department, if any? With the luxury of time, you can make them aware of your dedication, experience, and accomplishments. Don't discuss your hopes for a more flexible arrangement with them at this stage, however; your first meeting on that subject should be with your immediate supervisor, as I'll discuss later.

- **You work in the technology industry or another field that lends itself to part-time or flexible work.** Technology companies are often owned or managed by younger people, who tend to be open to unconventional schedules and arrangements; the work also lends itself well to working from home or at varied hours. Law, accounting, sales, science, social service, and government positions are also good candidates for restructuring, as are "24/7" businesses such as health-care facilities, convention centers, brokerage firms, resorts, and major law firms that work around the clock. The Association of Part-Time Professionals, for example, lists many job titles, from librarian to engineer, confirming the frequency with which these jobs are done part-time. Finally, arts and cultural organizations are often fairly open to unconventional working schedules, as they understand the creative mentality. In contrast, if you work in the field of advertising, public relations, publishing, or broadcasting—all media-related "glamour industries" that are in high demand and often work on intense deadlines—job flexibility may be much harder to secure.

- **You work for a small or suburban organization.** While it's by no means impossible to restructure a job within a larger urban firm, your chances are increased if you work in the suburbs or for a small company. Suburban companies must often work harder than big-city corporations to secure and retain talented employees. Small companies that cannot offer national prestige and wide promotion opportunities also tend to be more accommodating to valuable staffers.

- **Your company already has either a part-time, flex-time, or job-sharing policy (written or unwritten) or a history of offering such arrangements.** Carmen, a certified social worker, wanted to reduce her hours in order to return to an acting career. She met with her supervisor and had prepared a written request for a part-time schedule. Because her agency already had a policy for part-time workers, her request was easily approved. "The policy was actually put in place for those facing pregnancy and child-care issues, but it didn't matter. It was easy—all I had to do was ask."

- **Your responsibilities can be delegated, reassigned, and/or limited appropriately, leaving you an amount and type of work that will fit comfortably into your new reduced schedule.** Some jobs can be restructured from full to part time very neatly. Others can't. Typically, jobs that will work well in this regard involve self-initiated and directed work as well as tasks, clients, projects, or accounts that are defined relatively firmly and can therefore be re-assigned effectively. Dancer Neal, for example, was a part-time fitness instructor at his local Y. Over the years, his expertise and popularity ending up getting him promoted to be the director of that Y's overall fitness program. Unfortunately, this impinged on Neal's ability to dance. Having groomed a part-time associate during those same years, Neal was able to trade hours and position with his protégé, a simple solution that benefited everyone involved.

  Conversely, jobs that involve reaction to external factors rather than self-direction, are devoid of ample peer and subordinate support, or involve extremely various and interconnected tasks may not work well on a part-time or flexible basis.

- **You will be able to "let go" of your old level of responsibility as you let go of some of your tasks, roles, or hours.** "I was given a great flex-time version of my former full-time job, and *I* was the one who screwed it up," laments Penelope, an art weaver and former corporate marketer. "I admit it. I'm a type-A personality and I felt deeply committed to the projects I worked on. I just couldn't let go! I'd feel compelled to check my voicemail on my off days or attend meetings that weren't scheduled on days I was at work. Everybody at the company was so supportive. They were always telling me 'go,' 'relax,' 'do your thing,' but I'd been doing my job all-out for too long, and I wasn't able to adjust. Actually, it took my eleven-year-old son—I'm a single mom—to make me see the light. 'But you work just as much as before, even though we don't have money for movies any more,' he said to me one afternoon, and it was true."

As Penelope's story demonstrates, it's not always easy for a responsible, scrupulous professional to make a part-time transition. It requires the ability to compartmentalize—to "turn off" thoughts of the job and its responsibilities during all nonworking time—and also the willingness to achieve less than former levels of excellence. In essence, you must renegotiate not just your external working arrangement but also your internal expectations. If you suspect that you might be unable to do this, it may be wiser to find a new lifeline job—one that you begin fresh, knowing that your goal is to leave time for your creative work.

- **Your current work fits your basic needs, interests, and values reasonably well.** No matter how financially practical it may seem, renegotiating your current job will probably *not* serve you well unless you are at least moderately content with where you work and what you do. The stress of feeling truly out of place—doing work you strongly dislike or find antithetical to your values or working in an environment which is deeply uncongenial—is a profound drain on energy and confidence. Even if you are working a more minimal schedule, such a job may undercut your sense of momentum and leave you feeling conflicted or ambivalent. This can sabotage the entire goal of your transition: to be able to approach your art with new energy, integrity, and freedom. For this reason, I advise only those who are happy or content with their current work to attempt to renegotiate their job.

    Avoid emotions and peer pressure as you contemplate change. Don't allow your current frustration to overshadow your awareness of the positives of your current job. Try visualizing what it would be like if the frustration of being overcommitted to work and unavailable for creativity were to disappear. Would the other elements of the position then feel satisfying? If the answer is "no" even after careful reflection, don't allow others to make you feel irresponsible for deciding to make a clean and appropriate break. This is, after all, your life, and it is your right and responsibility to live it with integrity and commitment to the things you care about. Moreover, while it may be the most obvious one, renegotiating your current job is *not* the only practical means to making more time for your art without "breaking the bank." You can research and train for another career, check out opportunities for consulting arrangements for other firms in the field, and even commit to working full time for a fixed period—say, one more year—while you save every penny and plan an effective transition.

Researching Your Restructuring

The first step in restructuring your job, as in all career transitions, is research. You need to understand both your company's needs and position on unconventional working arrangements and your own needs in order to make an effective transition. Your research will enable you to create a strong restructuring proposal and to better handle subsequent negotiations effectively.

Restructuring Research Focus #1: Your Needs

Reduced hours typically mean a corresponding reduction in either income and/or benefits, if not both. (The most common exception is a shift to a consulting agreement in which your hourly rate increases while your hours worked drop, leaving you with a similar income level. Though by no means unheard of, such arrangements are usually available only for highly experienced professionals with specialized expertise in fields of high demand.)

What compensation do you need? What income or benefits could you give up without jeopardizing your own or your family's security? You may know immediately whether you can or cannot afford a cut in pay. More often, however, you won't be entirely sure how much you could afford to sacrifice. It's crucial to enter into the restructuring process with clarity on this issue. Unless you specifically negotiate a trial period, it may be difficult to go back to your old full-time routine once you've transitioned to flex- or part-time. You therefore want to make sure that you don't discover, six months down the road, that you're not making ends meet under the new terms of your job. Avoid the temptation to be so eager to get out of your working bind that you give up too much.

Use the worksheet on the following page to give you a more concrete idea of what kind of change you can realistically make. It covers the common categories of income, benefits, and expenses and will allow you to see how changes in one area affect the others.

You'll find that if you restructure your job, certain categories of expenses may decrease (commuting costs, clothing, dry cleaning), while others may increase (insurance-coverage costs). Sometimes, the changes may surprise you. "I wasn't extravagant, exactly—no more so than my peers—but I definitely treated myself: fine dinners out, upscale clothing, a nice car," says Marissa, a sculptor. "I called those things my consolation prizes, my rewards for working in a profession—law—that I really didn't like. When I started thinking about transitioning to a consulting arrangement with my firm, I realized that I had quite a bit of financial latitude if I went back to getting more of my satisfaction from my sculpture rather than consumerism! If I hadn't taken a hard look at my budget, I would have assumed I needed quite a bit more in salary than I actually do."

Make sure to factor such issues as well as more tangible ones into your personal equation.

Restructuring Research Focus #2: Your Organization

Assuming that you've discovered that you can indeed afford to reduce your income somewhat, it's time to look at your company. Use this checklist to make sure you find the right answers before beginning to work on a restructuring proposal. Some of this information may be available in your employee handbook or by asking the Human Resources department of your firm; other facts must be gained by exploration or dialogue within or outside of the company.

1. **Who if anyone at your company works a special, flexible, or part-time arrangement?** Get as much information as you can about why, how, and when.

2. **Who at similar or competitive firms works a special, flexible, or part-time arrangement?** Even if your own organization has few such staffers, pointing out that competitors do can be very powerful.

3. **Does your company have a written policy on this issue?** A written policy may or may not always define your restructuring entirely, as its provisions may be originally designed for lower-level staff or special situations such as maternity leave. However, you should know exactly what it specifies.

Personal Financial Worksheet for Job Restructuring

INCOME	FULL-TIME	PART-TIME
Gross Pay	$	$
Company's Pretax Contributions (401ks, etc)	$	$
Extras (bonus, overtime, freelance income, etc.)	$	$
TOTAL	$	$

BENEFITS	FULL-TIME	PART-TIME
Health, Dental, Life, Disability Insurance	$	$
Pension Contributions	$	$
Social-Security Contributions	$	$
Profit-Sharing Plan	$	$
TOTAL	$	$

EXPENSES	FULL-TIME	PART-TIME
Federal, State and Local Taxes	$	$
Transportation (nonauto)	$	$
Insurance	$	$
Rent/Mortgage	$	$
Charitable Donations	$	$
Medical and Dental bills	$	$
Household (furniture, supplies)	$	$
Car (insurance, gas, car loan)	$	$
Childcare	$	$
Debt (student loans, credit-card bills)	$	$
Food	$	$
Restaurants	$	$
Personal (clothing, cleaning, hair, cosmetics)	$	$
Professional Dues and Fees	$	$
Vacations/Leisure Pursuits	$	$
TOTAL	$	$

- **How long has it been in effect?** The longer its history, the more likely it is that your request will be accepted.

- **Are there any fixed time limits for flexible or part-time work?**

- **Will you need to work a minimum or maximum number of hours?**

- **How is compensation decided according to this policy?** Is it prorated, translated into an hourly rate, subject to any maximums, etc.?

4. **Are benefits available to part-time workers in your firm?**

5. **Can you retain your title?** This is often a somewhat flexible issue. Obviously, it is an advantage to keep your current title if you can.

6. **Are you eligible for promotions, bonuses, and/or raises as a part-time, flex-time, or job-sharing employee?**

Proposing Your Restructured Position

With all of this information in hand, it's time to begin work on a proposal for more flexible, or part-time, work.

Though you should make your request face to face with your boss, I strongly advise that you create a concise written document that outlines the terms you propose for your "new" position. Putting it in writing ensures that you have thought through all of the ramifications of the change, proves to your boss that you are thinking in a businesslike and responsible way, avoids future conflicts or unclear expectations, and helps you powerfully articulate the benefits to your employer.

This last element—the benefits *your employer* will gain by the change, or at least the assurance that the organization will lose nothing by it—is absolutely critical. This may sound self-evident, but I've found that it is frequently overlooked by creative individuals immersed in the excitement of making a transition to a life more consistent with their deep core passions and values. As with any other life "conversion," feelings of emotion and urgency can run high at these times, as when water that has been dammed up too long finally bursts free.

Personally, I have tremendous sympathy—and, in fact, admiration—for such feelings. You may feel that you have "given blood" to your employer for years; you may feel that finally getting a bit of time to do what matters to you is little enough to ask; you may feel that you can barely take your stultifying job as an accountant, lawyer, or manager one moment longer. And you may be right! Nevertheless, it's a tough and competitive job market out there. No matter how much your organization values you or how much you have given over the years, you are being paid (now and in the future) to serve the organization's needs.

Given this reality, do not take your employer's good will for granted. Treat this transition as though you were interviewing for a very attractive new job or competing for a highly lucrative account: Be just that thorough in your preparation, just that positive, and just that focused on your employer's needs. By making absolutely sure that you structure your transition as a win/win situation that benefits all parties involved, you will radically increase your chances not only to obtain, but to thrive in, a new and more flexible work arrangement. With that in mind, the following are the twelve steps to restructuring your job successfully:

1. **Using the financial worksheet provided, determine how many hours you want or need to work.**

2. **Using a weekly calendar, map out your typical week at work.** Mapping a typical work week will help you visualize what your tasks are and how they flow. Once you have a good weekly chart, you can build on it to add nonweekly items such as quarterly meetings, periodic deadlines, monthly budgets, and so on. You're finished with this when you have a comprehensive picture of your work and how it flows in your working time. If you have a personal account or client base, you'll also want to make sure your listing of it is complete and up to date.

   Susanna, a human resources executive who wanted more time to work on her photography, found doing this job grid very helpful. She immediately discovered that she could delegate weekly new-hire orientations, individual orientations, and paperwork to her assistant, who welcomed additional job growth. Over the course of six months, Susanna trained and promoted her assistant to a more senior position to make this delegation possible. In addition, she began to videotape her frequently repeated training and orientation presentations so that they could be used even in her absence. At that point, Susanna requested and was granted a reduced schedule.

3. **Decide which tasks, roles, or aspects of your job could be delegated, shifted, or relinquished and which you can continue to do within your altered or reduced hours.** The key here is specificity. You must be prepared to tell your superior exactly how you will

accomplish everything you say you can handle in the time you allot yourself and where the work you will no longer handle will go.

Although it's not your responsibility to make a final decision on the latter issue, a proposal that simply dumps part of your workload back on your boss's shoulders is unlikely to succeed. Instead, you should be able to suggest concrete ways part of your work can be accommodated by your support staff or other departments. Is there a junior manager itching for more visibility? A talented assistant who'd love to move up the ladder? A working parent who'd welcome job sharing? A consultant who could handle a specific project or task more cheaply on a freelance basis? A fellow lawyer, accountant, or executive with connections to some of your clients or a similar specialty to yours? A whole department—training, marketing, etc.— whose domain some of your tasks overlap? Technological tools (like Susanna's videotapes) that can pick up some of the slack? You may be surprised to find out how many creative solutions to your needs already exist within your working structure.

4. **Based on this information, decide when your working time should ideally occur.** Some jobs are easier to restructure on the basis of reduced daily hours; others work better if you work an ordinary day but take off one or two days a week. Your own proposed schedule will be based both on your particular creative needs (i.e., needing late afternoons off for rehearsals, wanting Fridays off to write) as well as the nature of your job.

5. **Determine what compensation and benefits package you will propose.** Based on your worksheets and any information you can glean about comparable situations, you should define benefits and compensation very clearly. Issues to be addressed include:

- **Salary.** Will yours be prorated, or will you work on an hourly basis?

- **Bonus.** Are bonuses, if any, based on performance? New revenue? Standard company bonuses are generally prorated if you begin to work part time.

- **Commissions.** Commission rates should not be affected by your change, though your overall commission earnings may drop if you are working fewer hours.

- **Increases and raises.** You will want to be eligible for these just as before.

• **Benefits.** In the old days, health and pension benefits were widely available from employers. Today, even full-time workers may receive limited benefits, and part-time staffers may receive no benefits at all. If you're lucky, your company will prorate benefits based on your new reduced work schedule. If not, your benefits cost may have to be built into your own budget. Jessie's company, for example, offered health insurance only to those who worked over twenty-eight hours each week. Jessie decided that her need to invest time in her fashion design was more important. She went on her husband's benefit plan; another creative person faced with a similar choice might explore purchasing her own coverage. On the other hand, Jessie's company did provide pension benefits to those working at least twenty-one hours a week, the work level she had chosen. Thus, she was able to continue receiving her 401(k) contributions as before.

6. **Draft your proposal.** You are looking for a succinct, powerful, positive document that preempts your employer's objections and demonstrates clearly that your responsibilities can be handled effectively despite the change you propose. It should not be overly legalistic or detailed at this stage; there is time to resolve minor issues (sick days, for example, or how and when the announcement of the change will be made) later, after an initial agreement has been reached. However, your proposal should cover any basic points necessary to clarify the new relationship and its impact on both you and your employer.

Though it may vary depending on your job level, field, etc., your proposal, which should be no more than two to three pages in length, might include the following:

• An affirmation of your openness to alternative suggestions on the points in the proposal. (Naturally, when the time comes, you can choose to stand your ground on important issues. However, indicating openness will prevent an employer from rejecting you simply because he or she disagrees with small, potentially resolvable points.)

• An emphasis on the advantages the new arrangement would give to the employer. Reiterate your existing value to the firm (experience, client base, expertise, involvement in special projects) as well as any benefits resulting from the restructuring (cost savings, outsourcing).

- A detailed outline of your responsibilities and how they will be handled (through outsourcing, reorganization, staffing shifts, redeployment of technology) under your new arrangement.

- If necessary, a proposal regarding new logistics such as office or phone usage. (This may be especially important in organizations where physical space is tight or offices are in high demand; your willingness to give up or share a big office, for example, can be offered as a benefit.)

- A formal schedule or, if more appropriate, a detailed explanation of how and when you would work, including a brief statement as to how emergencies or contingencies might be handled.

- A commitment to continue to be available for stated special projects. This is crucial. It might include information on how you can be reached in emergencies, your willingness to be called at home, and/or your willingness to work more hours when special needs arise. For example, Tyrell, a lawyer, decided to take himself off the "partner track" in order to reduce his eighty-hour work weeks. In his proposal, he made clear that he would be available by phone and e-mail in emergencies, present at all important meetings, and available to work extra hours when necessary.

- A plan for any training or retraining necessary to shift required tasks or roles to others.

- A request regarding new salary level, bonus, retention of benefits, or other relevant arrangements.

7. **Find one or more devil's advocates.** Look for bright, fairly assertive peers (from *outside* your organization) who will examine your proposal aggressively from both your own and your employer's perspectives. Are there potential employer objections unanswered? Issues or items you need to cover or rephrase for your own benefit? The purpose of this step is to provide a level of objectivity you may not be able to offer, no matter how thoughtful your proposal preparation has been. After all, you are very familiar with your job and emotionally invested in the outcome of the transition. Clarity is not always possible under those circumstances. Yet it is essential, since it may not be possible to change key terms of a renegotiation after a formal proposal has been made.

    In the opinion of Gianni, a successful salesperson for a large investment firm, this kind of brainstorming can save many headaches—and lots of money—later. "I wrote what I thought was a very good proposal," he explains. "I was especially careful to create a package that would be very attractive to my superiors, because I knew they wouldn't be crazy about having one of their longtime salespeople go to film school! I was too careful, in the opinion of my wife and two close friends, who loudly agreed that I was 'giving away the store.' They pointed out, for example, that suggesting that I shift to half salary and bonus just because I was planning on working half time was absurd. If I managed my assistant well and focused on key accounts, I would likely continue to produce at 60 to 70 percent of my former sales level—as has, in fact, been the case."

Gianni—whose first film is now in the editing stage—shakes his head and laughs. "Looking back, I can see how my eagerness—well, my desperation—to get on with finally making a film led me to abandon about twenty years negotiating savvy when I wrote that proposal. I was literally willing to do anything to make it work. I'm grateful that I at least had the sense to get some feedback before I committed myself."

8. **Develop a contingency plan.** Your employer may make a counter-proposal in response to your ideas. For this reason, you must develop a contingency plan covering the minimum you will accept and what you will do if you cannot get it *before* you present your proposal. Charlene Canape, the author of *The Part Time Solution*, offers the following suggestions, which I have adapted to the special needs of the creative person:

- Suggest a three- to six-month trial period that uses the terms of your proposal. If the arrangement does not meet your employer's needs during that time, you will return to full-time work. (During this period, you can research other positions, start a job search, and even make progress on your art.)

- If appropriate, consider other positions within the company that are offered on a part-time or flexible schedule.

- If appropriate, consider resigning as an employee and working on a project or consulting basis. Michelle, for example, left her job as writer and staff editor for a national magazine's health-and-beauty department and became chief editor of the magazine's annual health-and-beauty special edition. She now has more time for her own creative writing career. Maxene, an accountant, resigned her position but continues to help her firm on their annual audit and budget review.

• Resign completely. Once having submitted a proposal, you should be prepared to resign if your request is denied. You may wish to leave if your employer is adamantly opposed to your proposal and offers no flexibility; you have already determined that you are willing and able to leave; or you would be equally happy starting your own business.

9. **Present your proposal to your employer.** If you meet regularly, use that meeting. If not, ask to meet to discuss "future goals" and make sure it's scheduled for a time when your boss can focus for ten or fifteen minutes. (If the meeting is timed shortly after you have gained a new client, finished a terrific project, or completed a tough assignment, so much the better!) Present your need for change clearly but briefly—you don't have to explain or justify it at length. Be positive and upbeat; anticipate agreement, not refusal. Similarly, don't over-dramatize. The organization will survive without your full-time services, and people's situations change all the time. Finally, recognize that this conversation may come as a complete surprise to your boss. Don't demand an instant response; offer to leave the proposal and speak further about it at a specified later time.

Be prepared, however, to answer your superior's questions right at this first meeting, despite the fact that you will almost certainly not get approval at this point. Thus, you must go into the meeting with a clear idea of the minimum you will accept on each point you propose. In addition, you should be able to counter any arguments that are offered effectively. Some good responses are given below. They build on those in the book *The Part Time Professional* by Diane Rothberg, Ph.D., and Barbara Cook, in which the authors provide a useful guide for many elements of part-time professional work.

Q. Why do you want to do this?
A. In addition to my strong commitment to XYZ Company, I have a personal commitment as an artist, [and/or] I'm confident that I will perform even better with the balance this new schedule will offer in my life.

Q. How can you be serious about your profession and want to work part time?
A. I believe my history at XYZ demonstrates my dedication to my job and the firm, and that I will be able to perform even better with the life balance this new schedule will afford.

Q. Your coworkers will resent you.

A. I'm confident that there will be little resentment once they know of my reduced benefits, salary, and vacation time.

Q. If I let you work part time, everyone will want to do it.

A. My research on this subject has found that this is not the case. Many more people say they want to work part time than are actually willing to accept a cut in pay!

Q. Part-time work is only suitable for those in lower positions than yours.

A. Within our firm, Jane Doe has worked a very successful part-time schedule for over a year [and/or] ABC Company has used part-time arrangements for senior staff quite effectively with executives including John Smith.

Q. What happens when you are not here and someone needs you?

A. As you know, I've performed very effectively despite the fact that I am not always at my desk, travel one week a month, and take appropriate vacations. You'll see that my proposal includes what I believe will be an effective system for messages as well as calls to my home when necessary. In addition, I'll naturally be available for special meetings and projects as they arise.

Q. I can't visualize how this will work. I don't want to commit myself.

A. I'd like to propose a six-month trial period to see how the new arrangement will work. I believe you'll see that it will be effective over that time frame.

10. **Follow up.** Do not mention your proposal within the firm after your first meeting; continue working at your current hour and performance level. Follow up with your boss if you do not have an answer or response within two weeks. You want him or her to know that you are serious about the proposal and that the new arrangements are important to you.

11. **If you do not like a counter-offer, use your contingency plan.**

12. **Plan for a gradual, orderly, and effective transition.** Think of your old working status and your new situation as being two banks of a river. The transition period is the bridge between the two, and it must be handled thoughtfully to ensure a safe passage! Haste or sloppiness in this task can lead to resentful colleagues and support staff, nervous clients, and/or irritating logistical snafus—any or all of which can sabotage your ability to work successfully under the new terms. To avoid such problems, treat your transition with care. Depending on the complexity of your job, your length of tenure with

the organization, and other factors, a good transition may take several months to accomplish.

Work with your boss on how and when to notify colleagues and clients. Be sensitive to their need not to publicize your new schedule too widely in order to prevent many others from jumping on the bandwagon. Again and as always, be positive! This is not the time to demonstrate a "thank God I'm out of here!" attitude, even if it's true. Evince confidence in your new plans and gratitude toward the organization for making a change possible. After all, it is now supporting your need for a balanced life.

Building a Better Balance through Lifeline Self-Employment

Chapter Twelve

Envisioning and Establishing Your Own Lifeline Business

Genius is the ability to put into effect what is in your mind.
> —F. Scott Fitzgerald

Being good in business is the most fascinating kind of art....Making money is art and working is art and business is the best art.
> —Andy Warhol

The banks couldn't afford me. That's why I had to be in business for myself.
> —Samuel Goldwyn

The way I see it, if you want the rainbow, you gotta put up with the rain.
> —Dolly Parton

Thanks to the exploration you've done in response to earlier chapters, you now have a great idea for a business or an area of expertise in which you are ready to serve as a consultant. This is an extremely exciting venture, as well as the answer to your quest for meaningful lifeline work. But as you are almost certainly aware, it takes more than just creativity to turn your dream into reality. You'll need to be committed to your idea, have a distinct vision of what you'll do, and maintain the positive attitude that will actually make it happen. In addition, having a successful business will take planning, follow-through, sales skills, attention to detail, and careful record keeping. If being a freelancer still seems interesting in the face of these requirements, read on!

Alternatively, if the fact that running your own business requires you to market yourself constantly, take responsibility for scrupulous tax management and record keeping, *and* be chief cook and bottle washer at the same time seems daunting, you may want to reconsider traditional employment. If so, browse through chapter 4 again to clarify your choice. Before you set this chapter aside, however, keep in mind that *small business skills are also essential for your "business" as a performing or creative artist.* Even if you decide that employment rather than self-employment is the better choice for a lifeline career, you'll still be self-employed in the arts. Therefore, reviewing this chapter at your convenience may still be useful to you.

Your Own Business: Building on the Foundation of Reality

Entrepreneurs are widely admired in today's society. The individual who takes a risk, thinks outside the box, and makes a million with a novel product or idea is lavished with attention and praise. While such innovation and courage are certainly to be admired, the effect is often to idealize or glamorize self-employment in a way that does not reflect the reality most small businesspeople face. It is helpful to be aware of the discrepancy between image and reality *before* you plan and establish your new freelance business.

"The glamour and excitement that people imagine when they think of entrepreneurs couldn't be further from the truth," agrees Melanie, a musician who is also a self-employed deejay for dances, weddings, and parties. "It reflects the few ventures that are lavishly funded by venture capital or backers, not the vast majority who, like me, have small one-person operations with minimal capital at best. I love my business and wouldn't think of doing anything else, but the day-to-day reality of it isn't glamorous at all. I move all my own equipment, make my own bookings, keep my own records, send out my own invoices, handle my own gigs, and drop exhausted into bed at the end of the day!"

Melanie's experience does indeed represent the type of business most creative people have. It can be a fun and challenging life, but it also entails solving a multitude of problems; performing a wide range of roles well; working without the comfort of peer support or a supervisor's approval; marketing yourself constantly; and having little or no security or cushion. The chart below summarizes the basic pros and cons of self-employment.

Advantages	Disadvantages
Chance to be in control of your destiny	Isolation—no close peer support
Opportunity to be creative and innovative	Multiple roles, many "hats"
Scheduling flexibility	Long and unpredictable hours
Great potential financial gains	Fluctuating income and financial risk
Opportunity for social impact	Responsibility for business details

My goal in this rather brutal picture of the self-employed existence is not to discourage you. In truth, many creative people do thrive as freelancers. My hope in reminding you of the difficulties of self-employment is to help you develop realistic, achievable expectations and a sound business plan for your new venture. The more realistic you are at the start, the better you can overcome contingencies and challenges and the more likely you are to succeed.

Researching Your New Business

Just as with salaried employment, research is the key to initiating and operating a successful lifeline business. Many of the resources discussed in chapter 6 will help you research your new business. Supplementing that discussion, the following sources are particularly helpful for freelancers and small businesspeople.

- **Professional associations.** These organizations can be of great help, both through their regular meetings and through their Web sites or printed material.

- **Friends in similar businesses.** Direct competitors may be reluctant to share information, but those in similar but not identical businesses can be very informative.

- **Printed materials.** As self-employment becomes more and more popular in our culture, printed material on the subject—appearing in both general-interest and specialized publications—becomes more and more widely available. Relevant magazines include *Entrepreneur, Home Business Journal, Black Enterprise, Sales and Marketing Management, Contract Professional* (for computer consultants and contract workers), and more. Books on entrepreneurship and small business management are also extremely popular and widely available.

- **Web sites.** These encompass a truly immense wealth of information and services to small businesses and also provide an excellent way to study the competition.

- **Business classes and seminars.** College and adult education centers all over the country offer classes in business administration—marketing and advertising, finance, record-keeping, strategic planning, computers and information management, and other relevant subjects. Courses are often very affordable, especially if you are not taking them for credit.

- **The Small Business Administration.** Accessible on the Internet at *www.sba.gov,* this government agency is specifically designed to help people with smaller ventures. It offers a wide variety of information and assistance. Other government and nonprofit agencies can also assist you in various business areas, including strategy, business plans, and financing. A complete listing of these agencies can be found in the Resources section.

- **Local bankers, lawyers, and accountants.** Many of these professionals will offer an initial consultation and some advice for free (usually with the hope that you will retain their services at normal fees later on). It's useful to have contacts in each of these areas, since you may well need to use such services once your business is underway.

Asking the Right Questions

In chapter 6, I described the process of researching a new career. While some of the information the chapter contains is oriented to those seeking salaried employment, its guidance on networking is just as applicable to those forming a freelance or small business. In entrepreneurship as in employment, people are the best research tool of all. When you speak with those who own or work in small businesses—the B contacts described in chapter 6—you can get the benefit of real-life experience, which is invaluable.

It goes without saying that the most useful information will come from those in the same field you're intending to enter. In fact, your competitors can be great teachers. Knowing your competition and what they offer helps you shape and improve your services, price your product, and understand what your market wants. This information is invaluable at the start of your business and beyond.

Ryan was trained as a film and television actor and then learned Avid editing. After a few years of working for production companies, he decided to strike out on his own. His artistic dream was to write and direct his own documentary; to support himself he chose to form a business that creates interesting and artistic wedding and bar mitzvah videos. Ryan investigated this business possibility by pricing his own wedding video. "I was astounded at how much people charged for something I was sure I could do better," he says. "After interviewing three companies, I knew how long they spent on each project, how they got on the referral lists of caterers, hotels, and party planners, and a whole host of other information."

"Who has more relevant ideas about how to name, plan, or sell a product than the competition?" Juan, a party planner, agrees laughingly. "Several times a year, I update my knowledge of who's out there offering services similar to mine. I look at Web sites, send for brochures, ask friends to check out local competitors, and so on. I make sure that my prices and services are competitive that way, but I also get valuable ideas that I can adapt to my own business."

In order to get information from a competitor (assuming you don't actually need the services of one, as Ryan did) you can pose as a potential client, ask someone you know to do so for you, send for any information they distribute, or, if you have a mutual contact and the businesses are not too directly competitive, simply ask if they'd spend some time with you. You can also use the Internet. Carefully studying competitors' Web sites is an invaluable way to access competitor information anonymously.

Beyond the competition, anyone who has started or run a small business in a field or service area even somewhat similar to yours will also be very useful. Many of the basics of marketing, financing, freelance scheduling, pricing, and paperwork management hold true for small businesses in many fields. Expand your network of B contacts aggressively to get as much input as possible. Almost all of the clients I introduce in this chapter agree that talking to other freelancers, consultants, and small-business owners was invaluable in helping them avoid common mistakes and handle typical problems.

As you speak with these contacts, probe to get the fullest possible sense of both their business and their experience. The following are some questions that are helpful to ask.

- How did you decide to start your own business? What factors made you decide on your field and services?

- How does your business fit into your overall career plan? Is it your final goal, or a stepping-stone to other or larger ventures?

- What prepared you for this business? What training or preparation is necessary in general?

- How has your business progressed and changed?

- How long did it take before you felt that the business was fully "up and running"?

- What about your business gives you the most satisfaction? Frustration?

- How could I become most competitive if I started a business in this or a related field?

- What are the characteristics of successful business owners in this field?

- What is the market like for this type of business venture?

- What is your fee structure and how did you determine it?

- How do you advertise and market yourself?

- How do you plan and manage your time?

- How do you gain assistance if you're not able to hire full-time staff?

- Do you use an accountant? A lawyer?

- Do you have plans for expansion? What are the opportunities for growth?

- What would you change if you could restart your business again today?

- What advice would you give someone just starting out?

The Benefits of (Simple) Business Planning

The basis for a new business of any size is, naturally enough, the business plan. A typical business plan will be anywhere from 15 to over 100 pages in length depending on the scope of the business, the amount of capital involved, and a host of other factors. It will include subsections on topics such as customer and market analysis, sales forecasts, organizational and hiring plans, and more.

There are a variety of books and computer programs that can help you write such a plan. But let me hasten to say that unless you are looking for investor backing or bank financing, you *do not need* a formal business plan of this type. A simple overview and consideration of some basic financial questions are all you need to get started.

Although, strictly speaking, it is not necessary, I do encourage you to put your overview and financial ideas down on paper. The benefits of writing down the basic details of your business plans, even in a relatively brief or informal way, can't be overstated. They are so important that I'm going to take a moment to review them here, before going on to explain what should actually be included in the overview and cost analysis you create.

Business Planning Benefit #1: *Momentum*

As discussed in detail in the section on goal setting in chapter 2 (material you might wish to review as you write your business plan), having a concrete plan inspires action, while merely having vague dreams or ideas induces paralysis. Ryan, the Avid editor we met earlier, confirms this value: "I was getting married when I began my business, and I knew I needed something that would help support us steadily—in fact, our hope was to move into a larger house. Even though the business overview I wrote was quite brief, defining my market and product clearly really helped me take action. Because I now knew who my customers were and what I would provide, I also knew where to market, what equipment to purchase, who to network with, and so on. Otherwise, I would have been paralyzed by big dreams I had no way of achieving. This way, it was a series of clear, simple steps."

Business Planning Benefit #2: *Achievability*

An important part of being creative is to have big dreams. This quality has its advantages—it encourages risk and ambition, for example—but it is also dangerous, as it may lead you to have grandiose expectations unsupported by sufficient planning or research. The act of writing down what you intend to do, how you will go about it, and what it will cost immediately grounds your business goals. Unrealistic plans are much easier to spot in black and white! Plus, a written business plan can be reviewed by friends, family, or close business contacts, who can further troubleshoot your ideas.

"I wanted to leave my full-time medical editing job and start a freelance business as a yoga teacher," says Shari, a dancer. "I felt that it would leave my time more flexible for dancing roles, and yoga is a real love of mine. But when I started writing my costs down, I quickly found out that the class fees I had envisioned would not be enough to support me or pay for the studio and advertising the business would require. Unfortunately, higher prices seemed more than the local market would bear. I felt down when I realized this, but now that I've had time to recover I'm glad that the planning process revealed this flaw before I quit my job! I'm now exploring ways to solve this problem—for example, offering my classes through a local gym or spa."

Business Planning Benefit #3: *Specificity*

Small businesses tend to succeed best when they are specific and focused. With limited capital and staff, you simply will not be able to target every market segment, provide every possible service, and utilize every potential marketing tool within your chosen field. Creating a business overview with a clear mission helps you define and focus your services and market. You'll thus be able to use your resources in a more concentrated and effective fashion and define your services far more clearly to others as well. "When I started thinking about my new business, I envisioned it simply as weight-loss consulting," says Rosie, who loves acting but was employed for years at a large health-food company. "But as I tried to write about my market, I realized that I actually wanted to do weight-loss management *for women.* This level of specificity has brought the whole business into focus! It's affected how I designed my flyer and marketed my services . . . it's even gained me some local press, since it has that extra 'hook.' I never would have gotten so specific without the prompting of having to create a written plan."

Business Planning Benefit #4: *Measurability*

Owning your own business can be overwhelming. It is easy to end up with so much responsibility that you feel like a failure no matter what you accomplish or how hard you try. Having a business overview or plan relieves you of this particular form of distress by defining specific goals against which to measure your performance. Even if you don't quite make your targets, you'll have a concrete idea of how close you came, what stood in your way, and what you can do to either create a more realistic goal or meet your original plans. This is a much more comfortable feeling than vague unease.

Casey, a writer, has published two novels and some nonfiction but is waiting for his big break, the novel that will hit the best-seller lists, make lots of money, *and* gain him a rave review in the *New Yorker!* Until then, his lifeline business is ghostwriting. "My goal is to have a continual flow of ghostwriting assignments. I work hard to market myself when I see my assignment calendar thinning out and to keep my name visible in general. When my schedule is full, I know that I am meeting my goal. I also have an annual income goal I measure myself against. It's hard work, but in that sense it's simple, and very satisfying. Knowing that I am in business for myself keeps me much more focused than if I had a regular job," he adds. "This way, I feel more responsible, and I find that I'm more productive."

Business Planning Benefit #5: *Focus*

In the rush of operating your own business, it is easy to become sidetracked. You take on projects even though they are not really "what you do," or you react to others' needs and ideas in a way that may or may not serve your own goals. A business overview helps you avoid these problems by giving you a concrete, tangible reminder of how you articulated your mission at the start.

"I didn't create a plan when I began my freelance editing business," Jennifer, a poet, says ruefully. "I basically took any kind of work at more or less whatever fee was being offered. At the end of my first year, I was burned out and frustrated. I'd worked very hard, for many long hours, but I made little money. I sensed that this was the right business for me, but I knew I was doing something wrong! Luckily, someone encouraged me to create a simple business overview along with a summary of costs and revenues. In the process, I set a fee range based on figuring out my overhead, specified a minimum total project price, and defined what kind of editing work I would aim for. I can't even begin to explain how helpful this has been. Now, when I'm offered a job, I have clear criteria against which to evaluate it. I am doing less work, but actually making more money as a result."

Business Planning Benefit #6: *Profitability*

No, a business plan does not guarantee that your business will be profitable. But without any kind of clear overview or plan, you can be pretty sure it *won't* be! Underestimating costs, underpricing products and services, and failing to have a sufficient financial cushion to keep you going during a slow start-up or periodic business lulls are among the most common reasons small businesses fail. In fact, a full *40 percent* of new businesses fail due to poor planning. A detailed overview helps you avoid such pitfalls by forcing you to do at least some simple budgeting and pricing *before* you open your doors.

Michelle, an actress, is a case in point. She has expertise in computers from working years in an information-technology job. She plans to develop a business as a computer consultant. "I will help individuals become more comfortable with their personal computers; install, repair, and upgrade systems; and teach computer applications. My fee will be $75 per hour. I will keep my current job until I can generate a steady ten hours per week of freelance work, which will also give me extra income with which to fund start-up items such as letterhead and business cards, a second phone line for my home office, a brochure, and later some advertising in local papers. I expect to meet the ten-hour weekly goal within six months and target a $35,000 income in my first full year of business." Michelle may need to adjust some of the specifics of this plan, but you can no doubt see how a clear outline makes it much more likely that her new venture will be profitable.

Business Plan Benefit #7: *Flexibility*

The notion of flexibility may sound odd, since you may think that writing your plans down gives you *less* flexibility. In fact, the opposite is the case. Because it gives you a concrete basis to start from, a business plan or overview makes it easier to identify what is not working in your business and decide how exactly it should be changed.

In other words, a business plan is not a static or unalterable document. Business plans, like all of your goals, can mature and evolve over time. In fact, it almost certainly *will* change, as it is virtually impossible to predict all variables accurately before you have actually operated a while. This is as true of successful businesses as it is of fledgling start-ups. In 1946, for example, Henry Bloch and his brother Richard formed the United Business Company, which provided bookkeeping and management to businesses. They soon found that they were spending most of their time helping customers fill out tax forms! You already know the rest of this story. The brothers refocused their business on tax preparation, renaming it after themselves but changing the spelling to reflect the way their name is pronounced and to provide a solid, dependable image. Today, H&R Block helps prepare an astonishing one out of every ten income-tax forms filed each year! It has been so successful precisely because the brothers built on the foundation of a concrete business plan by adapting to new information, experience, and insight.

I've found that the business plans of creative individuals evolve in varied and interesting ways over time. The opportunity to refine and adjust your plan to make your business more satisfying or rewarding as you proceed is something you can look forward to—a natural outgrowth of getting to know yourself as well as your market better.

Jose, for example, became a magazine editor when he left college. More or less by chance, he got a freelance job as a script editor. He was hooked.

"The work with scripts was so interesting and exciting to me that I soon made a plan to leave the magazine business for the entertainment industry. I now take every script that comes my way and average an income of $60,000 each year. Just as I hoped, this feeds my work as a screenwriter—I've even had one of my screenplays produced. My evolution feels very natural, but it has been successful partly because I have tried to keep my focus pretty concrete at every step of the way."

The Small-Business Overview

By the time you have completed your business overview, you have envisioned virtually all of the key elements of your new business. The overview is a succinct summary of your entire business plan. As a concise statement of all key elements, it helps you envision and reach your goals. The summary will include a description of your service, an explanation of those you are selling to (customers), how you will make yourself known (marketing) and your projected earnings or profit (financial). Just as the lead line of a traditional news story answers "who, what, where, when, and why," your business overview will answer some basic questions—six, in this instance.

What Will I Be Selling?

This may be a product, a service, or both. Priscilla began providing image-consulting services but then wrote a book. After a number of successful years in business she is now considering creating a cosmetics line to further build her business and reputation. Marketing of her personalized services and her book "product" reinforce each other, and the cosmetic line would add further synergy.

To Whom Will I Be Selling?

The age, gender, geography, interests, and needs of your potential customers, among other factors, will enter into this description. Your particular business may target a broad market or hone in on a niche audience. Josefina, for example, who runs a personal business as a motivational teacher and coach, defines her market as "anyone who wants to change." Because what she does is in fact widely applicable to people of many ages, income levels, and interests, this is specific enough to serve her needs well. On the other hand, Robert, a printmaker who does freelance murals as a lifeline business, must define his market much more specifically. "My customers are institutions, municipalities, or very affluent individuals with a strong concern for individual style and status; I contract with them through top-level interior designers," he says, paraphrasing part of his business overview. "With only a few exceptions, marketing to any other group just doesn't make sense, since a mural tends to be too expensive for the average person to commission."

Who Are My Competitors?

This is an area of consideration on which many neophyte business owners skimp, but it is very important. As I suggested earlier in this chapter, your competition helps define what your customers expect and what prices are considered acceptable. If you do not understand your competition, you will not be able to distinguish yourself from them effectively. Take the time to get a good sense of the marketplace within which your business fits. For each competitor, study products/services offered, prices, style, target customer, advertising or marketing strategy, and any other factors that impact the business strongly.

"As a private writing teacher and 'coach' who helps aspiring creative writers write and market books, I had almost no local competition," says a writer named Rita. "However, there are several large online writing schools and services. By studying them I was able to price myself competitively and define what I could offer that they could not: personalized at-home meetings. I've now shaped my marketing around that quality."

In addition, taking the time to learn about the competition can actually help you *gain* clients. How? By widening your source of referrals. "When I completed my social work degree and established a counseling business in my home town, I familiarized myself with other counselors, therapists, and also doctors there. I wanted to focus on couples' counseling, and I'd refer clients with special needs that didn't fit my business to others. As a result, they now refer couples to me! Everybody wins," says Katie, a painter who is now a successful therapist.

How Will People Find Out About My Services?

Networking, advertising, targeted mailings, introductory courses, a Web site—your options in the area of marketing are very broad. Chapter 13 presents a variety of marketing ideas which you might review as you complete this section of your overview. It is best to try to select a limited group of marketing tools—perhaps two to four basic strategies. This will prevent you from spreading yourself too thin, as it's more effective to use a single strategy thoroughly than to scatter your sales energies too widely. You can add more later if you need to or if your budget permits.

What is My Fee?

You may have a single hourly rate, a variety of fees for different services, a flat fee, or some variation or combination of all three. Your fee will be defined by your cost analysis, coupled with your study of the competition and what they charge. Though it's usually best to keep your fee structure fairly simple, it can also be helpful to arrange your pricing so that a customer has options at several levels. Rita, the writing coach mentioned earlier, offers personalized consultation at $100 per hour, but also editing at a lower rate. By offering both options, she broadens her client base, and the editing provides her with a "break" from the more intense business of consulting. In addition to the basic fee structure, you may also want to define a minimum job size, a rush surcharge, and a volume discount, depending on your business and needs.

What Do I Expect to Make in a Week, a Month, and a Year?

You will probably need to establish a preliminary target for your start-up phase, then a higher goal for the time after your business is established. As with your fees, your overall income from the business should reflect both what is realistic in your market, and also what you need. It, too, flows from your cost analysis.

Congratulations! With these questions answered, you're almost finished with your overview. All you have to do now is to state it in a clear and succinct form. Following are some brief business overviews written by my clients, some of whom have already been introduced. Your own overview may be longer than these if it incorporates additional items from the above questions; the ones here are meant simply to give you an idea of what an overview sounds like.

> **Cheryl, writer:** My freelance business will ghostwrite books and articles for business professionals who wish to gain more visibility in their fields. For the first year, I will market myself to potential clients through referrals from my existing business contacts; local networking resources including chamber of commerce meetings and professional women's groups; the National Writers' Union technical-writing job hotlines; and a biannual brochure mailing. During the second year, I plan to advertise in professional journals as well. I will charge $75 per hour and aim to complete two to three books the first year depending on the length and complexity of each book. *Cheryl's business requires relatively few clients each year; at the same time, relatively few people*

have the ability and money to have a book ghostwritten. Therefore, her emphasis on marketing is appropriate.

Jason, full-time accountant and aspiring opera singer: I will specialize in tax preparation and bookkeeping for creative and performing artists. I will market my services through artistic associations, groups, and guilds. My projected earnings are $25,000 per year. *Jason's emphasis on artists is an excellent way to distinguish himself from the many other accountants who perform similar services. It gives him useful marketing opportunities and even increases the value of the service he provides, since artistic clients will work better with an accountant who "speaks their language."*

Ryan, Avid editor: I produce videos for weddings, bar mitzvahs, and other events and celebrations. My videos differ from those of competitors by virtue of their more artistic, innovative quality. My services will be promoted by word of mouth recommendations and by referrals from several party planners. My fee is $2,000 per event, with a target of two events per month to start.

Marianna, jewelry designer: I will use the knowledge of the market gained in many years in jewelry sales and buying to produce a line of rings, bracelets, and pendants made from birthstone gems. Items will be sold to the preteen and adolescent markets. I will begin by producing a sample line for shops serving these demographics. The business will begin while I am still employed at my current job with somewhat reduced hours. At the end of the first year, I will assess its performance. If I clear a profit of over $5,000 the first year, I will continue my designs and possibly even expand. Otherwise, I will return to work full time. *Marianna's gradual entry into her new business is a type of plan that can make sense for someone with a good, longstanding lifeline career. Her clarity about what the business needs to accomplish for her will stand her in good stead, as it gives her a clear way to evaluate whether or not she is successful.*

C.J., writer and organizer: My business provides organizational consulting to visual artists and writers in order to help them better manage their creative and business workflow. I charge $30 per hour with a minimum commitment of one day, although my goal is to work for the same clients at least one day a month over time. The start-up costs for my business are $975, including the installation of a second phone line usable for the business; letterhead and cards; a brochure which I will mail to all of my existing contacts and distribute through art museums, schools, libraries, and writers' groups and workshops; and the food and drinks for a monthly creative artists' salon, which I will host for the first three months of business in order to generate visibility and goodwill. I expect to generate six days of business a month for the first three months, rising to a minimum of twelve days a month by the end of the first year. *For a professional organizer, CJ's business plan is, not surprisingly, detailed and clear!*

Jake, cellist: My business is that of an SAT test-preparation tutor. My fee is $100 per hour and I expect to make $35,000 in my first year. In addition to customer referrals, I will advertise in local newspaper listings of services for students and parents. I will also propose my own course in test preparation at community centers and local adult-education centers as a means of generating additional visibility and clientele. *As Jake's overview shows, tutors in areas of high demand such as test preparation are well compensated. For more information on proposing a course as a means of marketing yourself, see chapter 13.*

Financial Considerations

Financial thinking is territory in which many of my clients are rather uncomfortable. (If you're the exception—for example, if you are a "closet creative" who has had budgeting, forecasting, or financial analysis experience—my apologies! You may wish to skim this section or move on to the marketing information in chapter 13.) Creative people often feel that they are "not good at numbers." They may also fear that the numbers will not support their business vision. But as Aldous Huxley wrote, "Facts do not cease to exist because they are ignored." You will find out sooner or later if your business is not financially viable; it's better to find out sooner than later, before you have committed large amounts of your energy and time.

A true cost and revenue analysis can be extremely complex and is beyond the scope of this book. For our purposes, a relatively simple set of questions will suffice to give you a sense of your new business' financial picture. For information about doing more elaborate financial plans, see the Resources section at the end of this book.

What are My Start-Up Costs?

No matter how small it is, a new business involves a number of one-time initial costs. These can include letterhead and business cards, office supplies, a new phone line and possibly a new computer or printer, a fax machine, incorporation fees, initial marketing materials such as advertisements or brochures, and the like. It is helpful to estimate these costs right from the start. If your budget will be tight, you can also figure out which expenses among them can be delayed and which must be incurred right up front.

Can I Afford to Start This Business?

To answer this question, you need to add up any funds you have in reserve (savings and other unearned income) to your income from your current work and your art, assuming there is income from the latter. Then, you need to add up the living expenses in chapter 11's worksheet plus any start-up costs. Then, compare the two figures. These computations should at least equal each other—hopefully your income and funds will be greater than your total expenses.

Relatively few creative people gain formal financing to start up their ventures. Instead, they fund their start-up costs as well as their early months of operation using money they have saved (sometimes from working extra hours in preparation for opening the business, sometimes from their normal compensation package if they are white-collar "closet creatives") or by continuing to work at another job during the start-up period.

What is My Overhead?

Overhead includes all of the costs involved in running your business. Supplies, phone and Internet usage, copies and faxes, rent if any, medical insurance you provide for yourself, electric costs for your home office, legal or accounting services, the cost of any other services you use, advertising, brochures, professional memberships and dues, professional journal subscriptions, and, potentially, the self-employment tax—all of these and potentially more are overhead costs. It is difficult to break these down in the early days of your business planning, since some expenses are irregular or unpredictable. Make the best guess you can, add on a margin for error, and re-calculate again at the end of six months and then a year. You're simply looking for a "guesstimate" at this stage.

Even if your initial guess is wrong, the process of coming up with a figure will be immensely helpful. Again and again, I hear freelancers confess that their failure to accurately assess the costs of running their business puts their income estimates wildly off track. "I ran my business so minimally that I never thought about overhead costs or how they impacted my profit," Cheryl says sheepishly. "I worked from home, I spent nothing on marketing. The way I saw it, it cost nothing to operate. But when you add in my medical insurance, phone calls, and the price of items I use in large volume such as laser printer toner and copies, my overhead was actually large enough to cut into my earnings quite substantially. That explained why I seemed to have so little to live on despite charging what seemed like a very lucrative hourly rate!"

What Price Must I Charge?

Your price will ideally cover your overhead and (once the business is established and you're fully "booked") include a percentage on top of those costs to bring you home a sufficient profit to meet your personal needs and goals. It's not always easy to guesstimate this at the beginning, but it's still useful to make the attempt. As Cheryl's experience shows, it is possible to price at a level which can never support you if you do not attempt to set your own figure.

Obviously, the proposed price must then be tested against norms in your market. If it is considerably higher than fees for similar services, you may need to adjust, either by figuring out ways to cut your costs and make a lower fee viable, or by finding ways to provide a "value added" in the form of an extra benefit which will justify a higher rate.

If your fees are considerably lower than those of other similar businesses, beware. You may have assessed your overhead unrealistically. Also, lower than normal fees may also give the impression that you are less desirable or qualified than your competitors. Your goal should be to charge fees similar to others in your field and at your experience level. If you feel that you need a pricing advantage to compete at the start, you can offer a "first-timer" discount of 10 percent or some similar promotion. This has the advantage of making you very competitive with other providers of your service as you build your clientele while leaving your regular rate appropriately higher.

The better you research your competitors' prices and understand your own pricing needs, the more firm and professional you can be about what you charge. Sam, a dancer who has a small business catering and creating theme parties, tells a relevant story. He started catering free of charge for friends and thus wasn't sure how much to charge clients. "I would cost my materials for food and decorations, but I wasn't sure how much of a markup I should figure in order to make a profit. I asked friends in related businesses and they gave me a good idea of where to start. But I came in too high a few times at the beginning and agreed to lower my fee because I got embarrassed. That's not the image I want to project. Now, after additional research, I'm very confident about what I charge, and it must come across, because no one ever questions me any more."

Of course, you may not always be able to earn the ideal rate your calculations establish. A high-volume client may ask for a volume discount, or a prolonged dry spell may cause you to be willing to take on somewhat lower-paying work. Nevertheless, you should try to keep this to a minimum. Having a clear target figure in mind will help keep you from radically under- or overpricing in your early days of operation.

Establishing Your New Business: Some Final Considerations

Small businesses have always been a healthy part of American commerce and are only becoming more prevalent in this era of corporate downsizing and increased emphasis on personalized service. This means that there are scores of resources to help provide you with guidance on the practical aspects of forming and managing your business. I strongly urge you to seek out those resources; here I'll simply review a few final issues you should have in mind as you start your new venture.

Location

Most creative people run their businesses from home. Several clients with home-based businesses have emphasized to me how important it is to set up your home office or work area as carefully as you can from the start, as this helps you organize your business records and save time. "The temptation, which I gave in to, is to stick everything on your existing desk and make do," says Melanie, the freelance deejay. "But as your business takes off and your time becomes more pressured, it just doesn't work. About two months into my freelance business, I had to set aside a whole weekend to buy filing cabinets, reorganize my office area, clean up the piles of paper that had accumulated. And then I still had to catch up on the bills, records, and tax forms I'd let slide because it was so hard to find anything. It's easier to set it up right from the get-go."

You should also decide from the start how you will separate your personal and creative space and time apart from your business. Will you close the door, use a voice-mail system to answer the phone, or set some other boundary? "Even though my budget was tight when I started, I had a second, business-only phone line put in my home office fairly soon," says Glenda, the writer we met earlier. "That way, I could choose to let the answering machine pick up at night and on weekends. It helped me keep some semblance of a personal life even though I work at home."

Business Name

The variations here are endless. As you're probably aware, white-collar and consulting businesses are likely to operate under the name of the owner, as in law and accounting firms where it is the specialized expertise of one or more individuals that is being sold; businesses related to leisure or lifestyle and those which provide products more typically operate under a name related to their service or theme. A trade name will help brand and identify your product and can remind the customer of its prime benefit or appeal to a particular market. Whether you name your business after yourself or your product is up to you; your business name can succeed either way. Gourmet cook Patricia Nelson, for example, did party planning under the name Patty's Parties; in the same business, Martha Stewart used her own name.

If you do use a name other than your own, of course, make sure that it's suitable to your market demographics and that it's flexible enough to allow your business to evolve. An interesting example of the problems this latter issue can produce is the retail chain Calico Corners, which sells discount home-furnishing fabrics. Today, the store's wares include costly (although discounted) silks, damasks, and chintzes—a far cry from its lowbrow, homey name!

Business Certificate

You must register your business in order to operate under a trade or assumed name. This is done at the County Clerk's office in the county in which the business is located.

Business Structure

Most businesses owned by creative people are operated as sole proprietorships; less frequently, legal partnerships or corporations are formed. It is worth considering this issue before you open, in case there is a tax or liability advantage in choosing a structure other than sole proprietorship. The following brief summaries give you an overview of each and will point you in the right direction. Because tax and legal issues are complex, however, be sure to obtain advice appropriate to your business needs and location.

Sole Proprietorship

A sole proprietorship is a business owned by one person. It is the most popular structure in part because it is so simple to set up. It may require state and local licenses but needs no other paperwork to be formed. Profits or losses for the business are factored into your personal tax return rather than filed separately. This means that there are a variety of legitimate tax deductions that may be offset against your personal income. These include membership dues, legal and accounting bills, printing and postage, some education expenses, office supplies, rentals, work-related subscriptions, travel, and so on. The drawbacks of sole proprietorships are, first, that the owner assumes personal responsibility for any debts or lawsuit judgments and, second, that there may be less capital and teamwork available than with a partnership.

Partnership

A partnership is a shared business ownership between you and one or more individuals. Partnerships are often compared to business "marriages." Their advantage is the sharing of workload, financing, and ideas, but problems can arise when the relationship between the partners sours, the line of responsibility is not clear, differences arise about operational decisions, and so on. For this reason, if you consider a legal partnership, you will want to choose your partner very carefully. Consider factors such as similarity of values, goals, and business style. In addition, you will need a formal written (not oral) agreement that sets forth quite specifically how the business will be managed, how authority will be shared, what capital each partner will contribute, and how revenues will be shared. The advice of an attorney is important in planning and setting up a partnership.

Corporation

A corporation is a complex business structure (a separate entity from owners and their financial assets) which can yield tax benefits in certain circumstances and which also shields the owner(s) from personal liability for debts and lawsuits. In other words, your personal assets cannot be touched if the company goes bankrupt. Unless either of those issues are a consideration or the type of business you do demands it, creative people typically do not form corporations, since their formation and operation require legal and accounting advice, which adds to expenses. If you think you should incorporate, consult with your attorney and an accountant. They can explain the advantages and drawbacks of the regular corporation, the subchapter S corporation, and a new variant known as a limited liability company (LLC)—all of which offer the protection of limited personal liability.

Letter Agreements

Unless your business involves very small transactions or simple, one-step product sales, you will need some formal arrangement to confirm the working agreement you have with a client or customer. This will ensure that you and your client are actually in agreement on all terms from the start and protects you if there is any problem with expectations or payment later on. Though it takes some time to do, investing attention in this agreement is essential to a well-run business.

Typically, a simple one- or two-page letter agreement, to be signed by both yourself and the client, will suffice. You should draft a standard letter agreement which gives you room to describe the nature and timing of the services to be rendered; which reviews the amount and deadline for payments; which details how to cope with various contingencies (such as specifying that changes must be made in writing), and which clarifies the ownership of copyrights and other intellectual property when applicable.

Ghostwriter Cheryl's letter agreement, for example, explains what she will provide to a client (one first and one final draft), specifies how she will accept changes to the first draft (in writing only, and at one time), sets a timetable, absolves herself of responsibility should the book being written not sell to a publisher, reviews terms under which she will be credited, and assures the client that the notes and material will remain confidential. "I try to refine my basic letter form over time to cover contingencies and potential problems. My experience has been that the clearer I am up front, the more likely it is that things will go smoothly later." Most creative people who freelance—many of whom have had problems with clients who do not pay on time or other conflicts—would agree.

Whether or not you have your letter reviewed by a lawyer—either as a standard boilerplate form or as an agreement tailored to each new client—depends on your preference, the complexity of your business, and the size of each transaction. If you can have your letter reviewed, it may save you headaches down the road. I strongly advise that you consult an attorney to review any large or complex transactions.

Record Keeping

The final decisions you must make right at the outset have to do with how you manage your operation's money, file taxes, and keep records. You can either do most of these tasks yourself or hire others to do everything:

setting up your filing system, managing your finances, organizing your papers, setting up your bookkeeping system, and computerizing your records. Whether you do everything yourself, very little yourself, or somewhere in between, it is very much in your best interest to take responsibility for keeping track of your income and operations.

Stories abound of creative people who end up losing everything, merely because they did not pay attention to what was happening with their money. Following the runaway success of *Jonathan Livingston Seagull*, author Richard Bach, for example, discovered that his tax bill alone amounted to more than a million dollars due to poor management on the part of those to whom he had delegated virtually every aspect of his finances. He lost nearly everything before resolving this debt. Musician Willie Nelson, too, is a celebrated artist with legendary tax and financial problems. Authors Patricia Cornwall and Colette Dowling also let their inattention to record keeping and management lead them to near ruin. As these examples demonstrate, huge incomes and artistic success do not exempt one from attending to these concerns. Whether your business income is abundant or tiny, it is crucial to recognize that the ultimate responsibility for managing it is in your hands. As Star Jones says, "I have a business manager I can trust. He's worked for me for years. Besides, I'm a lawyer. Nobody's going to steal any money from me." This kind of attitude is much healthier for your small business than a shrug and an "I don't know."

In addition to experts and freelancers you can turn to for assistance, today's marketplace offers excellent book and computer resources that can help you manage the business and financial end of your operations. For a thorough discussion of contracts for artists and entrepreneurs, see the Business and Legal Forms Series (Allworth Press), referred to in the Resources section of this book. Excel and QuickBooks are both excellent programs for small businesses. If your accounts receivable (incoming revenues) and accounts payable (outgoing expenses) are not numerous or complex, you may choose to record them manually or on a simple computer spreadsheet, including such items as dates, amounts, vendors, customers, purpose, and so on. Invoices, bills, letter agreements, receipts for taxable items, and so on can be stapled into your appointment diary, filed into accordion or Pendaflex files, or organized by some other simple system. Consulting with your accountant could certainly be a wise step in setting up your system. It doesn't matter how you choose to handle your paperwork and record keeping. It only matters that you set up a system that will work for you and that you will be able to maintain over time.

Chapter Thirteen

Your Business Selling Tools

A businessman is a hybrid between a dancer and a calculator.
—Paul Valery

Nothing except the mint can make money without advertising.
—Thomas Maculay

Once your new business is chosen, planned, and structured, it's time to work on promoting it. As I mentioned in chapter 4, salesmanship and promotion are an essential part of any small business, no matter what the field. Whether you become a tutor or a massage therapist, an interior designer or a computer engineer, the more active and innovative you are in getting the word on your business out, the more successful you will be. Conversely, if you do not promote your business, you have only a slim chance of thriving—or even surviving—in today's competitive marketplace.

Basic Market Terminology
Target Market
This is simply the primary customer base you identified in chapter 12. It's helpful continually to identify and refine your sense of what your target market is and any subgroups it has. If you can visualize and pin down your average customer's age range, income, gender, product preferences/buying habits, and qualifications desired from a provider of your services, you will increase your ability to market powerfully to their needs.

For example, Rosie, the actress and weight-loss consultant we met in chapter 12, discovered that marketing her weight-loss consulting service to women involved a whole different slant than selling to men or mixed groups. "The physical process of weight loss may be the same for everyone, but women's fears, concerns, and personal issues are quite distinct. I always remember that whenever I create any kind of promotion, be it a speech, an ad, a newsletter or a brochure. Everything I produce is directed specifically at those concerns."

Market Survey

Again, this is just the industry name for the process of finding out what customers in the target group want. While national organizations do this very elaborately, with focus groups and tests, you can do your own market survey quite simply and informally. Either in person or by mail, just describe your product or service briefly, then ask the following questions.

- Overall, what is your opinion of the product/service?
- What do you like about it? Dislike about it?
- What might you change or add?
- What would be the best way for others to learn about it?
- Would you be interested in purchasing this product? Why or why not?
- What price would you be willing to pay for this product/service?

You can use such information both at start-up or periodically thereafter to evaluate your services and how they meet your market's needs.

Competitive Advantage

This is simply an attempt to articulate as precisely as possible what makes you *different* and *better* than your competition. Your competitive advantage may be in the area of price; quality; special features; customer type; manner of purchase, i.e., store, phone, Internet; personal qualifications or experience; or specialty/niche. For many creative people who choose self-employment, personal qualifications and/or niche comprise a competitive advantage. For example, you'll notice that a number of the people discussed in this book slanted their services toward the artistic community. I do that myself as well, as I am a career counselor specializing in the needs of creative and performing artists. From the very beginning of my practice, this separated me from my colleagues and enabled me to be easily identified with a specific area of expertise. Over time, my personal qualifications and my niche specialty began to overlap more and more. Having this type of competitive advantage can help you get referrals, public-speaking engagements, and other promotional opportunities such as press coverage.

Spheres (Also Called Centers) of Influence

These are individuals with connections who could refer clients or customers to you. Centers of influence for a tutor might include pastors, private and public school principals, and teachers; centers of influence for a massage therapist might include doctors, fitness trainers, and athletic coaches; centers of influence for a dog walker or groomer would include vets and pet store owners. For Ryan, the Avid editor and wedding videographer we met earlier, they would be caterers, still photographers, hotel managers, party planners and so on; for Shawna, the Lamaze instructor whose broadcast letter appears at the end of this chapter, key spheres of influence are obstetricians.

Names and addresses of such individuals can be accessed through easy sources such as the white and yellow pages as well as through networking. It is well worth your time to cultivate your awareness of which people or groups are spheres of influence for your business and to keep in touch with them—through special mailings of broadcast letters, a newsletter, or a phone call—periodically. You can simply write a note mentioning any new accomplishments ("I am delighted to have formed a partnership with Rhoda James, a C.P.A., who specializes in complex tax filings and who will allow me to better serve large businesses"; "You have been so supportive that I know you'll be pleased to learn that we served our five hundredth customer last month"). You can also remind them that you appreciate any referrals they can give ("I would appreciate your willingness to refer clients to me and hope you will continue to keep me in mind when those you know are in need of presentation coaching").

Promoting and Marketing Your Business: Your Selling Tools

Business marketing can take forms so diverse it is impossible to even list them here, much less provide a thorough discussion of them. In my work with creative professionals, however, I've found that the business commercial is the foundation for selling your services and, once written, can then be used as a basis for a variety of advertising and marketing materials.

The Business Commercial

The business commercial consists of several sentences, prepared and even practiced in advance, which allow you to communicate the key points about your business, its benefits, and its market powerfully and succinctly in conversation with others. Like the personal commercial, its purpose is to allow you to introduce yourself well at business meetings, in social situations, or in any setting where you may meet individuals who could use or refer your services.

The business commercial answers several questions.

- What is my business or service?

- Who is it sold to?

- Why should the customer buy it?

- In addition, it may cover other issues, such as where the business is located or when you started operating, if these details strongly support the above answers or enhance your salability in some way.

Your new business will likely be very closely identified with *you*—your personal talents, training, and skills. Thus, the best way to begin working on your business commercial is to work through the information on personal commercials I shared in chapter 8, keeping in mind that the crucial difference is that as a small businessperson, you will be trying to sell your new service or product to many clients rather than to a single employer. When you're finished, you should actually be quite close to having a good business commercial in hand. All you'll then need to do is look at your "draft" commercial with these special business perspectives in mind.

Emphasize Service or Benefits

Emphasize the service or benefits you provide and the clientele you provide it to, rather than points of personal background that do not relate to the service you are selling. This accomplishes two things: It links the content of your commercial to the potential needs of the listener and his or her circle of influence, and it helps you negotiate the difficulty of "talking yourself up" without appearing egotistical and arrogant. Because you are presenting yourself as a conduit of knowledge, skills, or products to your clientele—a means, not an end—it will feel more comfortable to display confidence and enthusiasm than if you were extolling your own professional virtues.

Mention Links to the Community

If possible or appropriate, mention links to your community and/or one or more constituencies. Again, this allows you to display a sense of connection to something outside yourself and thus gives your commercial power without risking self-absorption.

Thomas, a teacher who, after many years of planning, started a community theater company, is emphatic on this point: "Though I phrase it differently depending on whether I'm asking for donations, volunteers, subscribers, or program advertising, I never, ever forget to emphasize that this is our community's first theater company. I truly believe that the company is a vehicle for community expression, connection, and culture—and that's how I present it.

"I think it's entirely that focus," Thomas continues, "that has allowed me to build such great local support. It's been incredible. The parents and students who ran the school drama club helped me make promotional materials very cheaply—they even gave me the student roster to start my subscription list! A local lawyer who really believes in our community's need for the arts helped me file for my government nonprofit status at a very reasonable rate. I didn't ask these people to help *me*; I gave them a way to support something larger than that: their own love for our town and belief in the arts." If your business has no local or area connection, the same purpose can be accomplished by emphasizing the special groups you serve.

Emphasize Uniqueness

It is infinitely easier to create a powerful commercial if your business has a distinct or unusual focus, clientele, service, or "hook." Mind you, I'm not talking about a gimmick, which is an angle or feature contrived purely for sales effect. Instead, I'm taking about an element of distinction that arises naturally from your own unique skills, interests, and passions.

Theo had been a struggling actor for years and had earned his money as a word processor. When computer graphics came on the scene, he knew he had found his niche. "I learned a lot of graphics software, but particularly liked those programs that incorporated photography," he says. "I developed what eventually became my business niche while I was looking for a graphics job. I didn't get much luck until I added the phrase, 'Using photographs, I find creative solutions to computer-graphics needs.' I got three immediate responses! Now I use that in my freelance business commercial, which is, 'I run a computer-graphics business for individuals and businesses. Using state-of-the art techniques that incorporate photographics with print and artistic borders, I specialize in finding creative solutions to your graphics needs.'"

Stay Focused

A commercial is very short, and as with a personal commercial it is therefore important to keep it very tightly focused. You won't be able to mention all of your services or benefits; if you try, you risk sounding scattered or distracting the listener with too much information. Choose the ones that are crucial in the particular situation at hand and stick only to those. If necessary, prepare several different commercials to suit the needs of the situations or audiences you might face. For example, consider these two different commercials, developed by the same freelance writer:

1. "I'm a consulting writer and editor, helping both individuals and businesses shape their written materials effectively. As a Wall Street executive for ten years, I'm well versed in business and can write effectively about financial and technical issues. I'm currently working on the operating policy for a regional manufacturing company."

2. "I'm a consulting writer and editor. My own writing deals with women's issues, and I especially enjoy helping women set down their stories and memories. In fact, I'm teaching a women's journal workshop beginning next month."

Notice that these commercials, though quite different, do not contradict each other. In one, Susan highlights an aspect of her business that arises from her past experience; in the other, she emphasizes a specialty that relates to a personal passion. If the man and woman to whom she addressed these commercials happened to be a husband and wife who compared notes at the end of the day, they would find nothing duplicitous in Susan's different presentations. *Yet her ability to present her business in two very different lights will make it memorable to its particular audiences.* Susan has a quite generalized business, but at any given moment her tightly focused commercial makes it sound specialized—specialized to her current audience's needs.

To get you started on your business commercial, here are some strong business commercials that have been used by my clients. Notice the way each "spins" his or her business in a way that sounds interesting and focused.

From Tina, whose tap-dancing school fills a unique niche in her community, which had not previously offered any tap lessons: "I own and operate Top Tap, a dancing school specializing in tap lessons and musical theater productions for children at beginner, intermediate, and advanced levels. We use techniques and repertoire based on the years I spent with the Rockettes and as a cast member in several Broadway shows."

From Priscilla, whose highly successful image-consulting business was introduced earlier: "I am a professional image consultant, advising clients on business and social dress. I also provide a personal shopping service. My mission is to make my clients as beautiful as possible and to enable them to have the impact they desire."

From Michelle, the computer consultant introduced in a previous chapter: "I am a friendly computer consultant who helps clients feel more comfortable with their personal computers. I install, repair, troubleshoot, and teach computer applications in a way that lets people like and rely on them. I can change a fearful or skeptical person into an advocate of personal computing!"

From Natalia, an aspiring children's book writer who works with children: "I am a certified child psychologist offering groups and workshops for parents of toddlers, preteens, and adolescents. I focus on teaching parents the techniques of effective listening, interaction, and discipline of children based on my hands-on experience in the field. I also see individuals and families in my private practice."

From Ivan, an actor and ESL teacher who uses his lifetime hobby of world travel in his business: "I act as a language and communications consultant for individuals, corporations, schools, and universities. I teach English and business etiquette to foreign executives and work to help a variety of companies improve their intercultural communications."

Overview of Marketing

As I have said, there are a wide variety of marketing strategies open to you as a small businessperson. The brief overview that follows will give you a sense of what's out there and where you might start. The Resources section lists a number of books and other sources that specialize in marketing and advertising issues for small businesses. Note that whatever medium or strategy you choose, all of your marketing communications, both verbal and written, should be based on your commercial and should be consistent in terms of the message they proclaim.

Business card

This is not generally perceived as a marketing tool per se, but it is. In fact, it's the single most important piece you'll use for name recognition and contact information. It can be used almost anywhere, so don't leave home without it. In addition to the obvious facts, make sure that it explains what you do if the business operates under your own name. Something simple like "Michelle Blank, Computer Consultant" or "Cheryl Stanley, Ghostwriting and Editing" will do fine.

Brochures

Though the word "brocher" is French for "to staple," in the United States the term "brochure" might cover anything from a small folder to a lavish four-color booklet, whether or not staples are involved. In practice, it is rare for a small or freelance business to need anything much more elaborate than a small two- or three-fold flyer—something which can fit into a small or medium business envelope (or folded and addressed on one of its own panels to save envelope costs). In fact, making your brochure larger or more complex brings several disadvantages, including increased printing and postage costs and greater storage bulk. Further, clients are actually suspicious of brochures that appear too elaborate, costly, or slick, as they know that it's their payments that fund such luxuries! The only major exceptions are graphic-design businesses (where your brochure demonstrates your talents and therefore serves as an additional portfolio piece) and businesses that involve extremely high-end services or clients, where a more upscale brochure than usual may be appropriate.

The brochure builds on your business commercial and includes information on who you are (focusing on background that is relevant to your services), what you provide, why it is unique or distinctive, what your market is (to make a link to your customers' needs), and any special services and resources you provide. It is a valuable tool for any freelancer or small businessperson because it can be mailed, distributed, given to clients, and otherwise widely used.

Newsletter

As the "news" in the word implies, a newsletter focuses on providing information rather than on a hard sell of goods and services. Its advantage is that it positions you as an expert in your field. Writing articles or interviewing others about related business issues (which often is the type of material included in a newsletter) also pays off in letting you make new contacts and stay on the "cutting edge" of your field. Along with their informational content, newsletters are used to inform new, old, and prospective clients of your accomplishments, new services, and anything else you wish to highlight. A newsletter may simply be formatted and printed front and back on standard size paper for easy distribution. E-mail newsletters are also becoming common.

Print Advertisements

Ads may be placed in newspapers, magazines, playbills, and many other printed materials. They are priced according to size, with charges reflecting the prestige and circulation of the publication. Local advertising is often quite affordable and will work well if your business targets primarily local customers.

TV and Radio Advertisements

Television and radio commercials have historically been very expensive due to the huge audience they reach. However, the advent of cable television and its proliferation of channels has made TV advertising more affordable for the small business than previously; your cable system may well have one or more local or regional channels, for example. As with all advertising, of course, media advertising is a good investment only if it will clearly reach your target audience. If your customers are especially upscale or exist only in a narrow niche or subgroup, you may be better served with marketing strategies that focus more precisely on your target market.

Web Sites

Web sites are one of the newest forms of advertising, yet are becoming increasingly common. Your site can include the information covered in your brochure, plus images or excerpts that communicate your philosophy or sell your services. Fees may be listed, though many business people prefer to wait until a client has contacted them to give specifics. Though your site can support e-commerce, it does not necessary have to, and the sites of many small businesspeople do not. It is crucial that your site, if you choose to have one, be clear, concise, friendly, and professional in appearance; unless you are very expert in computer graphics and Web site creation, it is almost always necessary to get professional assistance with its design in order to achieve a sufficiently polished and attractive site.

Broadcast Letters

Broadcast letters for your small business are very similar to those I described for job hunting in chapter 9. Used with a follow-up phone call, they can be mailed to contacts gleaned from the yellow pages, business directories, organizational/professional membership lists, or personal referrals. Tailor the letter as specifically as you can to the particular needs of the recipients and address all recipients by name. Naturally, if you have a referral, mention it right at the start of the letter. A sample broadcast letter appears on the next page.

Guidelines for Powerful Communications

Whether your communications materials encompass brochures, proposals, flyers, booklets, and manuals or are limited to only a flyer or two, these guidelines will help you ensure that they effectively represent you in the marketplace.

Make sure your marketing communications style matches your business style and market

This sounds obvious, yet it's a precept that is often ignored. Businesses that rely on an image of innovation or creativity produce dull, conventional materials; businesses that serve traditional or business markets create inappropriately playful, whimsical, or colorful pieces. Think carefully about your customers and their concerns before choosing colors, papers, fonts, and layouts and before finalizing any text. Are you a caterer promising festivity and style, or a massage therapist working with clients who must trust you? What would make your brochure reassuring or appealing to your particular customers?

If you can't produce high quality illustrations, don't use them at all

We've all seen small-business brochures and flyers that include poorly reproduced clip art or fuzzy black-and-white photographs of the owner or facility. These images do little to sell services and in fact can substantially lower the professionalism and appeal of your business. In many business materials, photography and illustrations are not necessary. Exceptions might include fields such as image, color, or fashion consulting, where a photograph that demonstrates your own personal image or style can help establish credibility—or catering, event planning, landscaping, and graphic design, where illustrations of projects can convey uniqueness, elegance, and other qualities that are difficult to describe in words. If you feel that photos or illustrations are a must, make sure both the quality of the original and the quality of the printing are top-rate. Computer programs, digital cameras, and color printers can produce quite sophisticated products. You can also check with local designers and printers to see what kinds of reproduction and printing are available in your price range.

Shawna Barrie
8 Coxley Court
Belltown, VT 32000

May 3, 2000

Dear Dr. OB/GYN:

I would be pleased to offer classes in the techniques of Lamaze childbirth to your patients in the last trimester of pregnancy. Whether or not the patient chooses to deliver by natural childbirth methods, learning what to expect and how to prepare can decrease anxiety and increase her sense of control and well-being. My services therefore benefit not only mothers but also fathers, physicians and the hospital staff.

I generally conduct these lessons for four to six couples in four two-hour sessions. They are offered in the doctor's office after office hours. The fee is $250 per couple.

As a yoga instructor and certified Lamaze instructor, I have conducted classes in hospitals, clinics, and yoga institutes and also work with clients privately. I would be glad to provide references and testimonials from clients and colleagues.

I welcome the chance to discuss these services with you further and will call you next week to see if they may be of interest.

Sincerely,

Shawna Barrie

Leave yourself room to maneuver

While your communications must describe your market and services specifically enough to be clear and compelling, it is unwise to be too specific.

Linda, who has a successful business teaching American etiquette to foreign business people working for or with U.S. corporations, smiles ruefully as she underscores this point. "My first brochure said that I offered three-hour hands-on manners classes. I sent it out to a potential client who seemed very enthusiastic, but I never heard back. When I bumped into him a month later, he said that the classes interested him, but that his executives would never be willing to give up almost half a day just to learn how to hold a fork! Needless to say, I felt very foolish to have turned off a potential client due to such a silly, overly specific statement. I scrapped that brochure and created a more flexible one; it wasted some money, but I felt that it just wasn't worth risking more problems of that kind. I'm glad to say I did eventually land the man's account—under a contract to give his company nice, brief, *one*-hour manners seminars!"

Give enough information to pique the interests of your market but remain flexible enough to ensure that neither you nor the client feel "boxed in." Avoid any references that might date quickly. Where appropriate, make clear that various options or variations on your basic service are available. Linda, for example, now offers "seminars ranging in length from one hour to a full day." Use bullet lists where potential services are numerous—listing, for example, brochures, articles, flyers, reports, and newsletters for a business writer; headshots, portraits, wedding photos, baby photos for a freelance photographer). Don't put prices into more expensive communications tools such as brochures unless you reprint very often; otherwise, keep them to an inexpensive price list or card that can be updated quickly.

"Putting your fees down in a brochure tends to be a lose/lose situation," Linda explains. "If you state a specific fee in your printed material, you really can't change it without looking a little sleazy or unprofessional. If a potential client feels that your fees are too high, you've lost them from the start, and you don't even have the option of negotiating. On the other hand, if a potential client feels that your fees are fine, you haven't gained anything—and in fact you might have been able to charge more based on actual personal discussions with that client. My solution is to list my prices on a separate card which I identify by season—Spring 2002, for example. A line at the bottom of the card tells the customer that if the season header is not current, prices may have changed and they should ask for a new price card. That way, I can alter my prices quarterly if necessary without seeming unprofessional."

Instead of stating actual rates, you might also offer text that explains how pricing is figured (by the project, by the hour, etc.) and invites the client to find out more. Something like "Hourly fees are based on the timetable and complexity of the work. Estimates for your project will be provided free and without obligation" works well in many types of brochures. Finally, you could give a range rather than a fixed amount: "Fees for editing range from $30 and up, for writing from $50 and up," for example. Make the number cited just a fraction lower than your typical low fee and do not state an upper range.

Hire or "borrow" professional help when needed

Poorly formatted graphics, small grammatical errors, or typos can put big doubts in clients' minds about your professionalism and attention to detail. Yet such mistakes are very easy to make. The solution is professional support, either hired, bartered, or borrowed. If none of your friends or family have excellent writing, graphics, or editing skills, you can find freelancers to help. It is well worth a small investment to ensure that your communications are professional. Whether or not an editor works on your printed materials, have several people—including some who have never seen your brochure before—read all text carefully before you go to print. That includes address and phone information as well as promotional material. "My zip code changed right around the time I did my business brochure, and I put the old one in the text without thinking. When I proofed the brochure, I didn't even glance at that section. It's not that big a deal, but it bothers me that I've had to correct my own brochure right from the start," says Scott, the freelance paralegal we met in chapter 3. "I'm going to have the brochure reprinted as soon as I can, but it was a silly and unnecessary mistake to make."

Make yourself widely known

The more visible you are, the more successful your business will be. Try these distribution outlets to ensure that you and your services get seen as much as possible.

- **Mailing lists.** Develop your own, and consider looking into the rental or purchase of the lists of one or more businesses in your field. Mail to your combined list periodically—every six months or every year, depending on your budget. Don't be afraid to mail a brochure to individuals or businesses who did not contact you upon the first mailing. Sometimes they just haven't needed your services yet but will eventually use you if you jog their memory at the right moment.

- **Media coverage.** Utilizing your specialty in creative ways can get you coverage in local, regional, or even national media. This in turn can not only help you gain clients, but also enhance your reputation as an expert in your field or service. Though media coverage is not always easy to secure, it has the great advantage of being free! The key to getting media coverage is a combination of uniqueness, timeliness, and service. Media outlets will not typically cover mere products, unless they are very unusual or especially timely or trendy; instead, they feature items they deem useful or newsworthy to the community. As you do business, look for ways you can offer newsworthy special services. Party planner Sam, for example, collaborated with the owner of a Mexican restaurant to create a Monday school lunch with a Mexican theme, served to the music of a mariachi band at the restaurant. Different schools participated each week to learn more about Mexican culture, and the restaurant got extra business on a slow day. Sam used the experience to build his credentials; as an added bonus, the local news station picked up the story and did a feature on it. Sam and the restaurant owner both built their clientele thanks to this exposure, and Sam can now promote his services with the phrase, "As seen on Channel 6 news . . . ."

- **Local establishments.** Libraries, museums, coffee houses, gyms and health clubs, restaurants, shops, and other area businesses will often let you post a flyer on their bulletin boards or even, if your service may help their clientele, leave a stack of brochures on their counter. Jerry, a veterinarian who used his love of photography to open a business specializing in pet photographs, says, "I display my work in pet stores, pet supply and specialty shops, and my office. This gets me work both as a photographer and a vet— one of the benefits of having an artistic and professional life that are so closely related."

- **Meetings or conferences.** These are ideal times to network, distribute business cards, hand out your brochure, and otherwise make yourself visible. They need not even be in your field to be useful. A freelance business writer, for example, could attend any number of professional open houses, meetings, and conferences to prospect for business with professionals in various fields.

- **Social events.** Though it's inappropriate at social events to do business in any hard-sell or direct way, you should certainly let people know you are a small businessperson.

- **Your existing customer base.** Don't neglect to market with those already familiar with your services. You can ask for referrals gracefully by saying something like, "I'm able to keep my prices low because referrals bring me new clients without the high cost of advertising. If you've been pleased with my work, I hope you'll think of me when your friends or colleagues are in need of tax assistance."

The Course Proposal

As they are starting up their new businesses, many creative professionals propose to teach a workshop or class at a school, agency, business, or other setting. Teaching a class is a powerful marketing and business-building tool, because it helps you

- Meet individuals who may be potential customers for your personalized services;

- Build a client base by giving you local exposure;

- Establish credibility as someone with expertise to share in some aspect of your new field;

- Practice presenting key concepts relating to your field;

- Provide publicity by giving you free mentions in course catalogs, brochures, and company newsletters; and

- Build your income in the long run, though you may have to charge little or nothing for your first few classes.

The types of potential classes you might teach is limited only by your imagination and the nature of your business. Almost every field, both creative and professional, offers some potential for a course, seminar, or workshop. (I'll be using those terms more or less interchangeably in the course of this discussion; strictly speaking, however, a seminar lasts anywhere from a few hours to a full day and a workshop implies a course that uses more than just lectures as a means of information delivery.) A few examples of many include:

Investments for Beginners	Fitness for Seniors
Retirement Planning	Creating a Successful Theme Party
Improving Your Fashion Sense	Gourmet Cooking for Beginners
Stress Management	Positive Parenting
Introduction to Computers	Internet Shopping for Beginners
Buying Your Dream House	Self-Defense Workshop
Assertiveness Training	Presentation Skills
Journal Writing	Writing Your Family History
Law for the Layman	Basic Photography

As you can immediately see, it is possible to teach a class that straight-forwardly utilizes your professional skills (such as Basic Photography) or one that more creatively makes a particular niche audience (such as Fitness for Seniors) aware of you and your expertise. Once you have developed one course proposal, you'll likely find it fairly simple to adapt it to different groups and to different settings, such as adult- or continuing-education centers, churches, women's clubs, senior centers, Ys, retirement homes, hospitals or rehabilitation centers, museums, arts centers, and country clubs. In some cases, even retail establishments will sponsor a course; an upscale fashion boutique, for example, might agree to offer a one-hour seminar in scarf tying, choosing colors, and so on.

Just as when you were researching your new lifeline field, you'll need to do some preliminary information gathering before you develop a course or program. Specifically, you'll need to answer several questions.

•**Do similar programs exist in your area?** Review school or organizational brochures and check newspapers for listings from local clubs, professional organizations, and so on. (Specialized newsletters and/or the Internet can also post classes outside your area that can help you get ideas.)

•**How is your class different and/or better than others like it?** Do you have a special niche, an unusual or powerful angle, or exceptional credentials? Why should people sign up for your class rather than another, similar one?

•**Who is your potential market?** How will this course attract potential customers for your business (which is, after all, your ultimate goal)? How can these customers be grouped or described? Note that this question can offer many different answers depending on your business. For example, let's say you are a massage therapist. Your potential market may include senior citizens, those with sports injuries, and athletes. Each market might inspire a different course in a different setting.

•**Where should the course be taught?** What setting will best attract the type of potential customer you have just identified?

•**What duration best suits your subject, market, and potential teaching setting?** Most subjects can be appropriately taught in anything from a few hours to a full twelve-week semester; the secret is simply the ability to slant and limit the information involved. A journal-writing class offered as a single three-hour program at a community center, for example, might promise that "participants will learn what the four main purposes of a personal journal are, learn six basic guidelines to fun and productive journal writing, and hear examples from the published journals of writers, both well-known and unknown." A ten-week journal-writing program, in contrast, would offer much more hands-on guidance and feedback, as well as more theoretical background.

To some extent, then, your duration depends mainly on how you feel the course can best serve *you*. Can you commit to five, eight, or ten weeks at a community college? Or would you prefer a brief, "punchy" one-day seminar? Will it be easier to get hired by a college for a standard term-length course, or by a business for a shorter class?

•**What are your costs, and how will you need to price your services?** If you are not yet visible in your new field, you may need to provide your first class or program on a volunteer or unpaid basis, just to get the credentials on your resume. Thereafter, you'll have to determine your fees or be ready to be paid the going rate.

Your costs can vary considerably depending on the setting you are teaching in. Teaching in a school or business where the room, any equipment, advertising, and registration are handled for you costs you little; renting a room and advertising for participants yourself is considerably more costly. Thus, you'll need to be paid considerably more to make such programs worth your while. Many creative individuals therefore start out teaching in community colleges or similar venues, then "move up" to seminars they sponsor themselves after they have built up a sufficient reputation and clientele to ensure profitable enrollment.

Teacher fees and salaries, too, vary. Continuing-education centers, adult-education units, community colleges, and Ys often pay instructors $25 to $50 per teaching (not preparation) hour. Programs offered to businesses or agencies can be considerably more lucrative, especially if you are expert or highly visible in your field; fees can range from $50 to $100 an hour and total as much as $1,000 for full-day programs. Networking in your area can give you a sense of the going rates there; contacting the

American Society of Training and Development can also be helpful.

Of course, it's important to consider more than just up-front profit when you decide to propose a class. Ann, a lawyer who developed a passion for photography after the birth of her first child, explains. "My community-college course in photography pays only about as much as working in McDonald's by the time all the planning and preparation are finished!" she jokes. "Nevertheless, it's been an incredible way to help establish my photography business. I've gotten many new clients and an equal number of referrals; I've been written up in the area newspaper; and I've become quite well-known as a photographer in my community. People I've never seen before will meet me and say, 'Oh, you're the photographer,' and I'll find out that a student has talked about me. That's invaluable. I don't look at teaching as a way of making money; I see it as someone paying me to advertise my services!"

Writing a Successful Proposal

A course proposal may vary in tone, style, content, and level of detail, depending on the subject you intend to teach and the environment in which it will be taught. However, it always includes three basic elements: a cover letter; a summary of course objectives, design, and schedule; and a personal biography. Each element is described below. Two full sample proposals then follow, showing you how each element was handled by a particular creative individual with a small business.

The Cover Letter

The cover letter is similar to the broadcast letter I discussed in this chapter and in chapter 9. It should be a powerful, one-page summary of the body of the proposal. It includes an "umbrella" statement broadly describing the purpose of your program or course; a statement of need, perhaps with supporting facts, that explains why the course is necessary; a brief description that explains how you'll conduct the program; highlights of the personal credentials that qualify you to teach the course; and a conclusion, which explains what you'll do next to further the possibility of teaching.

The Course Outline

This is similar to the material you may have received for some or all of your college courses. It may be one to three pages long and should include:

- **A course description.** This is a short summary (30 to 50 words) of your course *as it will appear in a catalog or brochure.* Some schools or businesses will write this themselves, but it is best at this stage to provide something they could use and to make your own succinct, focused statement. Review school, business, or agency catalogs that might have similar courses and model your description on entries there. Here is the course description for a workshop called "Power Presentation." As you can see, it is short, powerful, and clear.

The Power Presentation workshop prepares participants to make strong presentations to business and professional settings. Through lecture, discussion, and written materials, the elements of communicating powerfully are imparted. Each participant will have an opportunity to test his or her new skills by making a short "power presentation" at the conclusion of the session.

- **Course objectives.** These are tangible, specific, or measurable outcomes of the course. (In this context, objectives are outcomes that are more concrete—less conceptual and abstract—than educational goals.) Commonly used types of objectives include:

  - **Behavioral objectives,** which specify a type of behavior the participant will acquire by course completion, such as "the ability to define the elements of making a strong first impression."

  - **Performance objectives,** which define an expected proficiency level at a specific time during the class (midpoint, ending) and/or list verbs that describe the skills and actions the class will allow students to perform. For example, from a course on using the software program Excel, "upon completion of the three-week program, participants will be able to perform beginner through advanced functions of the Excel program."

  - **Product objectives,** which define a product that will result from the course of the program. A journal-writing course might state that "students will have written six weeks of a daily journal"; an arts-in-education program might promise that "participants will plan, write, and make a three-minute presentation on a topic of their choice."

The objectives for the Power Presentation course introduced above were given as follows in the proposal:

Upon completing the workshop, participants will be able to:

- List the elements of a powerful presentation

- Describe three methods of better understanding and connecting with their audience
- Make and/or analyze a three-minute speech demonstrating knowledge of all elements of a power presentation

- **Course design.** This section describes the specific *methods* you'll use to achieve the stated objectives of your class, as well as the *schedule* for specific tasks or topics that may be included. Optimal or maximum class size should also be included here if the nature of the course makes limits necessary. Finally, this section might also list materials you plan to distribute or any visual or media aids (films, slide shows) you might use.

  Your reference to methods helps the reader visualize and understand how you will impart information and structure class sessions. For example, "the first half of each session will consist of a lecture, followed by a period of discussions, and ending in a fifteen-minute role-playing exercise." Other methods include "workshopping," in which students share and offer feedback on each other's work, and oral presentation, in which each student is responsible for one or more brief reports on specific topics.

  Your review of the schedule—which is similar to a course outline or curriculum for college classes—details the particular topics or tasks you'll cover, the time you'll allot to each, and the sequence in which they'll be covered. A Wall Street for Women class outline, for example, might begin with "Week One: Introduction to the Stock Market" and end with "Week Ten: Review of Student Investment Results," giving two or three brief subtopics beneath each general weekly header. It's best not to be overly detailed here, as the person responsible for hiring teachers may wish to have some input in how the class can be further slanted to meet the school or organization's needs. Instead, simply try to give a clear and reasonably complete assurance that the course will be thoughtful, useful, and effectively structured. You may also wish to point out possible variants from the basic duration and schedule you have chosen, in case the course sponsor wishes to structure the length or timing of the course differently. Here is the Power Presentation course-design summary.

  This three-hour workshop includes lecture material, group discussion, and exercises. Students are led through a step-by-step understanding of key elements of power presentations that allows them to apply concepts to their own speaking and presentation needs. Relevant written material is provided to supplement student understanding of key concepts. Video-taping of presentations, followed by replay and group feedback, is an extremely useful optional activity and could be added if time and facilities permit. Class size should be limited to eight to ten individuals if individual presentations are included, but may be larger if presentations are limited to several volunteers, who will be critiqued by all participants. Without the hands-on presentation component, the course could be limited to two hours' duration.

- **Personal biography.** Building on your commercial and your brochure bio, this includes all relevant skills, training, experience, and any other related credentials. If it fills less than a quarter of a page, simply continue it from the main body of your course outline; if it is longer, put it on a separate page. As I have said in many different contexts, relevance of credentials is essential. By all means include accomplishments that speak to your ability to present the course you're proposing effectively; however, to add to your credibility, omit references to those items too distant from the topic at hand or from your current business.

Congratulations and Closing Thoughts

I began this book by introducing the concept of balance. If you have followed the recommendations and taken the actions suggested in the preceding chapters, your life should now reflect that crucial quality in a whole new way.

Perhaps you have found satisfying and remunerative lifeline employment after many years of living precariously in order to follow your artistic dream.

Perhaps you've opened your own business, and are now bringing your innate creativity to bear on your career as well as your artistic pursuits.

Perhaps you've finally taken the leap of judiciously cutting back from a stifling business career in order to make time for your art.

Whichever path you followed, you've proved that your life can accommodate both your artistic goals and a stable, meaningful career.

And with that goal achieved, the work of this book is completed. In closing, let me leave you with two brief additional thoughts.

First, know that by bringing your creative and career needs into balance, you've accomplished something quite special. It would be impossible to quantify the numbers precisely, but my years of work in this field have shown me that a considerable percentage of those with creative aspirations at age twenty have given those dreams up entirely by age forty, tired out by the endless struggle of living without either time for their art or a stable financial base. And in truth, even people without the added complexity of an artistic dream to juggle often bemoan their lack of life balance. Disproportion between work and personal life, inner satisfaction and external success are endemic in our driven, materialistic society. So don't forget to take a moment to savor your accomplishment, even if you have only just taken the first steps of the journey described in this book.

Second, remember that balance is not achieved through a single act, a single step, or a single moment. Instead, it is an ongoing process.

Picture for a moment an old- fashioned scale . . . the kind the personification of Justice holds in countless courthouse statues. The two arms do not swing into balance immediately when such scales are used; instead, they dip and hover for a while before settling into equilibrium. Don't be concerned if your own life follows the same pattern, if you have periods of uncertainty during the early days of these new challenges or if you need to make a series of changes and adjustments as you go along.

Such concerns and corrections are totally natural, and in fact are to be expected. Bringing your art and your career into balance is a tremendously complex task. It requires you to bring a wide range of skills—interpersonal, analytical, creative—to bear. It forces you into new and untried arenas. No matter how well you do the research and self-analysis I've recommended, there is going to be a period of trial and error.

Finding the right career/creative balance is also work that is unique to each person. No other individual's strategies or solutions are guaranteed to work for you. The career/creative balance a fellow writer, dancer, painter, or actor thrives on may make you utterly miserable; *your* choices, however successful they are for *you*, are unlikely to work well for anyone else. In this sense, the process described in this book has ushered you into uncharted terrain. The exercises, resources and stories I've shared will, I hope, have given you a wealth of ideas about possible directions and the inspiration of knowing that a balanced life is indeed possible. But the decision about what feels right for you is ultimately in your hands alone, and will continue to require attention, experimentation and honesty as you live with your new choices over time.

For many years now, helping artistic people find a satisfying creative and career balance has been not just my career, but also a source of great personal joy. As someone with a creative gift, you are part of a truly extraordinary group of people! Day after day, I am awed by your energy, moved by your courage, edified by your integrity, and inspired by your imagination. Thank you for sharing this journey of discovery and transformation with me—and may your life always be rich with the creative and career satisfaction you so truly deserve.

Resources

Books and Workbooks

SECTION I:
Finding – and Creating – a Better Creative/Career Balance

Barranger, Jack. *Knowing When to Quit.* San Luis Obispo, Calif.: Impact Publishers, 1988.

Bolles, Richard N. *The Three Boxes of Life.* Berkeley: Ten Speed Press, 1981.

———. *What Color Is Your Parachute?* Berkeley: Ten Speed Press, 1999.

Bridges, William. *Job Shift.* Reading, Mass.: Addison Wesley Publishing, 1994.

———. *Transitions: Making Sense of Life's Changes.* Reading, Mass.: Addison-Wesley Publishing, 1980.

Bryan, M., and J. Cameron. *The Artist's Way At Work.* New York: William Morrow and Company, 1998.

Cameron, J. *The Artist's Way.* New York: G. P. Putnam's Sons, 1992.

———. *The Vein of Gold.* New York: G. P. Putnam's Sons, 1996.

Campbell, David. *If You Don't Know Where You're Going, You'll Probably End Up Somewhere Else.* Allen, Texas: Tabor Publishing, 1974.

Charland, William A., Jr. *Life Work: Meaningful Employment in an Age of Limits.* New York: Continuum Publishing, 1986.

Crystal, John, and Richard Bolles. *Where Do I Go From Here With My Life?* Berkeley: Ten Speed Press, 1974.

Dent, Harry S., Jr. *Job Shock.* New York: St. Martin's Press, 1995.

Edwards, Paul & Sarah. *Finding Your Perfect Work.* New York: G. P. Putnam's Sons, 1996.

Elusorr, Suzanne, and Charles Cameron. *T.G.I.M/Thank God It's Monday: Making Work Fulfilling and Finding Fulfilling Work.* Los Angeles: Jeremy P. Tarcher, 1986.

Helfand, David. *Career Change: Everything You Need to Know to Meet New Challenges and Take Control of Your Career.* Chicago: VGM Career Horizons, a division of NTC Publishing Group, 1995.

Katz, S. J., and A. Liu. *Success Trap.* New York: Ticknor & Fields, 1990.

Levinson, Harry. *Career Mastery: Keys to Taking Charge of Your Career Throughout Your Work Life.* San Francisco: Berrett-Koehler Publishers, 1992.

Maisel, E. *Staying Sane In the Arts.* New York: G. P. Putnam's Sons, 1992.

Rogers, L. *Working in Show Business: Behind the Scenes in Theater, Film, and Television.* New York: Back Stage Books, 1997.

Rosen, Stephen, and Celia Paul. *Career Renewal.* San Diego: Academic Press, 1998.

Schlossberg, N. K., and S. P. Robinson. *Going to Plan B.* New York: Simon & Schuster, 1996.

Sher, Barbara. *How To Get What You Really Want.* New York: Ballantine Books, 1983.

———. *I Could Do Anything If I Only Knew What It Was.* New York: Dell Publishing, 1994.

Simon, S. *Getting Unstuck.* New York: Warner Books, 1988.

Sinetar, Marsha. *Do What You Love, The Money Will Follow.* New York: Paulist Press, 1987.

Tieger, P. D., and B. Barron-Tieger. *Do What You Are.* Boston: Little, Brown & Co., 1992.

SECTION II: Exploring and Expanding Your Work Options

Bly, Robert W., and Gary Blake. *Dream Jobs.* New York: John Wiley & Sons, 1983.

Canape, Charlene. *The Part-Time Solution.* New York: Harper Perennial, 1991.

Eikleberry, Carol. *The Career Guide For Creators and Unconventional People.* Berkeley: Ten Speed Press, 1995.

Field, S. *Career Opportunities in Theater and the Performing Arts.* New York: Facts on File, 1992.

———. *Career Opportunities in the Music Industry.* New York: Facts on File, 1995.

Grant, Daniel. *The Fine Artist's Career Guide.* New York: Allworth Press, 1998.

Haubenstock, S., and D. Joselit. *Career Opportunities in Art.* New York: Facts on File, 1995.

Henry, Mary Lyn, and Lynne Rogers. *How To Be A Working Actor: The Insider's Guide to Finding Jobs in Theater, Film, and Television.* New York: Watson-Guptil, 2000.

Kennedy, J. L., and D. Laramore. *Joyce Laine Kennedy's Career Book.* Lincolnwood: Ill., VGM Career Horizons, 1994.

Rogers, Lynne. *Working in Show Business.* New York: Back Stage Books, 1997.

Rothberg, Diane S., and Barbara Ensor Cook. *Part-Time Professional.* Washington, D.C.: Acropoks Books, 1985.

Rozakis, Laurie. *The Complete Idiot's Guide To Making Money in Freelancing.* New York: Alpha Books, 1998.

SECTION III:
Building a Better Balance through Lifeline Employment

Bostwick, Burdette E. *Resume Writing.* New York: John Wiley & Sons, Inc., 1985.

Figler, H. *The Complete Job Search Handbook.* New York: Holt Rinehart Publishing, 1989.

Fortgang, Laura Berman. *Take Yourself to the Top.* New York: Warner Books, 1998.

Fry, R. *101 Great Answers To The Toughest Internee Questions.* Franklin Lakes, N.J.: Career Press, 1996.

Harris-Bowlsby; Margaret Riley Dickel; and James P. Sampson. *The Internet: A Tool for Career Planning.* Columbus, Ohio: National Career Development Association, 1998.

Kelley, Robert E. *How To Be A Star At Work.* New York: Times Business, division of Random House, 1998.

Petras, Kathryn, and Ross Petras. *The Only Job Hunting Guide You'll Ever Need.* New York: Fireside, 1995.

Potter, Beverly A. *Maverick Career Strategies.* New York: AMACOM, a division of American Management Association, 1984.

Richardson, Bradley G. *Job Smarts For Twentysomethings.* New York: Vintage Books, 1995.

Tullier, L. M. *Networking For Everyone!* Indianapolis: JIST Works, Inc., 1998.

Wendleton, K. *Through the Brick Wall: How to Job Hunt in a Tight Market.* New York: Villard Press, 1992.

Yate, Martin. *Beat The Odds.* New York: Ballantine Books, 1995.

———. *Knock 'Em Dead.* Holbrook, Mass.: Bob Adams, Inc., 1994.

SECTION IV:
Building a Better Balance through Lifeline Self-Employment

Crawford, Tad. *Business and Legal Forms for Authors and Self-Publishers.* Revised Edition. New York: Allworth Press, 1999.

———. *Business and Legal Forms for Crafts.* Revised Edition. New York: Allworth Press, 1998.

———. *Business and Legal Forms for Fine Artists.* Revised Edition. New York: Allworth Press, 1999.

———. *Business and Legal Forms for Graphic Designers.* Revised Edition. New York: Allworth Press, 1999.

———. *Business and Legal Forms for Illustrators.* Revised Edition. New York: Allworth Press, 1998.

———. *Business and Legal Forms for Photographers.* Revised Edition. New York: Allworth Press, 1997.

Gerber, Michael E. *The E-Myth Revisited: Why Most Small Businesses Don't Work and What To Do About It.* New York: Harper Business, 1995.

Hall, Daryl Allen. *1101 Business You Can Start From Home.* New York: John Wiley and Sons, 1995.

Levenson, Jay and Godin, Seth. *The Guerrilla Marketing Handbook.* New York: Houghton Mifflin, 1994.

Paulson, Ed with Layton, Marcia. *The Complete Idiot's Guide to Starting Your Own Business.* New York: Alpha Books, 1998.

Peters, Tom. *The Tom Peters Seminar: Crazy Times Call For Crazy Organizations.* New York: Vintage Books, a division of Random House, 1994.

Reirson, Vickie, ed. *Start Your Business: A Beginner's Guide.* Central Point, Oregon: Oasis Press, 1995.

Tiffany, Paul, and Steven Peterson. *Business Plans For Dummies.* Foster City, Calif.: IDG Books Worldwide, Inc., 1997.

Internet Career Information Resources

Below are a few suggestions of Internet resources for career exploration and information. These listings are predominantly national. Many provide links to state and regional labor market information, professional association chapters and local resources.

Career Information Websites with General and National Information
Changing Course: *www.changingcourse.com/links.htm*
California Job Search Guide (with many national links): *www.jobstar.org*
The Career Action Center: *http://careeraction.org*
Occupational Outlook Handbook online: *http://stats.bls.gov/ocohome.htm*
The Riley Guide: *www.jobtrak.com*
Richard Bolles, author of *What Color is Your Parachute*: *www.jobhuntersbible.com*
NY State Dept of Labor Career Resource Library: *www.labor.state.ny. us/html/library.htm*
Small Business Administration: *http://sbaonline.sba.gov*

Arts or Cultural Administrator/Manager
Association of Fund Raising Executives: *www.nsfre.org*
ArtsWire, a program of the NY State Council for the Arts: *www.artswire.org*
The Foundation Center: *www.fdn.org*
Meeting Planners International: *www.mpiweb.org*

Arts-in-Education Teacher
National Endowment for the Arts: *http://arts.endow.gov/federal.html*
National Association of State Art Agencies: *www.nasaa.org*
The Kennedy Center ARTSEDGE: *http://artsedge.kennedy-center.org/*
The Getty's Art Education: *www.artsednet.getty.edu/*
Music Educators National Conference: *www.menc.org*
American Association of Museums: *www.aam-us.org*
Arts Education Partnership: *http://aep-arts.org/aephome.html*
American Music Therapy Association: *www.namt.com*
American Dance Therapy Association: *www.adta.org*

Business and Technical Writer/Editor/Journalist
About Technical Writing: *http://technwriting.miningco.com/careers/techwriting*
Society for Technical Communication: *www.stc-va.org*
Jobs and recruiting for media professionals: *www.mediabistro.com*
Editing and writing jobs: *www.newsjobs.net*
Writers Guild of America: *www.wga.org*

The Association for Women in Communications: *www.womcom.org*

Chef
The American Culinary Federation: *www.acfchefs.org*

Computer Specialist
High Tech Careers: *www.hightechcareers.com/*
Careers in Computing: *www.tcm.org/html/resources/cmp-careers/cnc-support.html*

Corporate Trainer
American Society for Training and Development: *www.astd.org*
The Society for Human Resource Management: *www.shrm.org*
National Association of Workforce Development Professionals: *www.nawdp.org*

Film/Video/Electronic Media
Entertainment and New Media Career Guide: *www.skillsnet.net*
World Wide Web Artists' Consortium: *www.wwac.org*
International Film & Television Production Directory: *www.mandy.com*
Webgrrls Interational: *www.webgrrls.com*
New York New Media Association: *www.nynma.org*
Web developer info: *www.webdeveloper.com*

English as a Second Language Teacher
Literacy Organizations: *www.lacnyc.org/other/index.htm*

Fitness Trainer
Aerobics and Fitness Association of America: *www.afaa.com*
American Fitness Professionals Association: *www.afpafitness.com*
International Fitness Association: *www.ifafitness.com*
International Fitness Professionals Association: *www.ifpa-fitness.com*
Professional Fitness Training Information: *www.ideafit.com*

Graphic Designer
Graphic Artists Guild: *www.gag.org*
Desktop publishing info: *http://desktoppublishing.com*
Desktop Publishers Journal: *www.dtpjournal.com*
Trends in graphics, publishing, electronic media: *www.trendwatch.com*
Communications Arts Career Links: *www.commarts.com/career/car_links.html*
ACM SIGGRAPH – Computer Graphics: *www.siggraph.org*
Visual Effects Society: *www.visual-effects-society.org*

Massage Therapist

Associated Bodywork and Massage Professionals: *www.abmp.com*
NaturalHealers: *www.naturalhealers.com*

Office Administrator/Manager

International Association of Administrative Professionals: *www.iaap-hq.org*

Paralegal

National Federation of Paralegal Associates: *www.paralegals.org*
American Association for Paralegal Education: *www.aafpe.org*
National Association of Legal Assistants: *www.nala.org*

Real Estate Salesperson

National Association of Realtors: *www.nar.realtor.com*

Sign Language Interpreter

Registry of Interpreters for the Deaf: *www.rid.org*

Social Worker

National Association of Social Workers: *www.naswdc.org*

Speech or Language Pathologist/Audiologist

American Speech-Language-Hearing Association: *www.asha.org*

Teacher

Teaching jobs Online Directory: *www.teaching-jobs.org*

Volunteer

Volunteers of America: *www.voa.org*
Virtual Volunteering Project: *www.serviceleader.org*
Volunteer Match: *www.volunteermatch.org*

Index

A

achievements, 36
   goals and, 41
acquisitions editor, 134
Actors' Fund of America, The, xii
Actors' Work Program, xii
advertisements, 275
agreements, 265
alternative(s)
   advantages/disadvantages of, 74
   choosing, 74-75
   research your, 73
American Society of Training and
   Development, 284
analytical skills, 167
   check list for, 60
applications, 168-169
appointments, 120
artist(s),
   career problems of, 3-5
   marketable, 9-10
   objective standards of competence
     for, 7-8
   risks of, 15
   starving, xii
   vision of, 28-31
art(s)
   four realities of life in, 7-8
   balance in, 6-7
   life in the, 7-8
   purists in, 29-30
arts/cultural administrator/manager,
   127-128
arts-in-education teacher
   pros/cons of, 128-129
Association of Part-Time Professionals,
   The, 228

autonomy, 55

B

balance
   finding the, 9-10
   inventory, 16-17
   lack of, 5
   payoffs of creative/career, 14-15
   striking a better, 11
   value of life, 6-7
bankruptcy, 264
barriers, 30
   analyzing, 38-40
   breaking, 31-33, 34, 38-44
   concrete goals and, 40-43
   questionnaire for overcoming, 45-46
   target dates and, 43-44
beliefs, inner, 21
benefit(s), 55, 235-236, 270
   reduced, 231
   restructuring job, 231
biography, personal, 287
bonuses, 234, 236
books, 108, 124, 291-294
brainstorming, 84
   skills and, 63
   small business ideas and, 93-94
   values and, 56
brevity, 149
brochures, 274, 276, 278
budgets, 235
business cards, 273
business certificate, 263
business clients, 119
business commercial, 11, 270, 273
   uniqueness of, 271-272
business plan

benefits of, 250-255

C
calling, 29
candidate(s), 217-220
  job restructuring for, 227-231
  qualified, 199
career cluster(s)
  applying, 104
  artistic, 102-103
  conventional, 101-102
  enterprising, 100-101
  investigative, 99-100
  realistic, 98-99
  six, 98-103
Career Guide for Creative and Unconventional People, The, 103
Career Information Delivery Systems (CIDS), 107
Career Renewal, 115
career(s), 5. *See also* lifeline careers
  consolidation of, 156
  counseling, 177, 202, 211
  difficulties in path of, 96
  discovering new, 105-106
  driven, 11-13
  security, 226
  stability versus satisfaction in, 96
  subordination of, 96
caterer, 129-130
centers of influence, 269
certificates, 126-127
challenges
  meeting the, 9-10
change(s), 22
  goal, 40-43
  overcoming barriers to, 19-20
  readiness for, 23
  reasons for, 31
  subtle, 23
  turning points and, 26-27
chef, 130
classes, 281-282
classified advertisements, 177, 195, 202
"closet creatives," 27, 51, 259-260
clubs, 108, 282

cold calls, 150
commercials. *See* business commercial
commissions, 236
commitment(s), 11, 29, 39, 211, 236, 238, 240, 245
  creative, 9
  professional, 166
communication skills, 167
  skill check list for, 57
compensation, 201-202, 231, 236
competition, 6-7, 20, 36, 247-249, 256
  job, 235
competitive advantage, 268-269
competitors, 256
Complete Idiot's Guide to Making Money Freelancing, The, 92
compromises, identifying, 36
computer graphics designer, 131
computer network engineer, 131-132
computer programmer, 131-132
computer specialist, 130-131
computer trainer, teacher, or tutor, 131-132
conferences, 280
confidence, 6, 10, 14, 39, 87
  building, 49
consolidation, 156
consulting, 227, 249
  hidden job market and, 179
contact(s), 114-116, 191, 200
  A (primary), 115, 116-119, 180-181
  B (bridge), 115, 119-122, 148, 180-181, 202, 248-249
  C (VIP), 122-123, 148, 180-181
  calling, 191-192
  expanding, 115
  guidelines for making, 120-121
  hiring, 116
  jobs and, 183-184
  keep in touch with, 194-195
  meeting with, 192
  thank you notes to, 192-193
  writing to, 184-186
contentment, false, 33
contingency plans, 239, 241
control

lack of, 199
copy editor, 134-135
corporate trainer, 132-133
corporations, 264-265
course (workshop) proposal(s), 281-282
    design, 286
    objectives, 285
    outline, 284
    writing a successful, 284-287
cover letters, 150, 196. *See also* letters
"creative commitment(s)", 9
creative people
    ambiguity versus clarity in, 84-85
    capacity in, 48
    popular lifeline careers for, 125-144
    self-employment and, 245-247
credentials, 152, 194, 282
credibility, 209
criticism, 88-89
customer base, 255, 281

D
deadlines, 235
    setting specific, 43-44
decision maker(s)
    follow up letters and, 194-195
    jobs and, 183-184
    interviews and, 214
    letters to, 183-191
decision making
    balanced, 73
    consensus versus lone, 84
    delaying, 72
    dependent, 70-71
    fatalistic, 71-72
    impulsive, 69-70
    intuitive, 72
    quiz, 68-69
    realistic, 70
    reassessing, 47-54
    style, 68-73
decorative painter/muralist, 133
degrees, 126-127
Department of Labor, 123
design/planning skills, 168
  check list and, 60-61

disappointment, 20, 33
dissatisfaction, 26
dreams, 34
dress standards, 202-204

E
editor (film/video), 133-134
editor (text), 134-135
education
    adult courses in, 114
emotions, 234-235
employee
    entrepreneur or, 80-81
employer(s)
    job restructure and, 234
    resumes and, 153-176
employment. *See also* jobs
    agencies, 177-179, 179
    eight contrasts of, 82-83
    flexible locations for, 51
    gaps in, 169
    history, 168
    initiative or maintaining operations
      in, 85
    job applications for, 168-169
    mentality chart, 89-90
    resumes and, 164-165
    self-employment versus, 79-80
    sequence of, 164-165
entrepreneur(s), 246. *See also* self-
    employment
    common ventures for, 91-92
    confidence as, 87-88
    consensus and, 84
    decision making and, 84
    employee or, 80-81
    future, 92-93
    initiative and, 85
    inventory, 81-82
    optimism and, 88 89
ESL (English as a second language)
    teacher, 135-136
expectations,
    realistic, 33

F

failures, 20, 27, 88
fear of, 21, 33
fear, 20, 27, 31
  unbalancing effects of, 32-33
fees, 257, 261
financial aid, 114
financial plans, 259
financial security, 24
fitness trainer, 136
flexibility, 126, 254
flex-time. *See* part-time
flyers, 276
focus, 149
follow up, 241
freelancing, 11, 13, 20, 68, 80-81, 87,
  94, 225, 247, 249, 255, 257, 260-
  262, 266
  ambiguity of, 84-85
  hidden job market and, 179
  resumes and, 162, 166
friends, 114-116
frustrations, 35

G

goal(s), 38, 116, 147, 151, 152, 182,
  191, 282
  business, 251
  internships and, 111-112
  resumes used for, 156
  setting concrete, 20, 34, 40-43
graphic designer, 136-137

H

human resource service(s), 228
  job applications and, 168-169
  job restructuring and, 232
human services skills,
  check list for, 59

I

illustrations, 276
imbalance(s), 5
  creative/practical, 19-20, 26, 28
  fear of failure, 33-37
  long-term/unconscious, 20

perfectionism and, 35-36
  temporary, 19-20
  warning signs of, 15-17
income, 257
  reduced, 231
information management skills, 167
  check list for, 57-58
instincts
  interview and, 215
interests
  shifts in, 63
Internet, 183, 282
  online material on, 106-107
  Web sites on, 108-109, 294
internship(s), 110-112, 123, 127-128,
  206
  questions to ask for, 111-112
  resumes and, 162
  shadowing programs and, 112-113
interviewer(s), 200
  behavior with, 205-210
  dress and, 202
  thank you notes to, 211-213
interview(s), 11, 148-150, 154, 191-
  192
  action plan for, 199-200
  after the, 210-211
  anatomy of, 216
  appropriate behavior at, 205-210
  closing of, 220
  confirmation letter and, 221-223
  dress at, 202-204
  five fundamental realities of, 198-
    199
  introduction to, 197-198
  lack of control in, 199
  opening of, 216-217
  portfolio and, 201
  positivity at, 204-205
  preparation for, 199
  reference list and, 201
  relating skills to, 198
  resumes used for, 155
  salary/compensation and, 201-202
  thank you notes after, 211-213
  timeliness of, 204

unnatural situation of, 199
intuition, 27, 72

J
job(s)
application for, 168-169
artistic, 102-103
confirmation letter and, 221-223
conventional, 101-102
decision makers and, 180, 183-184
dress at, 202-204
enterprising, 100-101
hidden market for, 177, 179, 180
interviewing for, 199-200
investigative, 99
matching, 217-220
newspaper ads and, 177-179
offer with/without negotiation, 119,
   220-221
official market for, 177, 179, 195-
   196
other sources of, 196
realistic, 98-99
salary/compensation and, 201-202,
   225, 236
search, 214
shadowing, 127
social, 99-100
survival, 11-13
job(s), restructuring of
contingency plans and, 239, 241
counter-offer with, 241
current position and, 225-227
likely candidate for, 227-231
personal financial worksheet for, 233
proposing, 234-242
researching, 231-234
resignation and, 240
transition and, 241-242
journal, xiii
journalist, 137

K
knowledge
"new professional" and, 50

L
letter agreements, 265
letter(s)
confirmation, 221-223
cover, 196, 284
follow-up, 194-195
sample "broadcast," 184-191, 215,
   275-276, 284
thank you, 211-213
libraries, 183, 200
licensing, 114, 126-127
lifeline career(s), 5, 9, 11-13, 17, 26,
   40-41, 127, 166, 178-179, 181, 185,
   192, 258
A B and C contacts for, 116-124
creative people in, 48-54
developing of, 47-54
educational programs for, 114
exercise, 13-14
internships and, 111-112
motivators and, 63-68
networking and, 114-116
perspective in, 97-98
popular, 125-144
powerful presentation for a, 152-153
researching, 105-106
resumes and, 153-176
self-assessment tools for, 51-61
six job clusters for, 98-103
skills and, 56-63
tasks in building a, 96-97
use of personal commercial for, 148-
   150
values and, 52-56
volunteering and, 109-111
limited liability company (LLC), 265
location(s)
flexibility in, 51
small business, 262-263

M
magazines, 124
general-interest and specialized, 107-
   108
mailing lists, 279-280
mailings, 195-196, 256

management
    resumes and, 166
managerial skills, 167
    check list for, 59-60
managing editor, 134-135
manual/physical skills, 167
    check list for, 58
market survey, 268
marketing, 255-256
    business, 269
    communication style and, 276
    overview of, 273-276
marketing survey, 294-295
massage therapist, 137-138
media coverage, 280
mentors, 36
microcomputer specialist, 131-132
motivations
    reassessing, 47-54
motivator(s)
    checklist, 65
    ideal work and, 67-68
    reviewing, 63-66
    subconscious/conscious, 64
    success summaries and, 66-67
    summary, 66

N
negotiation, 84
networking, 11, 36, 147, 180, 248,
    256, 269, 280, 283
    beyond, 196
    hidden job market and, 180
    lifeline careers and, 114-116
    research through, 182-183
    time lost in, 214
newsletters, 274-275, 278, 282
newspaper ads
    jobs and, 178-179
newspapers, 107
non profits, 128, 179-180

O
Occupational Outlook Handbook, The
    (OOH), 107, 123
offers, 119-121, 241

office administrator/manager, 138-139
optimists, 88
option(s), 21-22, 27, 72
    consider, 70
    expanding, 25
    identifying, 74
    self-employment, 91-92
    work, 78-93
organization(s), 199-200
    hidden job market in, 179-180
    information checklist for, 184
    nonprofit, 128, 179-180
    professional, 108-109, 124, 151,
        181, 247, 282
    self-assessment with, 214-215
    small or suburban, 229
overhead, 260-261

P
paralegal, 125, 139
Part Time Professional, The, 240
Part Time Solution, The, 239
partnership, 264
part-time job(s), 11, 160, 231
    restructuring, 225-227
    unconventional schedules and, 228-
        229
    written/unwritten policy for, 232,
        234
past
    and future values, 56
    understanding your, 38-40
peer pressure, 127, 230, 238
perfectionists, 72
    breaking barriers of, 35-36
personal attributes
    skill check list and, 58-59
personal commercial(s), 148-153, 177,
    184-185
    definition/usage's for, 148-150
    resumes and, 162
    sample, 152-153
    strengths/weaknesses of, 154
    writing your, 150-152
personality, 82-83
philosophy

all versus part, 86
ambiguity versus clarity, 84-85
business-minded versus project-
   minded, 86-87
eight contrasting, 82-89
initiative versus maintaining, 85-86
lone decisions versus consensus, 84
optimistic versus perfectionist, 88-89
sales-oriented versus non-sales-
   oriented, 87-88
self-starting versus teamwork, 83-84
photographer, 140-141
plan, action, 11
portfolio, 201
preparation, 149, 199
pride, 14
print advertisements, 275
procrastination, 20
professionals. *See* organizations
promotions, 234
proposals, 237
purist, 29-30

Q
quarterly meetings, 235

R
raises, 234, 236
reassurance, 17
rebels, 29, 50
recognition, 225
record keeping, 265-266
reference list, 201
referrals, 181
rejection, 20, 35
research, 147
   alternatives, 73
   job restructuring and, 231-234
   network through, 182-183
resentment, 32
resource(s)
   four categories of, 106
   research, 106
resume(s), 11, 120, 148, 151, 200
   chronological, 154, 162-166
   five basic characteristics of, 155

functional, 154, 162-163, 167-168
interviews and, 155
irrelevancy of, 157-159
mailing of, 195-196
power, 153, 177
rules for, 155-163
sample, 170
sample arts administrator, 171
sample functional, 176
sample highlight, 174
sample office, 172
sample qualifications, 175
sample teaching, 173
skills on, 62
strong summary in, 162-163
substance/form of, 155
various, 159
work history used for, 158
writing the power, 154-155
risks, 20
role playing, 84

S
sacrifice, 13, 32
salaries, 7, 201-202, 225, 236
sales, 255
sales calls, 198
scholarships, 114
security, 55
self-assessment
   career related, 47-61
   interviews and, 214-215
   organization and, 214-215
self-employment, 80. *See also* small
   business
   advantages/disadvantages of, 246-
      247
   eight contrasts of, 82-83
   employment versus, 79-80
   envisioning/establishing, 245-246
   options, 91-92
   questions about, 248-250
   researching, 247-248
   strategies, xii, 13
self-esteem, 14, 22
self-starter

teamworker versus, 83-84
seminars, 248, 281-282
services
    costs of, 270, 283-284
setbacks, 6
shadowing programs, 112-113
sign-language interpreter, 141
skill(s), 34
    brainstorming for, 63
    check list for, 57-61
    clusters of, 167
    developing, 63
    favorite/not so favorite, 62-63
    personal commercials and, 148-153
    power resume and, 153-154
    reassessing, 47-54, 56-57
    resumes and, 153-176
    transferable, 61-62
Small Business Administration, The,
    248
small business(es), 80
    brainstorming ideas, 93-94
    establishing a, 262-266
    financial considerations in, 259-262
    name of, 263
    overview, 255-259
    plan for, 250-255
    selling tools, 267-273
    structure, 263-264
social events, 281
social services, 128
social usefulness, 55
social worker, 125, 141-142
sole proprietorship, 264
special-interest groups, 181
speech or language
    pathologist/audiologist, 142-143
stability, 225
    financial, 12
start-up costs, 260
"stuck," 26-28, 39
    checklist for being, 22-23
    getting, staying and living, 20-22
substitute-teaching, 162
success, 108
    fear of, 21, 31-32

summaries of, 66-67
sustaining, 8
visualize, 33

T
talents, 158-159
target market, 267-268
teaching
    computer, 131-132
    resumes and, 165
teamworker
    self-starter versus, 83-84
technical or business editor, 134-135
temp work, 156, 186
    resumes and, 162, 166
thank you notes, 121, 181, 211-213
    contacts and, 192-193
timeliness
    interviews and, 204
tool(s)
    personal selling, 147-148
    resume as selling, 153
    small business selling, 267-273
training program(s), 113-114
    costs of, 123
    formal, 126-127
transition(s), xiii
    career, 147-148, 231
    creative, 10
    creative people in career, 48-54, 113
    gradual job, 241-242
    internships and, 111-112
    reassurance in, 17
    volunteering and, 109-111
trends, 8
trial periods, 239
tuition, 114
turning point(s), 23
    "been there, done that," 25-26
    good/bad news of, 26-27
    "Is this all their is?", 23-24
    milestone, 25
    mortality, 24
    nonturning-point, 25-26
    rock bottom, 24
tutors, 131-132, 143-144

pros/cons, 143-144
TV and radio advertisements, 275

U
unions, 108

V
value(s)
  brainstorming and, 56
  changing of, 56
  checklist, 53-54
  core, 54
  defining your, 52-53
  existing, 55
  missing, 55-56
  past and future, 56
  reassessing, 47-54
  restatement, 54-55
variety, 55
verb power, 159-162
vision(s)
  artistic, 9
  compromising, 37-38
  defending artistic, 28-31
  entrepreneurs and, 84
  fear of failure, 33-35
  fear of success, 31-33
  going it alone, 36-37
  limiting, 28-37, 33
  loner/stoic, 36-37
  perfectionism in, 35-36

volunteering, 109-111, 127-128, 206
  lifetime career and, 109-111
  questions to ask before, 110-111
  resumes and, 162, 165

W
Web site designer/developer, 125, 131-132
Web sites, 247, 249, 256, 275
When Smart People Fail: Rebuilding Yourself for Success, 39
word power, 159-162
work
  blending artistic and other elements in, 103-104
  dream, 67
  environment, 225
  experience, 109, 121
  history, 154, 158
  lifeline, 11-13, 68
  options in, 78-93
  part-time, 160, 180, 226-227
  temp, 156
  understanding, 95-96
  various resumes used for, 153-176
workshops. *See* course proposals
writer
  business/technical, 129

Y
yellow pages, 183

𝔄 Books from Allworth Press

The Money Mentor: Winning Your Financial Freedom
by Tad Crawford (softcover, 6 × 9, 272 pages, $14.95)

The Entrepreneurial Age: Awakening the Spirit of Enterprise in People, Companies, and Countries
by Larry C. Farrell (hardcover, 6¼ × 9¼, 352 pages, $24.95)

Promoting Your Acting Career
by Glenn Alterman (softcover, 6 × 9, 224 pages, $18.95)

An Actor's Guide—Your First Year in Hollywood, Revised Edition
by Michael Saint Nicholas (softcover, 6 × 9, 272 pages, $18.95)

Creative Careers in Music
by Josquin des Pres and Mark Landsman (softcover, 6 × 9, 224 pages, $18.95)

The Songwriter's and Musician's Guide to Nashville, Revised Edition
by Sherry Bond (softcover, 6 × 9, 224 pages, $18.95)

Careers by Design: A Business Guide for Graphic Designers, Third Edition
by Roz Goldfarb (softcover, 6¾ × 9⅞, 256 pages, $19.95)

Artists Communities: A Directory of Residences in the United States That Offer Time and Space for Creativity, Second Edition
by the Alliance of Artists' Communities (softcover, 6¾ × 9⅞, 240 pages, $18.95)

The Artist's Resource Handbook, Revised Edition
by Daniel Grant (softcover, 6 × 9, 248, $18.95)

The Fine Artist's Career Guide
by Daniel Grant (softcover, 6 × 9, 224 pages, $18.95)

The Business of Being an Artist, Third Edition
by Daniel Grant (softcover, 6 × 9, 352 pags, $19.95)

Selling Your Crafts
by Susan Joy Sager (softcover, 6 × 9, 288 pages, $18.95)

Writing.com: Creative Internet Strategies to Advance Your Writing Career
by Moira Anderson Allen (softcover, 6 × 9, 256 pages, $16.95)

Please write to request our free catalog. To order by credit card, call 1-800-491-2808 or send a check or money order to Allworth Press, 10 East 23rd Street, Suite 510, New York, NY 10010. Include $5 for shipping and handling for the first book ordered and $1 for each additional book. Ten dollars plus $1 for each additional book if ordering from Canada. New York State residents must add sales tax.

To see our complete catalog on the World Wide Web, or to order online, you can find us at *www.allworth.com*.